CAMBRIDGE STUDIES IN LINGUISTICS

General Editors · W.SIDNEY ALLEN · EUGENIE J.A.HENDERSON
FRED W.HOUSEHOLDER · JOHN LYONS · R.B.LE PAGE · F.R.PALMER
J.L.M.TRIM

The linguistic theory of numerals

In this series

Other volumes in preparation

THE LINGUISTIC THEORY OF NUMERALS

JAMES R. HURFORD

Lecturer in Linguistics, University of Lancaster

CAMBRIDGE UNIVERSITY PRESS

CAMBRIDGE
LONDON · NEW YORK · MELBOURNE

CAMBRIDGE UNIVERSITY PRESS
Cambridge, New York, Melbourne, Madrid, Cape Town, Singapore,
São Paulo, Delhi, Dubai, Tokyo

Cambridge University Press
The Edinburgh Building, Cambridge CB2 8RU, UK

Published in the United States of America by Cambridge University Press, New York

www.cambridge.org
Information on this title: www.cambridge.org/9780521133685

First published 1975
This digitally printed version 2010

A catalogue record for this publication is available from the British Library

Library of Congress Catalogue Card Number: 74-25652

ISBN 978-0-521-20735-5 Hardback
ISBN 978-0-521-13368-5 Paperback

To my parents
James and Muriel Hurford

Contents

vii

Preface

What we attempt to achieve in this book is an explication of the essential formal properties of natural language numeral systems. The book owes debts to two rather different scholarly traditions, one quite old, but recently neglected, and the other quite new and presently blooming. The older tradition is that of intrepid data collection by anthropologists, explorers, missionaries, and miscellaneous travellers, culminating in some impressive and widely researched typological treatises and catalogues of data (e.g. by Pott, Kluge, Seidenberg, Conant – see Bibliography). The newer tradition is that of generative grammar, in the broadest sense of that term, in which it is regarded more as a disciplined methodology for investigating linguistic phenomena than as any particular body of specific rules, conventions, etc. That is, we share the principal methodological assumptions about 'doing linguistics' professed in such works as Chomsky (1965) and Chomsky and Halle (1968) but do not necessarily agree with the specific conclusions about the form of grammars reached in those works. In line with our basic methodological assumption, we treat these conclusions as empirical hypotheses, susceptible to testing and to confirmation or disconfirmation. We have subjected some of the data collected by the older tradition to the formal analytical method of the newer tradition. The result, we believe, is a contribution to both traditions. On the one hand we arrive at a deeper and more exact characterization of the essential underlying formal organization of natural language numeral systems. And on the other hand we develop proposals for certain specific formal devices which are new to the theory of generative grammar and for which the data of numeral systems appear to provide evidence.

The book will be easier to read for those with a working familiarity with the principles of generative grammar, though it has been attempted to give in chapter 1 enough of a general introduction to these principles to make it feasible for a determined reader to grasp the arguments developed in the rest of the book. A reader with experience in constructing formal grammars may wish to skip this chapter and begin at the second. Chapter 2, which deals with English numerals and develops the main proposals in the book, is the densest and will be the slowest to read. This chapter does not presuppose detailed knowledge of recent scholarship in generative grammar, but it does assume a willingness to persevere in following a close, detailed, and abstract argument. The material presented in the second chapter forms a basis for discussion of the numeral systems of a variety of languages, Mixtec, French, Danish, Welsh, Hawaiian, Yoruba, and others in chapters 3–9. Although some new formal proposals are made in these later chapters, they are built in large part on the main theoretical framework developed in chapter 2 and therefore, given an understanding of chapter 2, should make relatively straightforward reading. Familiarity with transformational rules will be a definite advantage in reading chapter 6. Chapter 10 gives a brief summary of the main conclusions to be drawn from the preceding chapters. Chapter 11 reviews a number of other scholarly works on numerals with broadly generative aims. In reading this final chapter some familiarity with the main currents of theoretical linguistic debate over the past two decades is likely to be an advantage.

Our language can be seen as an ancient city: a maze of little streets and squares, of old and new houses, and of houses with additions from various periods; and this surrounded by a multitude of new boroughs with straight regular streets and uniform houses.

Ludwig Wittgenstein, *Philosophical Investigations*

I *Introduction*

This book is concerned with the numeral systems of natural languages – with the ways, that is, in which people in various parts of the world count with words. In this Introduction I shall give the reader an idea of the central purpose of the book and draw an outline of the principal methodological assumptions which linguists bring to the study of language and those which I have brought to the study of the numeral systems of languages. In subsequent chapters I shall describe in some detail the numeral systems of, first, English, and then a variety of other, more or less 'exotic' languages. The motivation for this book is to discover the deep and general properties exhibited by numeral systems, rather than just to look at the superficial facts. Learning to count up to a given point in as many languages as possible is a pastime that has given pleasure to many people, but our purpose is to delve deeper, to investigate the special ways in which linguistic counting systems are organized. To get an inkling of what we are up to, try to list as many possible ways in which the sequence of words *one, two, three, four, five, six, seven, eight, nine, ten, eleven, twelve, thirteen, fourteen* differs from the sequence of words that is pronounced as *ay, bee, cee, dee, ee, eff, gee, aitch, eye, jay, kay, ell, emm, enn.* Do not be content to list just the most obvious differences; say as much as you can, drawing on all of your knowledge of the use of these words and the use of corresponding words in other languages. If that exercise strikes the reader as sufficiently intriguing or bizarre, he may read the rest of this book.

Consider the list of words *one, two, three, four, five, six, seven, eight, nine.* It is entirely natural to us to think of this list of words as a series or progression; it is equally obvious that the fact that it is a series or progression has nothing to do with the phonetic or phonological properties of the words. A foreigner learning English could no more predict that the next word is pronounced *ten* than we can predict what the name will be of the tenth planet in the solar system, if one is ever

1

discovered. The knowledge that the other nine are called *Mercury, Venus, Earth,* etc., gives us no help at all. But the foreigner learning English will have very definite expectations about the reference of the next item in the list of English number words given above. He will expect it to refer to a number 'one greater' than did the last term given. It is, then, more appropriate to say that the list of English words *one, . . ., nine* REPRESENTS a series or progression and that this progression is one of distinct, yet closely related number concepts.

A foreigner learning English is not at the same time learning arithmetic. He already has a clear idea of the relationships between the concepts underlying the English words *eight, nine, ten*; he is merely learning new names for them. In his own language he uses different names. Every known language has a way of naming at least a few numbers. The notion of numeration and the concepts of particular numbers seem to be universal, i.e. a comprehension of them is accessible to every healthy adult. A theory of language must contain the means for describing how each particular language associates arbitrary phonological sequences (words) with these universal concepts. We need a natural and 'neutral' notation, independent of any particular language, for representing number concepts.

The most natural and neutral form of representation to adopt is one from which one may actually 'count off' the number which is being represented in any given case. Thus, to represent the concept underlying the English word *three*, for example, I shall use three marks /// ; similarly, the meaning of the English word *nine* will be represented as /////////. The actual shape of the marks has no significance; all that is important is the number of marks in a given representation. I shall call these sets of marks 'semantic representations'. The particular form selected for the semantic representations of numbers is entirely appropriate to the nature of the arithmetical operations, such as subtraction, multiplication, etc., in which numbers may be involved. All such operations can be defined in terms of the basic arithmetical operation, namely 'adding one', and this basic operation can be represented simply by the analogical operation, performed on the semantic representations we are proposing, of 'making another mark'. Thus arithmetical operations involving number concepts can be described quite simply if we adopt these semantic representations. These semantic representations are linguistic universals. They will figure in the descriptions of any language which deals with numbers, that is to say of every language.

Just as human beings are universally capable of distinguishing between different number concepts, e.g. between //// and ///, so I assume that they are also universally capable of distinguishing numbers as a class of concepts from all other classes of objects, abstract or otherwise, in the universe. Number concepts are the only ones that may be combined with each other by arithmetical operations such as addition, subtraction, multiplication, and exponentiation. Although little can be said with clarity on the subject, it is certainly clear that number concepts interact with other concepts in a unique way. Colour concepts, for example, do not interact with the concepts of concrete objects in the same way as do number concepts.

Similarly in most, if not all of the world's languages, the phonological sequences (words and longer expressions) which are used to represent number concepts form a class with unique distributional properties. In English, for example, the set of contexts where one might possibly use a number expression, e.g. *six, twenty nine, eight hundred million and two*, etc., is not just that set of contexts in which one might also use an adjective, or a noun, or a verb, or a member of any other recognizable syntactic class. The word which in English comes closest to the number expressions in its distributional properties is probably *many*, but there are contexts in which *many* may be used but where a number expression would be unacceptable. Compare *too many, very many*, and *how many* with **too six, *very six* and **how six*. Again, there are contexts where number expressions may occur, but where *many* may not occur. Compare *exactly six, less than six* and *almost six* with **exactly many, *less than many*, and **almost many*.

We should not be surprised that a unique class of concepts is correlated by a language, and probably by all languages, with a unique class of expressions. This amounts to saying that probably all languages have as a component something that can be called a numeral system, a system distinct from all other systems in the same language. Let us postulate the abstract category NUMBER, representing in the theory of languages generally all that is peculiar to numeral systems as distinct from other language systems, such as the Verb system or the Noun system. Thus to associate a particular phonological form, say English *seven*, in some way with the universal category NUMBER is to express the fact that this form is an element in a numeral system. Similarly, to associate a particular semantic representation, say ///////, with NUMBER is to express the fact that it too is an element in a numeral system. The purpose of this book is to define the correlation between the universal class of number concepts and the class of number expressions found in several languages, and, moreover, to define the correlation in a way that seems likely to be appropriate for all languages. In short, we are setting out to express significant generalizations about NUMBER.

Now it can be argued that the class of number expressions in any given language is infinite. Intuitions of language users differ on the matter of whether the set of number expressions in their language is infinite. The crux of the matter is the question whether the names for very high numbers are in fact wellformed. In English, for example, the expression *two billion billion, five hundred and five* may be felt by some speakers to be quite wellformed, though of course unlikely to be observed, whereas other speakers may object that it is not wellformed. It is significant, however, that there are some high number expressions which are unacceptable for all speakers, e.g. *five trillion thousand and ten.* We shall see later that we can formulate statements which predict accurately that expressions of this latter sort are illformed. These statements will, furthermore, also correctly characterize as illformed certain lower number expressions such as *two hundred hundred* and *twenty ten*, over which there is no disagreement at all between speakers of English. In short, the unacceptability of some high number names seems to be systematic, whereas there does not appear to be such a systematic way of predicting the acceptability of the unclear cases in which there is disagreement between native speakers of the language. It will become obvious as we proceed that the particular systematic characteristics which are evident in natural language number-name systems tend to project the existence of infinite sets of number-names and a higher limit to the value of wellformed number-names can only be stated in a fairly *ad hoc*, arbitrary manner. We need, therefore, some device which is capable of generating, or specifying precisely, the entire set of number-names in a language without actually listing them. The idea of simply listing all the number-names in a language is unacceptable. To do so would be to miss the obvious generalizations which hold true about number-name systems, as we shall see; we are committed, in fact, by the nature of the data to describing an infinite set and it is obviously impossible to make a list of the members of an infinite set.

The set of number concepts is, also, of course, infinite. Therefore we definitely cannot proceed by simply listing the semantic representations of all numbers and correlating each item on the list with its appropriate

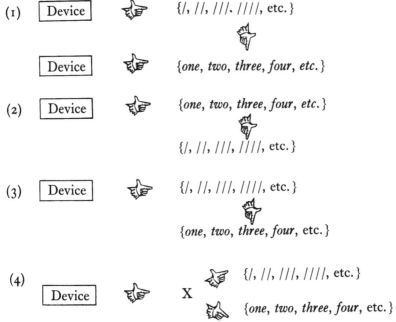

phonological form. We must again postulate some device which is able to generate, or define, the class of semantic representations for number concepts without listing all its members. What we are setting out to do might be represented schematically in a variety of ways. Diagrams (1)–(4) show some of these ways. In diagram (1) separate devices are postulated to define the two infinite sets with which we are dealing and the outputs of these devices are related by a set of statements represented by the downward 'hand' sign. In diagrams (2), (3), and (4), on the other hand, a single device is postulated. In (2) the device is one which specifies an infinite set of number-names for some language and uses this set as the basis for specification of the universal infinite set of semantic representations. In (3) the device generates the universal and infinite set of semantic representations for numbers, which is used as a basis for the specification of the infinite set of number-names in the language we happen to be dealing with. In (4) the device specifies an infinite set of abstract objects which are neither semantic representations nor the phonological specifications of number-names in any language. This set is represented by the letter X. X is used as a basis for the specification of both the infinite sets of semantic and phonological representations.

It should be obvious that the 'hand' signs in diagrams (1)–(4) do not necessarily stand for the same thing. They symbolize only whatever sets of statements are necessary to relate the sets and/or devices between which they are placed in a given diagram. Consider, for example, the set of statements needed to specify the set of number-expressions in a particular language using as a basis the already defined set of universal semantic representations (i.e. the set of statements represented by the downward 'hand' in diagram (3)). This set of statements is not likely to look the same as the set of statements needed to specify the universal set of semantic representations using as a basis the already specified set of number-expressions from some language (i.e. the set of statements represented by the downward 'hand' in diagram (2)). Some of the 'hands' in diagrams (1)–(4) do represent identical sets of statements, e.g. the leftmost hand in (3) and the top leftmost hand in (1).

The descriptive frameworks schematically represented in diagrams (1)–(4) are not the only possible ones, but they are among the most obvious. Two of them, namely (3) and (4), correspond to possible views of what a linguistic description should look like, the rival merits of which are being hotly debated at the time of writing. Diagrams (1) and (2) do not represent views of the way a language description should look that are held by any well-known linguistic theorists and we shall decline to investigate these possibilities. The two possibilities represented by (3) and (4) will, however, continue to concern us. The choice of a particular descriptive framework should not be a matter of the investigator's caprice: rather, it should be dictated by the nature of the data he is analysing. The linguist sets himself the goal of describing a language or some part of it by making true statements of the greatest possible generality, without thereby implying any falsehoods. Since, as we have noted, the sets of statements represented by the 'hands' in diagrams (1)–(4) are not necessarily identical, the individual statements which comprise these sets may quite possibly differ in generality. For example, the individual statements in the set represented by the downward 'hand' in diagram (1) may possibly be necessarily much less general, i.e. much more specific, than the individual statements in the set represented by the bottom rightmost 'hand' in diagram (4). The very nature of the framework presupposed may force some loss of generality. The descriptive framework which permits the expression of all the clearly significant generalizations that hold true about a language is the optimal framework.

Let us look at a concrete and simplified example of the type of problem we are facing. Consider for the moment just the English number-names from *one* to *nine* and the corresponding semantic representations /, ..., /////////. We will temporarily ignore the existence of higher numbers.

A device which has been used in linguistic theory for specifying sets whose members are sequences of identical elements of any length is that of designating the repeated element and marking it with an asterisk. Thus the formula in (5) could be used to generate the infinite set of semantic representations for numbers.

(5) /*

Remembering that we wish to associate each member of the universal set of semantic representations for number concepts with the category NUMBER, we may extend (5) to (6).

(6) NUMBER → /*

For our purposes the arrow sign in (6) may be thought of simply as representing the association we wish to express between NUMBER and each member of the set of semantic representations characterized by the formula /*. A formula such as (6) is known as a *rule schema*. It expresses what otherwise could only be expressed by postulating an infinite number of *rules* of the form (7).

(7) NUMBER → /
     NUMBER → //
     NUMBER → ///
     NUMBER → //// etc.

Rule schema (6) has, as we see, a dual function: it is a device which generates an infinite set of objects (in this case semantic representations) and at the same time associates each of these objects with a linguistic category (in this case the universal category NUMBER). The association between a category and an object (whether it be a semantic representation or not) specified by a rule schema naming that category on the left-hand side of the arrow is conventionally represented in the form of a *phrase marker* or labelled tree diagram. (8) is an example of a phrase

(8) NUMBER

marker derived from rule schema (6). This represents formally the association characterized by (6) between the semantic representation //// and the category NUMBER. An infinite number of such tree diagrams can, of course, be derived from rule schema (6) by means of a simple algorithm. This algorithm provides that for any application of a rule or rule schema the symbol on the left-hand side of the arrow be written and joined by downward lines to each of the elements on the right-hand side specified by that particular application of the rule.

We can now associate with each of the semantic representations from / to ///////// the appropriate English phonological form. (Remember that we are temporarily ignoring the existence of higher numbers.) This association can be expressed formally by simply writing the appropriate phonological form beneath a tree diagram such as (8), thereby simultaneously expressing the desired connection between the phonological form and the category NUMBER. An example of such a statement is (9). A statement such as (9) is known as a *lexicalization*

(9)   NUMBER

six

rule. Phonological sequences such as English *one, two, three, . . ., nine* are known as *lexical items*. To account for English number-names up to *nine* we will obviously need nine lexicalization rules such as (9). These will include, for example, those of (10). If English had no higher number

(10)   (a) NUMBER   (b) NUMBER   (c) NUMBER

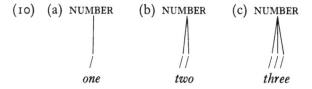

one   two   three

expressions than *nine* we could be content with this description. We have specified the universal set of semantic representations for numbers, associated each such representation with the category NUMBER and provided the necessary rules associating arbitrary phonological forms with semantic representations and the category NUMBER. The nonexistence of any higher number-names is expressed adequately by the nonexistence of any further lexicalization rules. This description, consisting of rule schema (6) and nine lexicalization rules of the form shown in (10), is roughly of the shape shown in diagram (3). Rule schema (6) and the algorithm for constructing phrase markers fulfil the functions of the boxed 'device' and the leftmost 'hand' in (3). The description we have provided does not appear to fail to express any obvious generalizations that hold true of English number-names from *one* to *nine*. For this limited purpose, then, the framework shown in diagram (3) is quite adequate.

Now let us consider another way of stating the same facts. Another method available within linguistic theory of specifying a set with infinite members is to use a rule that is *recursive*. In such a rule the symbol used on the left-hand side of the arrow reappears on the right-hand side along with other elements specified by the rule. A single application of a recursive rule generates a set of elements of which the symbol on the left-hand side of the rule is a member. This symbol can be used as a basis for a second application of the same rule, and so on *ad infinitum*. An example of such a rule is (11).

(11)   NUMBER → / NUMBER

One application of rule (11) and the tree-building algorithm connected with rules produces the phrase marker (12). The lower NUMBER in

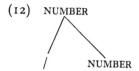

(12)   NUMBER

/   NUMBER

(12) may now be used as a basis for a second application of rule (11), yielding (13). Clearly rule (11) will not be of any use to us unless we have

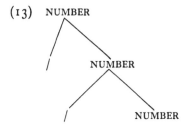

(13)   NUMBER

/   NUMBER

/   NUMBER

some means of stopping it from reapplying *ad infinitum*. If we could not somehow prevent the reapplication of this rule we would only succeed in generating a single phrase marker of infinite size, whereas we want to generate an infinite set of phrase markers of finite size.

To do this we provide for the optional interruption of the cyclic re-application of (11) after any number of applications. That is, we make the presence of NUMBER on the right-hand side of the arrow in (11) optional. The notation conventionally used for this purpose is a pair of parentheses around the optional element. Thus we substitute (14) for (11).

(14)   NUMBER → / (NUMBER)

Rule (14) actually expresses two possibilities: either that the element / is generated or that the sequence / NUMBER is generated on a particular application of the rule. Thus rule (14) together with the tree-building algorithm specifies an infinite set of phrase markers whose members are as in (15). There are a number of ways in which the universal set of

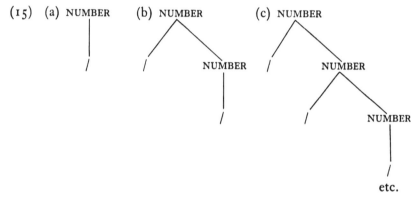

(15)   (a) NUMBER   (b) NUMBER   (c) NUMBER

etc.

semantic representations for numbers can be related to the set of structures as in (15). One simple and obvious way is to postulate a convention which reads off the bottom lines of phrase markers such as those of (15). This convention would correctly relate (15a) to the semantic representation /, (15b) to the semantic representation //, (15c) to ///, and so on. Another way is to postulate a set of conventions by which semantic representations are assigned to phrase markers and their subparts by the application of the arithmetical operation of addition. Let us say that if a NUMBER in a phrase marker is connected by a line to / lower down in the phrase marker and to nothing else, then the semantic representation we assign to that NUMBER is /. Let us also say that if a NUMBER in a phrase marker is joined by lines both to a lower / and to a lower NUMBER, then the semantic representation we assign to the upper NUMBER is that of the sum of / and the semantic representation of the lower NUMBER. These conventions will also correctly assign the semantic representation / to (15a), // to (15b), /// to (15c), and so on.

Since we will be dealing extensively with phrase markers, it is useful to introduce here some of the terminology used for convenience when speaking about phrase markers. Symbols in phrase markers are often referred to as *nodes*. If a node is connected to another node in a phrase marker by a single line, then we say that the higher of the two nodes *immediately dominates* the lower and that the lower node is an *immediate constituent* of the higher one. If some node A immediately dominates another node B, which in turn immediately dominates a further node C, then we may say that A *dominates* C. The relation *dominates* is transitive, so that if a node A dominates a node B and B dominates a node C, then A dominates C. If a node A dominates a node B, then B is a *constituent* of A. In these terms, we can express the conventions for assigning semantic interpretations to phrase markers as (16).

(16) The value of a NUMBER is the arithmetic sum of the values of its immediate constituents.

A statement such as (16) is a *projection rule*.

We can associate phrase markers such as those in (15) to lexical items in much the same way as before. We postulate lexicalization rules such as shown in (17). If we postulate nine such lexicalization rules, one for each of the English number-words from *one* to *nine*, then

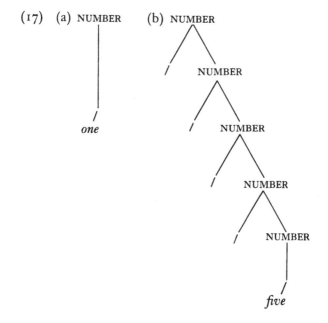

(17) (a) NUMBER (b) NUMBER

apparently we shall again have succeeded in stating all the significant facts about English number-names up to *nine*. In this way the universal set of semantic representations for numbers is characterized, its first nine members are associated with the appropriate arbitrary English phonological forms, and both semantic representations and phonological forms are associated with the category NUMBER. Again, the non-existence of lexicalization rules for further words adequately expresses the limitedness of the artificially restricted English example we are considering.

We have now presented a description of the English number-name system up to *nine* along the lines of the framework shown in diagram (4). Rule (14) and the associated tree-building algorithm correspond to the boxed 'device' and the leftmost 'hand' in (4), the infinite set of objects like those shown in (15) corresponds to the X in (4), the nine lexicalization rules like those of (17) correspond to the lower rightmost 'hand' in (4), and either the 'reading off the bottom line' convention or the projection rule (16) may be said to correspond to the upper rightmost 'hand' in (4). The description we have presented does not appear to fail to express any obvious generalizations that hold true of English number-names from *one* to *nine*. For this limited purpose, then, the descriptive framework shown in diagram (4) is also quite adequate.

If all number-name systems were as simple as, or simpler than, the artificially restricted system we have just been discussing, then the question of which framework of description was preferable would hinge on the relative overall simplicity of each framework. We should have to ask whether the framework of (3) is intrinsically more or less simple than that of (4). The preferable framework would be the simpler one. Such questions of relative simplicity are notoriously difficult to decide but probably most people would say that the framework of (3) is simpler than that of (4).

I must emphasize at this point that we are discussing just the frameworks represented in diagrams (3) and (4) because they appear, on consideration of the results of linguistic research over the past decade, to be the most likely candidates for selection as appropriate to the description of any language system, or indeed of any language. To introduce some more terminology at this convenient point, a descriptive framework as in (3) is frequently referred to as a *generative semantic* framework and a descriptive framework as in (4) as an *interpretive semantic* framework. Projection rules may be referred to as interpretive.

Phrase markers, such as those in (15), which are distinct from semantic representations, although these may be derived from them, are called *deep structures*. Within the generative semantic framework there are no deep structures. Semantic representations are related in a sense more directly, i.e. without the intermediate stage of deep structures (X in diagram (4)), to phonological sequences. Rules, such as (14), which generate deep structures, are known as *phrase structure rules.*

We have seen that an artificially restricted numeral system consisting just of the English numerals from *one* to *nine* provides no decisive evidence for choosing one form of descriptive statement over another. Let us now consider a wider set of data, though still artificially restricted (and distorted) for the sake of simplicity. Imagine some kind of pidgin English in which the expressions for the numbers from 10 through 19 are as follows: *onety, onety one, onety two, onety three, onety four, onety five, onety six, onety seven, onety eight, onety nine.* This variety of English expresses the other numbers up to 99 exactly as they are expressed in Standard English except that 20, 30 and 50 are pidginized to *twoty, threety,* and *fivety* respectively. This pidgin variety of English exhibits in a clear way the regularities which are somewhat disguised in the standard language by forms such as the *-teen* words and *twenty, thirty,* and *fifty.* Let us say that the dialect we are considering here counts only as far as 99. Now we will try to describe this pidgin numeral system within the descriptive framework we have set up in diagram (3).

Working within the framework of diagram (3), we can continue to use the rule schema (6) for generating the set of semantic representations and relating them to NUMBER. Schema (6) will generate the structure (18), which corresponds, in the dialect we are considering, to the expression *onety three.* Schema (6) will generate an infinite number

(18)   NUMBER

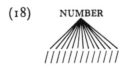

of structures like this and our task is to relate a finite subset of these to the set of expressions from *one* to *ninety nine.* We have already seen how to do this in the case of the numerals from *one* to *nine,* i.e. by the use of lexicalization rules such as those in (10). Now we could postulate another 90 such lexicalization rules to take care of the numbers up to 99. One of these extra lexicalization rules would look like (19). In a

(19)   NUMBER

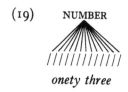

onety three

sense this approach is adequate. It succeeds in specifying the set of semantic representations and relating a subset of these to the appropriate numeral expressions in the dialect we are considering. But linguistics is more ambitious than this. We attempt to describe a language system and make explicit all the significant generalizations that hold true for it. Now with our 99 separate lexicalization rules for the numbers up to 99, we are missing at least one type of significant generalization. The phonological form *onety three*, for example, is quite obviously constructed out of three more basic forms, namely *one*, the suffix *-ty*, and *three*. Yet the lexicalization rule (19) does not make this fact explicit: it treats *onety three* as a single entity. This approach would similarly treat *onety four*, *onety five*, etc. as single entities, essentially neglecting the significant similarity between the subparts of these forms.

We can try to remedy this situation in the following way. We can relate a structure such as (18) to its phonological form in two separate steps. We can use two separate lexicalization rules, one corresponding to *onety* and another corresponding to *three*. We have already seen a rule for *three* in (10c) and this is adequate for our purposes here. The rule for *onety* would look like (20). Now we can envisage that lexicalization

(20)   NUMBER

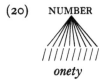

onety

rules apply in sequence, the rule for *onety* applying before that for *three* and applying, moreover, from the left-hand side of a given structure. In this way a structure as in (18) is related in two successive stages to the phonological form *onety three*. The first ten marks of the semantic representation are related to *onety* and the remaining three marks are then related to *three*.

This way of doing things is an improvement and still conforms to the general approach represented in diagram (3). In postulating that lexicalization rules apply in sequence and moreover from the left-hand side of a structure towards the right-hand side we have complicated the set of statements represented by the downward 'hand' in diagram (3), but what we are doing is still essentially what is shown in that diagram. We are generating directly a set of semantic representations and relating it by a set of statements, however complicated, to a set of phonological forms. Though we have complicated the form of the set of statements for relating semantic representations to phonological forms, we have nevertheless achieved some simplification, and hence some generality, as we have now eliminated nine whole lexicalization rules, namely those for *onety one, . . ., onety nine*. We can generalize this approach and reduce further the number of separate lexicalization rules. That is, we can arrange for lexicalization of expressions such as *twoty one, threety eight, fivety six, ninety nine*, etc. to take place also in two stages. In this way, we have only 18 separate lexicalization rules, i.e. those for *one, . . ., nine* and those for *onety, . . ., ninety*. A reduction from 99 to 18 lexicalization rules constitutes a significant simplification of the description and we have, moreover, now succeeded in making explicit the generalization that some numerals are constructed in two parts, e.g. *twoty three* is constructed by putting *twoty* and *three* together.

But the reader will have noticed that we are still missing a generalization just as significant as the one we have managed to capture, namely that forms such as *onety, twoty*, etc. are themselves constructed out of *one, two*, etc. plus the suffix *-ty*. Clearly, although a total of 18 lexicalization rules is an improvement on 99, it is still too many. It is an obvious fact that in the language we are considering there are really only ten separate lexical items, namely *one, . . ., nine*, and the suffix *-ty*. We must find a way around this difficulty.

Let us postulate a mechanism that takes semantic representations generated by schema (6) as input and segments them, beginning from the left-hand side, into groups of ten marks. For each group of ten marks this mechanism then substitutes some symbol, say A. In most cases there will remain after this mechanism has operated some residue at the right-hand end of the semantic representation. Thus, after the operation of this mechanism, the structure for, say, *threety two* would be as in (21).

(21)   NUMBER

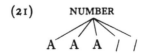

Now we can postulate a lexicalization rule for the suffix -*ty* that attaches it immediately to the right of a string of As after the operation of the mechanism we have postulated. Finally, we must generalize the lexicalization rules for the items *one*, . . ., *nine* so that these items are associated not only with appropriate strings of /s but also with strings of symbols or marks of any kind. In this way the lexical item *three* will be associated with the left-hand end of structure (21) by the generalized version of lexicalization rule (10c) and the item *two* is associated with the right-hand end. The ultimate effect is that structure (21) is associated with the expression *threety two*, as desired.

Now we have just ten lexicalization rules, namely those for *one*, . . ., *nine* and that for the suffix -*ty*. We have not missed making explicit in our description any significant generalizations that hold true of the data we are considering. But we have incurred a certain 'cost' in the complexity of our description in that we have been obliged to postulate certain 'mechanisms' and conventions pertaining to the method of application of the lexicalization rules. We have, that is, in trying to construct a theory about a set of data, been forced by the nature of the data to accept a certain complexity or richness in our theory.

I have given an example, within a generative semantic framework (i.e. as in diagram (3)), of how a linguist arrives at postulating certain theoretical constructs in preference to other logically possible ones (or simply not postulating anything). We have seen how certain constructs can be claimed, within a given framework, to be 'correct' in that they make it possible to express significant generalizations about language. It should also be possible to evaluate the rival merits of different 'frameworks', e.g. diagram (3) vs diagram (4), on exactly the same sort of grounds, since 'frameworks' are in fact just a rather basic kind of theoretical construct. The question of whether generative (diagram (3)) or interpretive (diagram (4)) semantics is the correct framework for the description of natural languages is the subject of much heated debate within linguistics, and it is a topic in which convincing evidence on either side of the argument seems especially hard to find.

The theoretical debate is very much complicated by several factors. In the first place, I have oversimplified the issue by implying that there are just two rival schools of thought, whose positions are illustrated in diagrams (3) and (4). In fact there are a number of intersecting, partly independent, partly interdependent issues, which I shall not confuse the reader by enumerating. Secondly, one cannot always be sure that two 'rival' theories are not in fact the same theory, expressed in different, though equivalent, notations. That is, for every statement in one theory, there may be a statement in the other theory which in effect makes explicit the same significant generalization, and vice versa. Languages, and correspondingly the theoretical constructs postulated by linguists, appear to be so complicated that it is not always easy to discern what are merely notational issues and what are not. Thirdly, we are not yet, nor will we be for a long time to come, in the position of having 'all the data' at our command. Linguists understandably seek out and cite data that tend to confirm, rather than disprove, the particular hypotheses they have an interest in. And frequently other linguists have only to dig around a little before they can come up with 'counterevidence' to these hypotheses. This is not to say that linguistic theorists are dishonest: but it is to say that they are often hasty.

We are in a position, then, of being able to reject some forms of description, of theoretical construct, as clearly incorrect, while being unable to arbitrate between rival forms of description in other cases. For example, if, in the generative semantic example I have used, we were to postulate that the mechanism for counting off groups of ten marks operated from the right-hand end of a semantic representation instead of from the left, that would clearly be incorrect, since it would predict the existence of forms such as *two threety* and would neglect the obvious fact that there are forms such as *threety two*. Again, if the description contained no such counting mechanism, but simply a long list of repetitive lexicalization rules, that would also be incorrect, as we have seen, for it would miss the obviously significant generalization that the numerals from *onety* to *ninety nine* are made up by putting together basic forms such as *one*, *nine*, and *-ty*. But on the other hand, the fundamental matter of the correct overall descriptive framework remains in the air.

In the ensuing chapters, in order to maintain what I think is the correct balance between an emphasis on data and an emphasis on theory, I have explored a variety of numeral systems which exhibit a rather wide range of 'exotic' (i.e. un-English) characteristics, besides several more 'typical' numeral systems. I have never given more than one analysis of a particular numeral system and each system is described within the same theoretical framework. I have, in other words, developed in as much detail as possible a single theoretical framework for the description of numeral systems and am satisfied that this framework makes it possible to capture all the types of significant generalization about numerals of which I am aware. The descriptions, furthermore, are not more complex than is demanded by the data. I have not adhered exclusively to any particular 'standard' theory current at the moment and the descriptive framework developed in the following chapters is quite eclectic and rich. This, I believe, is also demanded by the nature of the data. In reading on, then, the reader should constantly ask himself the following questions. Does this statement (or rule, or convention, or algorithm) make explicit a significant linguistic generalization? Does this description leave unexpressed any significant linguistic generalization? In what other ways, if any, could this generalization be made explicit?

2 The syntax and semantics of English numerals

The descriptive framework illustrated in (1) overleaf is adequate for describing the English numeral system and expressing all the significant generalizations that hold true of it. Boxes represent various sets of rules, or descriptive statements; arrows represent input and output of these sets of rules; broken lines between boxes indicate connections or dependencies between sets of rules.

2.1 The phrase structure rules

The phrase structure rules (the Base) appropriate to English number-names are given, in the familiar notation, in (2).

(2) (a)

$$\text{NUMBER} \rightarrow \left\{ \begin{array}{c} / \\ \text{PHRASE} \end{array} \right\} \text{(NUMBER)}$$

(b) PHRASE $\rightarrow$ NUMBER M

(c)

$$\text{M} \rightarrow \left\{ \begin{array}{c} ////////// \\ \text{NUMBER M} \end{array} \right\}$$

2.1.1. Terminal vocabulary. The symbols NUMBER, PHRASE, and M in these rules are syntactic category symbols. The symbol / is actually the semantic representation corresponding to the English word *one*; the symbol ////////// is the semantic representation corresponding to the word *ten* or the bound morphs *-ty* and *-teen*. It will be noticed that these semantic representations do not occur on the left-hand side of phrase structure rules, whereas each of the syntactic category symbols does so occur. The semantic representations / and ////////// constitute, then, the terminal vocabulary of this phrase structure grammar. These

19

(1) semantic representations

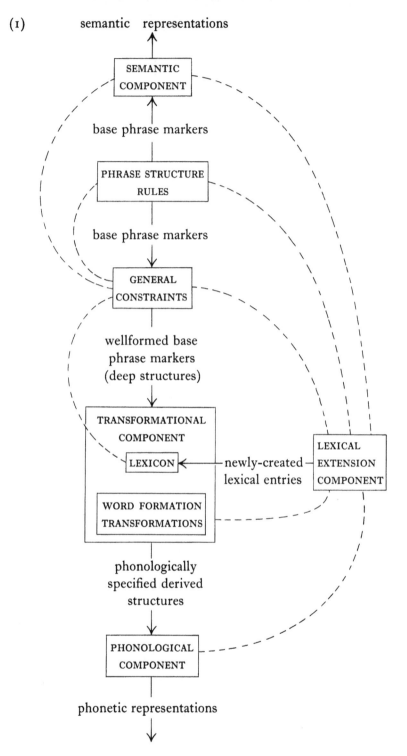

The various components in this diagram will be explained and justified
in detail in the ensuing sections of this chapter.

are not, of course, the only semantic representations generated by the grammar; the rest of the infinite set of semantic representations is projected by the interpretive semantic component, of which more will be said later. The inclusion of the semantic representations / and ////////// in the base component of the grammar reflects the obvious fact that the concepts behind English *one* and *ten* play a special role in the formation of English number-names. The concept behind *one*, of course, has a special role to play in any number-name system and it is true of the base component of the number-name grammar of any language that it explicitly specifies the semantic representation /. The majority of languages will also have in the base components of their number-name grammars the semantic representation //////////, since most languages use this number concept as a basis for higher counting.

At this stage, a word should be said about the nature of the semantic representations assumed here, although these will be dealt with more elaborately later. I assume the semantic representation of any positive whole number *n* to be *n* marks on whatever material medium we can agree to talk about. Linguists who prefer to think of linguistic de-scriptions as abstractions bearing no necessary relation to human physiology or psychology will surely be prepared to talk about marks on paper and linguists who see grammars as abstract approximations of systems realized physically (in some way) in human brains can also agree to talk about marks on paper with the mental reservation that what they are really talking about is something much more exciting. Let us say, then, that the semantic representation of *one* is /, that of *two* is //, that of *three* is ///, and so on *ad infinitum*. In these terms, the semantic representation assigned to *one million* would be a million marks on the medium and the semantic representation of *zero* would be a complete absence of marks. For obvious reasons, I will use Arabic notation when speaking of semantic representations, but it is to be understood as an informal means of abbreviating representations consisting solely of a number of identical marks. Clearly, no significance attaches to the particular size, shape, or colour of the marks we choose to use and the choice of / here is quite arbitrary.

The number-name grammars of some languages will refer explicitly in their base components to the semantic representations 2 (e.g. some Australian languages), 5 (e.g. Ainu, Khmer, Bantu languages), and 20 (e.g. French, Danish, Welsh, Ainu, Yoruba, Mixtec) reflecting the fact that these numbers play an obviously quite special role in the number-name systems of these languages. In a tiny minority of languages numbers other than 2, 5, 10 and 20 play such a special role as the basis (or one of the bases) of the number-name system. Note that the terminal vocabulary of the phrase structure rules (2) for English does not include the semantic representations 100, 1,000, or 1,000,000, as might possibly be expected. It will be shown later that the significance of these concepts is derivative from the fundamental significance of 10.

While it can be shown that just two number concepts, 1 and 10, play a special role in the English number-name system, i.e. that these are elemental concepts around which the system is organized, it cannot similarly be shown that there are just two basic phonological formatives which act as the building blocks out of which any English number-name can be constructed. The phonological shapes of the items *two*, *three*, *four*, ..., *nine*, *hundred*, and *thousand*, for example, cannot be predicted by any system of rules on the basis of just the two forms *one* and *ten*. The vocabulary of morphemes on which the English number-name system draws to construct long number expressions is obviously more extensive than the terminal vocabulary of the base, consisting of the two elemental concepts, 1 and 10, of the phrase structure grammar. Semantic representations of elemental significance are introduced, as we have seen, by the phrase structure rules; phonological information is introduced by a lexical attachment component, which I shall describe later.

2.1.2 Recursivity. The phrase structure rules (2) are recursive in four separate ways. The symbol NUMBER recurs in each of the three rules and the symbol M is also recursive. Transformational grammarians have traditionally been cautious with the use of recursion, but I believe that each use made of recursion in (2) can be justified. Recursion is a device which allows one to express the fact that a construction of a certain type has as a constituent a construction of the same type. The recursion of NUMBER in rule (2a), for example, allows one to express in a natural way the fact that (3) is a number-name, some of whose constituents are (4), (5), (6), and (7), all of which are also number-names.

(3)   one million, one thousand, one hundred and twenty one
(4)   one thousand, one hundred and twenty one
(5)   one hundred and twenty one

(6)   twenty one
(7)   one

As an example of a base phrase marker generated by the rules of (2), I give (8), which is the structure underlying the expression (4), and which illustrates the recursion of the node NUMBER in rule (2a).

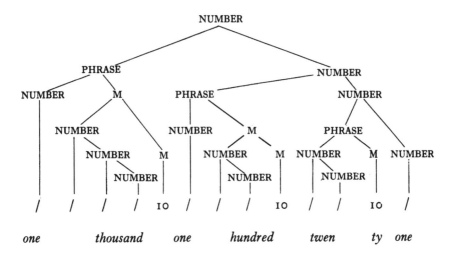

The English words below this tree structure are only included for convenience. They are not, of course, generated by the rules of (2).

The recursion of NUMBER in rule (2a) also allows one to capture a less transparent, but no less significant generalization. The English number-names after and including *ten* are analysed as containing PHRASES. Only the number-names *one, two, three, four, ..., nine* do not contain PHRASES. The semantic representations corresponding to these one-word expressions are /, //, ///, ////, ..., ///////// respectively. Simply to list these semantic representations in a phrase structure rule would be to fail to express the obvious similarity between them. The recursive use of NUMBER in rule (2a) expresses the fact that each successive semantic representation has just one more / than the last. Thus the underlying structure generated by the grammar for the English word *five*, for example, is (9). It might be thought that the similarity between the semantic representations corresponding to the English number-words from *one* to *nine* could be expressed better by an iterative rule schema, as in (10), rather than by recursion.

(9)   NUMBER

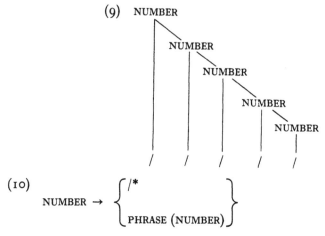

(10)

NUMBER → { /*
           PHRASE (NUMBER) }

If we adopted this rule instead of rule (2a), the structure underlying *five*, for example, would be as in (11). I do not think it is valid to argue

(11)   NUMBER

that rule (10) must be preferred to rule (2a) because structures generated by the former, such as (11), are simpler than structures generated by the latter, for example (9). Judgments of simplicity are notoriously deceptive; it is not true in this case that counting nodes in a tree diagram is a measure of simplicity that is likely to lead to significant generalizations about language. Indeed, it can be shown that postulation of 'more complex' structures such as (9), in preference to 'simpler' structures, such as (11), facilitates the expression of two significant generalizations about number-names. Both these generalizations can be expressed far more succinctly if it is postulated that a NUMBER has at most two immediate constituents, as in (9). These generalizations will be discussed in later sections; one has to do with the operation of the interpretive semantic component and the other has to do with 'deep structure constraints' or criteria for rejecting certain phrase markers generated by (2), but which do not correspond to wellformed English number-names. If these arguments are accepted in advance, the recursive use of NUMBER in rule (2a) can be said to be fully justified.

The strings *one million, one thousand,* and *one hundred* in (3) are analysed as constituents labelled PHRASE by this grammar. (The words *million, thousand*, and *hundred* belong to the category M.) It is clear that PHRASES can have whole number-names as constituents. Consider these examples:

(12) two thousand, three hundred and forty five million

(13) three hundred and forty five $\begin{Bmatrix} \text{thousand} \\ \text{million} \end{Bmatrix}$

(14) forty five $\begin{Bmatrix} \text{hundred} \\ \text{thousand} \\ \text{million} \end{Bmatrix}$

(15) five $\begin{Bmatrix} \text{hundred} \\ \text{thousand} \\ \text{million} \end{Bmatrix}$

The obvious generalization here is captured by the recursive use of the symbol NUMBER in the rule expanding PHRASE.

(16) below is the structure generated by the rules of (2) corresponding

(16)

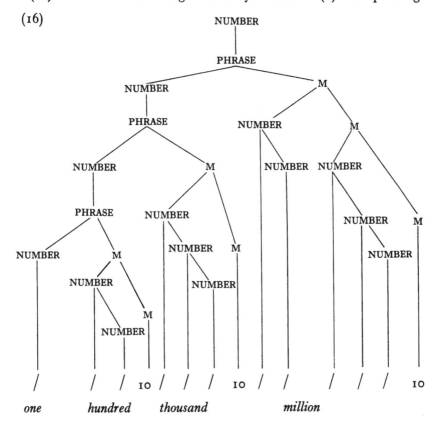

to the British English expression *one hundred thousand million*, and illustrating the recursion of the node NUMBER in the second rule. Again, the English words below the diagram are included only for convenience. The phonological forms of words are not at this stage associated with the base phrase markers generated by the rules of (2).

The recursive use of NUMBER in rule (2c) also captures a significant, though minor, generalization. M is the category to which *hundred, thousand, million, billion, trillion,* etc., belong. These words all represent powers of 10, and the series *million, billion, trillion,* etc., all represent powers (in American English) of 1,000 or (in British English) of 1,000,000. For concreteness, let us discuss the case of American English. The structure underlying *thousand* in this grammar is as in (17). The

(17)

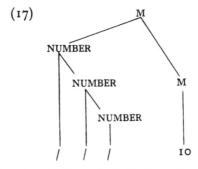

structure underlying *hundred* is as in (18). Postulating these structures

(18)

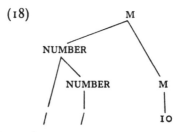

expresses the significant fact that *hundred* and *thousand* represent the second and third powers respectively of the base number 10. This fact could also be expressed by a rule such as (19).

(19)

$$M \to \left\{ \begin{matrix} 10 \\ \left\{ \begin{matrix} // \\ /// \end{matrix} \right\} \quad M \end{matrix} \right\}$$

But rule (19) fails to express a minor generalization, namely that of the similarity between the two semantic representations $//$ and $///$. This can be captured by using the symbol NUMBER recursively rather than listing the semantic representations $//$ and $///$ separately. There is in fact some slightly better evidence than this for the recursion of NUMBER in rule (2c). The words *million, billion,* and *trillion* represent the second, third, and fourth powers of 1,000 respectively. Structures built along the same lines as (17) and (18) can be generated to express these facts. The rule that generates them can either, as rule (19), list separately the values $//$, $///$, and $////$, or it can express the obvious similarity between them by using the recursive symbol NUMBER to generate the structures which in other contexts underlie *two, three,* and *four.* Most people's vocabularies of number-words do not go beyond *trillion,* but for those dialects in which terms like *quadrillion, quintillion, ...,* *decillion* are used, the force of this argument is stronger. In such dialects there are quite a number of successive powers of 1,000. It is in general true that if a dialect has a word for the nth power of 1,000, then it also has a word for the n-1th power of 1,000, where $n > 1$. The 1959 edition of Webster's *New Collegiate Dictionary,* for example, gives forms for each successive power of 1,000 up to the twenty-first, which it calls a *vigintillion.* Many other dictionaries of American English give forms for each successive power of 1,000 up to the eleventh, called a *decillion.* Parallel statements can be made about the successive powers of 1,000,000 in British English. The fact of this succession is expressed by using the recursive symbol NUMBER.

Finally, the recursion of the category M in rule (2c) also expresses a significant linguistic generalization. Items in the category M, which can be defined both in terms of syntactic distribution and in terms of semantic interpretation, as we shall see, do not represent all the possible powers of the base number, 10. There are systematic gaps. In American English, for example, there are forms for powers of 10 up to the third power. The form representing the third power of 10, namely *thousand,* belongs to the category M. After 1,000, the only powers of 10 for which forms exist are powers of 1,000; these forms, e.g. *million, billion,* etc., also belong to the category M. Thus we see that the higher-valued Ms must be specified not in terms of the base number, 10, but in terms of an M of intermediate value; this M of intermediate value is in its turn specified in terms of the base number, 10. This significant fact is expressed by the recursion of the symbol M in rule (2c). The facts of British English provide stronger evidence for the recursion of M. Here the 'first tier' of MS, namely *hundred* and *thousand* can be specified in terms of the base number, 10. The 'second tier' consisting of the word *million*, is specified as a power of a lower M, namely *thousand*, and the members of the 'third tier' of MS are specified as powers of *million*.

The facts I have mentioned justify the extensive use of recursion in the phrase structure grammar (2). The means by which the generative power of this grammar is curtailed will be discussed later. It will be shown that some quite general principles exist which define the conditions under which structures generated by the rules of (2) correspond to wellformed number-names. That is, the generative capacity of the rules of (2) is not counterevidence to their validity, as general statements can be made restricting this generative capacity. Most of these restrictive statements express significant generalizations about number-names, as we shall see, and their postulation is, therefore, in general, not *ad hoc*.

Provided, then, that they can be integrated with the rest of the description of English numerals, the phrase structure rules in (2) appear to be well-motivated.

2.2 The interpretive semantic component

I shall now describe the operation of the interpretive semantic component necessary to assign language-independent semantic representations to the base phrase markers generated by the rules (2). Language-independent semantic representations are necessary to provide the theory of numerals with the power to characterize numerals in one language as translations of numerals in another, even though the two expressions in question might have distinct base phrase markers. As we discuss the numeral systems of languages other than English in later chapters, we shall encounter many examples of numerals whose translatability into English expressions is captured in the theory by the assignation to the numerals in each language of common language-independent semantic representations of the type assumed in this study.

Within particular languages, additional justification for a component assigning semantic representations such as we assume here is provided by certain constraints on the wellformedness of base phrase markers. These constraints, which we shall discuss in a later section for English, and in later chapters for other languages, frequently make use of arithmetical notions such as 'is greater than' and 'is less than or equal to'. These notions are easily related to semantic representations such as /, //, ///, ////, etc., but it is not clear how they could be defined in any natural and simple way if use is not made of these representations.

Examples of structures generated by the rules of (2) are (20)–(22), corresponding to *twenty three*, *twenty*, and *thousand* respectively.

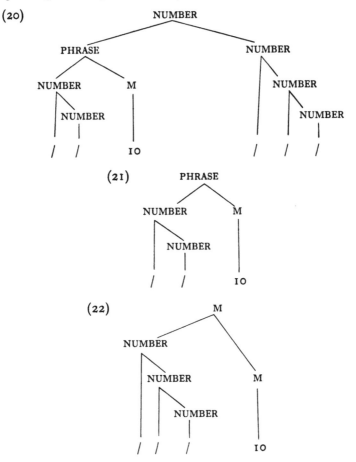

(20)

(21)

(22)

It is clear from these examples that three 'projection rules' are sufficient to assign semantic representations to structures generated by (2). These three projection rules can be stated as in (23).

(23) The value of a NUMBER is the sum of the values of its immediate constituents.

The value of a PHRASE is the product of the values of its immediate constituents.

The value of an M is the result of raising the value of its second
immediate constituent to the power of the value of its first
immediate constituent.

One could let the matter of the semantic component rest there, with
three separate projection rules postulated, but to do so would be to
ignore some impressive similarities between the processes by which
NUMBERS, PHRASES, and MS are assigned semantic values. The operations
of addition, multiplication and exponentiation are all defined in terms
of simpler operations, and ultimately all in terms of the basic arithmetical
operation, counting or incrementing iteratively by 1.

Thus to add x and y, one simply increments the value of y by 1 x
times. To multiply x and y, one adds y to itself $x - 1$ times. And to raise
y to the xth power, one multiplies y by itself $x - 1$ times. Describing
addition, multiplication and exponentiation in procedural terms
emphasizes the similarity between them. I give such descriptions
below. ((INCREMENT 1) = 2, (INCREMENT 2) = 3, etc. DECREMENT is
the converse of INCREMENT: (DECREMENT 1) = ø, (DECREMENT 3) = 2,
etc.)

(24)   (ADD x y) declare z as a variable for use in the pro-
                      cedure
                  set z to the value of y
              A if x = ø, return z as the value of the pro-
                      cedure
                  set z to (INCREMENT z)
                  set x to (DECREMENT x)
                  go back to the instruction labelled A and
                      continue
           (MULTIPLY x y) declare z as a variable for use in the pro-
                      cedure
                  set z to the value of y
              A if x = 1, return z as the value of the pro-
                      cedure
                  set z to (ADD z y)
                  set x to (DECREMENT x)
                  go back to the instruction labelled A and
                      continue

(EXPONENTIATE x y) declare z as a variable for use in the procedure

set z to the value of y

A if $x = 1$, return z as the value of the procedure

set z to (MULTIPLY z y)

set x to (DECREMENT x)

go back to the instruction labelled A and continue

The similarities here make it obvious that we should try to express the semantic interpretation of number-names as a single complex process, rather than as the three unrelated processes embodied in our three projection rules. (The procedure for addition could actually be described slightly more economically, using no procedure variable, but the similarity between addition and the other arithmetic operations is hardly less striking if this is done.)

Note that the arithmetical operations are ordered in complexity. The most simple operation is INCREMENT; next in complexity is ADD, followed by MULTIPLY and EXPONENTIATE, in that order. Note further that the definitions of the three more complex operations each refer to the operation one degree less complex at a certain point. Thus the description of EXPONENTIATE contains the statement 'set z to (MULTIPLY z y)' and so on. Now observe further that the degree of complexity of the arithmetical operation needed to interpret a constituent of a number-name phrase marker corresponds to the 'depth' of that constituent within the phrase marker. We can say that there are three degrees of depth in a phrase marker generated by application of all three phrase structure rules used here. Let us say that a NUMBER is a constituent at depth 1, a PHRASE a constituent at depth 2, and an M a constituent at depth 3. We can now define a general operation which I shall call CALCULATE. This operation is defined in essentially the same way as those defined above, except that it is sensitive to the depth of the constituent on which it operates. Thus where the other operations defined above refer at one stage in their definitions to the next less complex operation, the operation CALCULATE will refer to itself applied at the next lower degree of depth.

I shall define CALCULATE as an operation taking four arguments. The first argument may be either a +sign or a −sign and will barely concern us here. It is used to account for the interpretation of numerals in languages which make use of subtraction and division and will be explained more fully in chapter 5. The other arguments of operation CALCULATE as I shall define it are d, an index of the depth of the constituent being interpreted, and x and y as before, the two elements to be arithmetically combined in some way. I shall treat the operation I have called INCREMENT simply as a special case of the general operation CALCULATE, i.e. as operation CALCULATE applied at depth zero. Whereas addition, multiplication, and exponentiation involve two arithmetic values, the operation of incrementation by one involves but a single value. Therefore we postulate that when the general operation CALCULATE is applied at depth zero, the fourth argument is either irrelevant or is omitted. Thus the operation (INCREMENT 5), for example, is now stated as (CALCULATE $+ \emptyset$ 5 n), for any value of n, or simply as (CALCULATE $+ \emptyset$ 5). The operation I have referred to as DECREMENT I shall treat as the 'converse' of INCREMENT, indicating this by the use of a 'minus', rather than a 'plus' sign as the first argument of operation CALCULATE. Thus what we previously expressed as (DECREMENT 5), for example, we can now write either as (CALCULATE $- \emptyset$ 5 n), where n may again have any value, or simply as (CALCULATE $- \emptyset$ 5).

(CALCULATE $+ \emptyset$ x n) is not defined, except pragmatically as 'making another mark'. The value of (CALCULATE $+ \emptyset$ x n) for any x is here taken to be given *a priori*. (CALCULATE $- \emptyset$ x n) is defined as follows:

(25) If and only if (CALCULATE $+ \emptyset$ x n) $=$ z, (CALCULATE $- \emptyset$ z n) $=$ x

We shall see in ch. 5, where we discuss subtraction and division, that definition (25) is actually a special case of a more general definition that can be given with the notation that we are developing. Here, now, is the proposed definition of the general operation CALCULATE.

(26) (CALCULATE $+ d$ x y) declare z as a variable to be used in the
procedure
set z to the value of y
A if d $=$ 1 and x $=$ $\emptyset$, or if $d \neq$ 1 and x $=$ 1,
return z as the value of the procedure
otherwise,
set z to (CALCULATE $+$ (CALCULATE $- \emptyset$ d) z y)
set x to (CALCULATE $- \emptyset$ x)
go back to A and continue

The reader can check for himself that this operation works correctly, so defined. Thus (CALCULATE + 1 3 2) = 5; (CALCULATE + 2 3 2) = 6; (CALCULATE + 3 2 3) = 9. As an example of the operation of CALCULATE, let us 'compute' the value of 3^2. Below is a record of the values to which each variable is set during the procedure. The operation CALCULATE is, of course, called a number of times, at different depths.

(27)

$$(CALCULATE + 3\ 2\ 3)\quad x = 2, 1$$
$$y = 3$$
$$d = 3$$
$$z = 3, 9 \rightarrow \text{value of procedure}$$

$$(CALCULATE + 2\ 3\ 3)\quad x = 3, 2, 1$$
$$y = 3$$
$$d = 2$$
$$z = 3, 6, 9$$

$$(CALCULATE\ 1\ 3\ 3)\quad x = 3, 2, 1, \emptyset$$
$$y = 3$$
$$d = 1$$
$$z = 3, 4, 5, 6$$

$$(CALCULATE + 1\ 6\ 3)\quad x = 6, 5, 4, 3, 2, 1, \emptyset$$
$$y = 3$$
$$d = 1$$
$$z = 3, 4, 5, 6, 7, 8, 9$$

It should be remembered that we are using Arabic notation as an abbreviation for a cumbersome, but theoretically more significant notation for semantic representations. The 'basic' operation (CALCULATE + ø x) in terms of which operation CALCULATE is defined, can be thought of as adding a /. Thus the output of operation CALCULATE is always a sequence of /s, a member of the universal set of semantic representations for numbers. Operation CALCULATE is itself a universal, being relevant to the interpretation of numeral base phrase markers in any language. Operation CALCULATE is actually a basic part of a theory of 'natural mathematics' and to say that it is relevant to the interpretation of numerals in any language is merely to give an example of the not surprising fact that numeral systems generally are organized in accordance with the principles of what we can call 'natural mathematics'. We must now provide several statements showing how the mathematical operation CALCULATE is related specifically to the numeral system of English.

Operation CALCULATE is sensitive, not only to the values of the two immediate constituents of the constituent to which it applies, but also to the depth of that constituent. The depth of constituents must therefore be marked in phrase markers to which operation CALCULATE is to apply. This can be done by a convention associated with the application of the phrase structure rules.

(28)   Where there exists a phrase structure rule X → Y Z, and X is a constituent at depth *n*, all Ys and Zs in the phrase structure rules are marked as constituents at depth *n* + 1 unless they have already been assigned a depth by a previous application of this convention. All NUMBERS in phrase structure rules are assigned depth 1.

We can now formulate a single very general projection rule as a substitute for the three rules of (23). This rule states that the value of

$$(29) \qquad \begin{array}{c} X_d \\ \diagup \ \diagdown \\ x \qquad y \end{array} \qquad = (\text{CALCULATE} + d \; x \; y)$$

any constituent with depth *d* and immediate constituents with values *x* and *y* is to be computed by the formula (CALCULATE + *d* *x* *y*). To rule (29) should be added the convention that the value assigned to any node which has but a single immediate constituent is the value of the constituent.

The systematic relationship between the series of prefixes *bi-*, *tri-*, etc., and the series of simple numbers 2, 3, etc., is certainly a generalization worth capturing, but it is a generalization which is somewhat disguised in the American English number-name system. In American English all words ending in *-illion* have a structure containing as a subtree the structure for *thousand*; the correspondences between the prefixes and the appropriate powers of 1,000 are as follows:

(30)   bi-   3
     tri-   4
     quadri-   5
     quinti-   6   etc.

There obviously is a systematic relationship between the series of prefixes and the series of simple numbers here, but it is not the same relationship as that which obtains with all other uses of these prefixes. A grammar of American English must contain a statement to the effect that in the number-name system the normal relationships between these prefixes and the simple numbers are skewed by one digit. This can be done by an idiosyncratic statement applying after rule (29) and before the operation CALCULATE.

(31)   If $d = 3$ and $y > 10$, set x to (CALCULATE $+ \varnothing \; x$)

This rule is applicable just once in a given derivation, of course. With this statement in the grammar of American English the value $1,000^3$, for example, is assigned to structure (32) underlying *billion*, a treatment which is linguistically quite appropriate. Rule (31) expresses an obvious

(32)

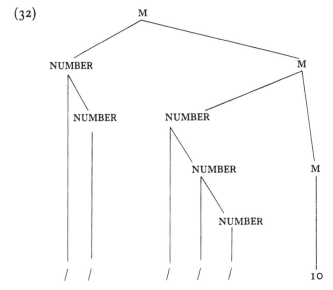

fact about American English in a clear way. The grammar of British English does not contain this rule.

Although the idea of an interpretive semantic component has been the subject of much debate, I believe that the interpretive semantic component proposed here for the grammar of English number-names is the first of which it can legitimately be claimed that it is clearly appropriate and complete. Projection rules proposed in the past have been tentative and programmatic.

Note that operation CALCULATE combines just two arithmetic values at whatever level (except at depth zero). The generalization expressed by operation CALCULATE and by the general projection rule (29) is only statable if it is the case that constituents of number-names at any level never have more than two subconstituents. This is one piece of evidence in favour of the first rule of (2) and structures such as (9) as opposed to rule (10) and structures such as (11). Structure (9), but not structure (11), is interpretable by rule (29) and operation CALCULATE, since the NUMBER in structure (11) has more than two immediate constituents.

2.3   The lexicon

This component of the grammar is responsible for attaching idiosyncratic phonological forms and syntactic specifications to constituents of phrase markers generated by the phrase structure rules. In the discussion that follows I shall at first be concerned only with the attachment of phonological forms and will leave the matter of idiosyncratic syntactic specifications until last. The lexicon, or lexical attachment component, comprises a set of lexicalization rules, or lexical entries; for these rules I use a modification of the notation proposed by Gruber (1967). Two simple lexical entries are given in (33) and (34). Rule (33)

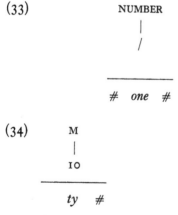

(33)   NUMBER

states the association between the structure specified above the line and the phonological form here represented as *one*. In constructing the derivation of a numeral expression, rule (33) is to be taken as an instruction to attach the phonological form *one* to any structure identical to that specified in the rule. This attachment is here represented by writing the phonological form below the entire structure, although writing it just below (or above) the NUMBER node would be equally satisfactory.

The essential claim being made by a rule such as (33) is that a given phonological form is associated with a given structure in its entirety and not just with some part (e.g. the 'bottom line') of that structure.

The two # signs in rule (33) are word boundary symbols, indicating that *one* is a word, rather than an affix. The introduction of word boundary symbols in this way is my own slight modification of Gruber's notation. These symbols are not introduced automatically, but are part of the idiosyncratic information given about each phonological formative by its lexicalization rule. In diagram (34), for example, which is the lexicalization rule for -*ty*, as in English *forty*, *fifty*, *sixty*, etc., only one word boundary symbol is introduced, after the formative. This indicates that -*ty* is a suffix.

At present this method of marking word boundaries, i.e. as idiosyncratic properties of phonological formatives listed in the lexicon, seems as likely to be correct as any other proposal of which I am aware, but a great deal more research needs to be done before an adequate theory can be put forward on this matter. The symbol # is the symbol used by Gruber and by Chomsky and Halle in *The Sound Pattern of English* to mark word boundaries. Chomsky and Halle remark that these boundaries must in some cases be deleted by irregular 'readjustment rules'. The example they give is of the vowel alternation manifested in the words *keep* and *kept*. They point out that the preconsonantal laxing evident in *kept* can only take place if the word boundary at the end of the verb *keep*, which separates it from the past tense morpheme, is deleted at some stage prior to the application of the laxing rule. It seems that something of the sort must also take place with some English number names. *Five*, for example, is definitely a word when used in isolation. Its lexical entry would have, below the line, #*five*#. The final word boundary here must be deleted in some cases. In the case where *five* occurs in a PHRASE immediately before -*ty*, the word boundary is not present. The evidence for this is the tense/lax vowel alternation and the voiced/unvoiced consonant alternation seen in *five* and *fifty*. Similarly the word boundary is not present when *five* turns up before -*teen*. Elsewhere *five* is a word and the final boundary is present. I will discuss the word formation processes of English number-names in more detail later. I wish only to claim here that the method of introducing word boundaries, some of which may later be deleted, by lexicalization rules is at least observationally adequate.

Consider now the lexical items *two*, *three*, *four*, ..., *nine*. Clearly the structures associated with these words are significantly similar and clearly also they are ordered in a natural hierarchy between 'highest' and 'lowest'. For these reasons lexical entries such as are given in (35) would not be satisfactory. These hypothetical lexicalization rules,

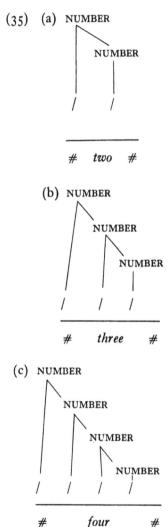

besides being implausibly cumbersome, do not explicitly capture the significant relationships between *two, three, four*, etc. A grammar should make explicit the fact that the existence of the lexical item *four* is in some way dependent on the existence of the 'more basic' item *three*,

and so on. I therefore adopt a format for lexicalization rules as in (36)–
(38). Taking rule (36) as an example, the structure specified above the

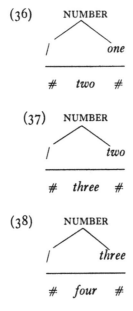

(36)   NUMBER

   /   *one*

———————————

  #   *two* #

(37)   NUMBER

   /   *two*

———————————

  # *three* #

(38)   NUMBER

   /   *three*

———————————

  # *four* #

line is in fact exactly the same as that specified in the hypothetical rule
(35a), but in (36) the notation expresses the significant systematic
relationship between *one* and *two*. In acquiring a competence in the
numeral system of English one could not master the use of *two* without
prior mastery of the use of *one*. This is reflected in the lexical entry
(36). Lexical entries as expressed in (36)–(38) are also simpler than the
hypothetical entries (35). This simplification becomes even more apparent if one considers the alternative ways of expressing the lexicalization
rule for *nine*, i.e. as in (39) and (40) overleaf.

Now consider the items *ten, eleven*, and *twelve*. Let us ignore for the
moment the possibility that *eleven* and *twelve* are in fact bi-morphemic,
i.e. let us say that the presence of *tw-* in both *twelve* and *two* and the
occurrence of both *l* and *v* in *eleven* and *twelve* are without significance.
Eleven and *twelve*, then, are to be treated as single lexical items. The
phrase structure rules generate two structures having each of the values
10, 11, and 12. Consequently we are faced with a choice between two sets
of lexicalization rules for *ten, eleven* and *twelve*, i.e. as in (41) and (42)
(p. 41). Rules (42) treat *ten, eleven*, and *twelve* as a straightforward extension of the series *one, two, . . ., eight, nine*. Rules (41), on the other hand,

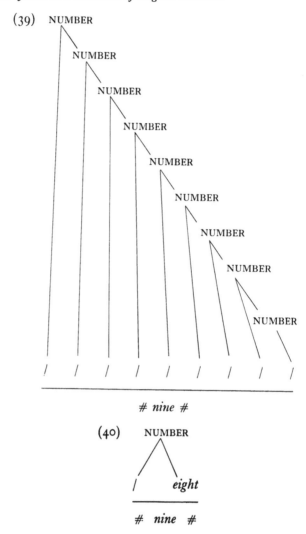

(39)

nine

(40)

nine

treat these as items with a different type of underlying structure from the items of the series *one, . . . nine*, in that they contain a PHRASE. We shall see that there are some reasons for preferring rules (42).

For the arithmetic values between 11 and 19, English has single lexical items for just the lowest two. We could perhaps conceive of a language L identical in all respects to English except that it counted the values from 11 to 19 as follows: *oneteen, twoteen, thirteen, blimp, fifteen, sixteen, glomp, eighteen, nineteen.* That is, in this language the values which correspond to single lexical items and those which do

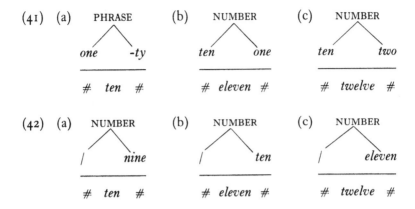

not appear to be randomly selected, rather than forming a natural class. It is significant that in English the values of the series 11, ..., 19 which are expressed by a single lexical item are the first two in the series. And this kind of pattern is found in other languages, e.g. Danish and German. A pattern such as that in the hypothetical language L referred to above is, on the other hand, quite untypical of natural languages and I do not know of any language exhibiting an unsystematic arrangement of this kind.

Thus the existence of the lexical item *twelve* can be seen to depend in a significant, and perhaps universal, way on the existence of the 'more basic' lexical item *eleven*, which in turn depends on the existence of the item *ten*. The form of our lexical entries should reflect these significant connections. It is clear that the lexical entry (42c), but not (41c), expresses the significant connection between the items *eleven* and *twelve*, so we must prefer (42c) over (41c) as the lexical entry for *twelve*. This choice dictates that we also select (42b) rather than (41b) as the lexical entry for *eleven*, since only the structure specified in (42b) can be generated by the phrase structure rules at the place occupied by the formative *eleven* in (42c), the lexical entry we have chosen for *twelve*. Similarly we must also prefer (42a) over (41a) as the lexical entry for *ten*. We shall return briefly in a later section to a problem incurred by our choice of (42) as the correct lexical entries for *ten*, *eleven*, and *twelve*.

We have now postulated a series of lexical entries for the items *one*, *two*, ..., *twelve*. The first in this series is (33), the entry for *one*, followed by the entries (36), (37), and (38), the entries for *two*, *three*, and *four* respectively. The entries for *five*, *six*, *seven*, and *eight* can be easily envisaged. The correct entry for *nine* is given in (40) and those for *ten*, *eleven*, and *twelve* in (42). These are all entries in the lexicon of the English numeral system.

It will be noticed that the underlying structure postulated above for *ten* is as in (43). When we consider the *-teen* words *thirteen*, . . ., *nineteen*,

(43)

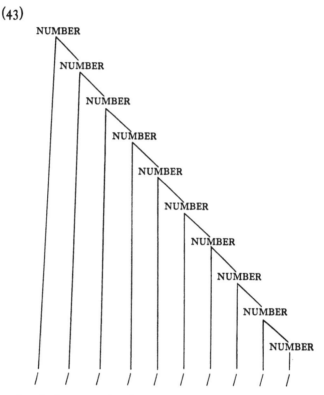

it is clear that (43) cannot be the structure underlying *-teen*. Obviously the phonological facts indicate that the structures underlying these words contain the structures underlying the simple lexical items *three*, . . ., *nine*. Thus we shall say that the structure underlying *thirteen*, for example, is as in (44). The phonological form *three* can be associated with the right-hand part of this structure in the desired way by lexicalization rule (37). If we assume the required phonological change from *three* to *thir*, all that remains is to specify the association between the left-hand part of structure (44) and the formative *-teen* and to formulate a permutation rule changing *-teen + thir* to *thir-teen*. A permutation rule such as this appears to be necessary and correct, but a problem arises if we assume a simple lexical entry for *-teen* such as (45). The problem

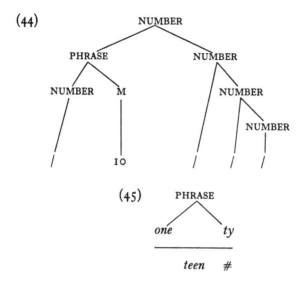

(44)

(45)

here is that the obvious phonological similarity between *-teen* and *ten*, both of which are associated by the grammar with the same arithmetic value, 10, is ignored. It is obviously more than a coincidence that *ten* and *-teen* both denote the same arithmetic value and are strikingly similar in phonological form, but this significant fact is ignored if we postulate two separate lexicalization rules (42a) and (45). I shall not offer a solution to this problem immediately but will return to it in the next section. For the moment it will suffice that the reader accept that some mechanism exists fulfilling the role of (45), i.e. that the grammar provides a way of associating the phonological form *ten*, alias *-teen*, with the structure specified above the line in (45) for the purpose of generating forms of the series *thirteen*, ..., *nineteen*.

Let us now consider the forms *billion* and *trillion*. These forms can be analysed as *bi + illion* and *tri + illion* respectively. We will postpone discussion of the somewhat problematic form *-illion* until later and concentrate on the prefixes *bi-* and *tri-*. In both British and American English these prefixes are associated with the same underlying structures as the words *two* and *three*, although as we have seen it is necessary to interpret *bi-* and *tri-* semantically as 3 and 4 in the case of American *billion* and *trillion*, since these words mean $1,000^3$ and $1,000^4$ in American English. We can postulate in (46) and (47) the lexical entries for *bi-* and *tri-* for both British and American English. These rules are context-sensitive. This is indicated by the fact that only half of the

(46)

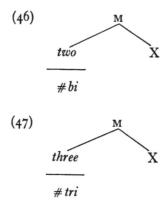

structure specified in each case is underlined. The phonological form
is associated by the rule with just the underlined constituent of the
specified structure. The part of the specified structure which is not
underlined states the context in which this association obtains. Rules
(46) and (47) associate *bi-* and *tri-* with *two* and *three* (or the structures
underlying these words) just when they are part of an M. The symbol X
in these rules stands for whatever constituent is also part of the M in
question. We shall see that we do not need to be more specific than this
about this constituent.

  I now give the lexicalization rules for *hundred* and *thousand.* By

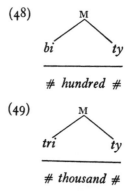

adopting this form for the lexical entries of *hundred* and *thousand* we
avoid the complication of having to stipulate an order in which these
and some other lexicalization rules apply. Consider the way in which
hundred, for example, is associated with its underlying structure. The
underlying structure, as generated by the phrase structure rules, is as
in (50). If we now apply to this structure any applicable lexicalization

(50)

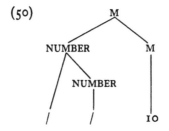

rule, we obtain, by applying rules (33) and (34), the only rules which are applicable at this stage, structure (51). The only lexicalization rule

(51)

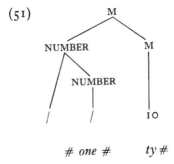

applicable to structure (51) is (36). Applying (36), we obtain (52).

(52)

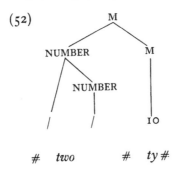

(I assume that application of rule (36) to structure (51) has the effect of suppressing the *one* already present in that structure, and that in general where a lexicalization rule applies to a constituent of which all or part is already associated with some phonological form, the application of the later rule 'overrides' the association with a phonological form specified by a previous rule.)

The only lexicalization rule applicable to structure (52) is (46). Applying (46), we get (53). Finally, applying (48) to (53), we get (54), in

(53)

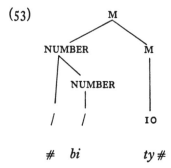

which *hundred* is associated with the entire structure. By a similar

(54)

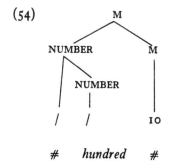

derivation, culminating in the application of rule (49), the phonological form *thousand* is associated with its underlying structure, which is as in (55). In British English, as in American English, the value assigned to

(55)

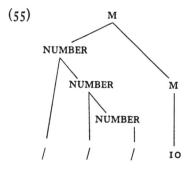

the word *million* is 1,000,000, i.e. the sixth power of 10. The underlying structures of *million* in British and American English are as in (56a) and 56b) respectively. For the moment we shall refrain from formulating lexical entries for *million*, as there is a certain complicating problem with this form to which we shall return later. Simply assume at present

(56) (a)

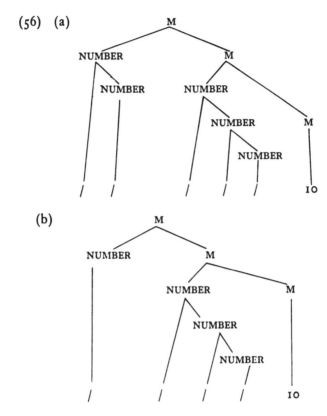

(b)

that the grammars of British and American English provide means for relating structures (56) to the word *million*.

The grammar of British English must associate the form *-illion*, as in *billion* and *trillion*, obviously phonologically related to *million*, to the underlying structure (56), since British *billion* and *trillion* are the second and third powers respectively of 1,000,000.

We shall also leave temporarily unformulated the means by which *-illion* is related to structure (56) in British English, but if it is assumed that this can be done, then it is clear how the derivations of British *billion* and *trillion* will proceed. Structure (57), for example, is associated, via rule (46) and the assumed processes relating *-illion* to (56), to *bi + illion*. The derivation of *trillion* will be similar. The strings *bi + illion* and *tri + illion* undergo a slight phonological readjustment to become *billion* and *trillion*.

In American English *million*, *billion*, and *trillion* represent successive powers of 1,000 and there is, as we have seen, a systematic relationship

(57)

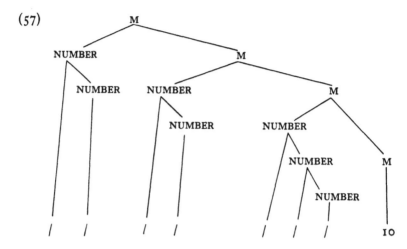

between the prefixes *bi-*, *tri-*, etc., and the simple number sequence. This leads to the conclusion that *-illion* in American English has the meaning 1,000 and is therefore associated with the same underlying structure as *thousand*, i.e. structure (55). The means by which this association is stated will be described in the next section. Assuming this mechanism to exist in the grammar, *billion*, for example, can be associated with its underlying structure, (58), via rule (46), the lexical

(58)

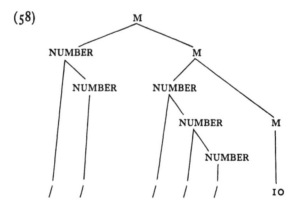

entry for *bi-*. In a similar way, *trillion* can be associated with its correct underlying structure in American English.

In summary, the lexicon is a list of rules, or lexical entries. Each rule states the association of a particular phonological form, together with information concerning word boundaries, with a particular structure generated by the phrase structure rules. The phonological form and word boundaries specified in each lexical entry are represented below a line. Above this line is a specification of the structure with which the phonological form below the line is to be associated. Once a lexicalization rule has applied, the phonological form in it can be regarded as constituting an additional specification of the structure with which it has been associated. Since the association of a particular structure with a particular phonological form is usually unique, a phonological form associated with a structure by a lexicalization rule can economically be used to specify that structure when it occurs embedded in other structures referred to by other lexical entries. This treatment permits rules which reflect significant relationships between different entries in the lexicon to be expressed in an economic notation. This treatment also allows one to avoid imposing an extrinsic ordering on the application of lexicalization rules in some cases. The lexicon is thus a set of mainly intrinsically ordered rules associating phonological forms with their underlying structures. The few lexicalization rules for which an extrinsic ordering statement must be made are discussed in the next section.

Some lexical entries are context-sensitive. In these lexical entries, only a constituent of the given structure is underlined and it is with the underlined constituent that the given phonological form is to be associated. The non-underlined part of such a context-sensitive lexicalization rule specifies the environment in which the underlined constituent is to be associated with the given form.

Some lexical entries, such as those for the English prefixes *bi-* and *tri-*, (46) and (47), refer to underlying structures which are only partially specified in that they contain variables. Partial specification of underlying structures in lexical entries of this sort is made possible by, and takes advantage of, certain predictable redundancies in the lexicon. That is, the class of constituents to which variable X in entries (46) and (47) can refer is limited by certain general principles governing the wellformedness of numeral structures. These general principles will be discussed in a later section.

We have described the lexical entries for the items *one, two, three, four, five, six, seven, eight, nine, ten, eleven, twelve, -ty, hundred, thousand, bi-,* and *tri-*. We restrict ourselves in this study to English dialects in which *trillion* is the highest valued number word, but the treatment followed here could be applied in an obvious way to dialects which have terms such as *quadrillion, quintillion,* etc.

I assume here certain idiosyncratic phonological processes, such as those converting *two* to *twen-* in *twenty* and *three* to *thir-* in *thirty*. I have not yet specified the means by which the forms *-teen*, *million*, and *-illion* are accounted for in the grammar of English numerals. This I will do in the ensuing section.

There remain the two lexical items *and* and the indefinite article *a*. I have not made an attempt to integrate the grammar of numerals into a grammar for the rest of the language. The items *and* and *a* fall into an area of overlap between the numeral system and the rest of the language. The question of a proper account of the 'indefinite article' is still quite open and rather complex, and the types of treatment that have been proposed for *and* and other conjunctions do not fit in in an obvious way with the grammar we have developed for numerals. Meanwhile, for completeness, I will sketch the treatment I assume for these items.

Perlmutter (1970) has argued fairly convincingly that the indefinite article is derived from a deep structure identical to that for the numeral *one*. Perlmutter's theory is that a very late rule, in fact a phonological rule, changes unstressed *one* to *a* or *an*. He does not go into the difficult question of the assignment of stress and explain the fact that some occurrences of *one* are stressed while others are not, but his account of the relationship between *a* and *one* is in general very plausible and I accept it here. Note that in the dialect described here the indefinite article only occurs initially in numeral expressions. That is, *a hundred and one* is grammatical, but **two thousand, a hundred and one* is not.

Rule (59) is adequate for inserting *and* into numeral phrase markers, though the formulation is obviously not applicable to other instances of *and*. This lexicalization rule differs from the others we have discussed

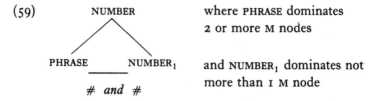

(59)   NUMBER   where PHRASE dominates 2 or more M nodes

PHRASE   NUMBER₁   and NUMBER₁ dominates not more than 1 M node

and

in that it attaches a lexical item between, rather than below, constituents of a phrase marker. There is no theoretical objection to this. It is clear that some lexical items denote semantic relationships, rather than semantic objects. The conditions on rule (59) guarantee that only well-formed expressions such as *two hundred and one, two hundred and twenty one, two million and one, two million and twenty one*, are generated, while illformed expressions such as **twenty and one, *two thousand and two hundred* are not. For dialects in which expressions like *two hundred four*, and *two hundred forty* are grammatical, rule (59) is an optional rule.

Finally, it is convenient to introduce at this stage a mechanism for expressing the fact that items belonging to the category M also possess properties of nouns. Interestingly, the stressing rules proposed by Chomsky and Halle (1968) can operate correctly only if the item *thousand* is categorized as a noun, rather than as an adjective or a verb. And in other respects MS appear to behave as nouns. For example, in some dialects MS may be pluralized, e.g. *three millions*; MS may sometimes be used as measure nouns, e.g. *hundreds of flowers, millions of flowers, masses of flowers, tons of flowers*. We shall see that in languages it is often the case that MS have the properties of nouns (see also, for example, the chapter on Welsh). To express this fact I propose the 'lexical redundancy rule' (60).

(60) M → noun

This rule is not to be understood in the same way as a phrase structure rule. Rule (60) operates on lexical entries and adds the specification 'noun' to any entry specifying a structure which is an M. It converts (61), for instance, into (62).

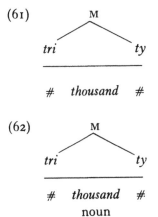

(61)

M

tri   ty

\# *thousand* \#

(62)

M

tri   ty

\# *thousand* \#
noun

By this means the specification 'noun' is introduced into phrase markers in association with the item *thousand*. Rule (60) applies similarly in the case of all other MS specified in the lexicon. We shall not have occasion, in connection with English numerals, to study further the interrelationships between the categories of the numeral system and other categories, such as noun, verb, and adjective, but this matter is touched upon in some more detail in connection with the Welsh numeral system, in ch. 6.

2.4   The lexical extension component

In the preceding section we postponed discussion of several problems involving the forms *million, -illion,* and *-teen.* We now return to these problems.

What is the morphemic makeup of the word *million?* Two analyses are possible, *m + illion* on the one hand, and *mill + ion* on the other. In favour of *m + illion* one can cite the fact that *million* is obviously part of a series with *billion, trillion,* etc., and that in this series *-illion* is associated consistently with a particular meaning, 1,000 in American English, and 1,000,000 in British English. Furthermore, the form *-illion* is somewhat productive, since we have coinings like *centillion* and the humorous forms *skillion, jillion,* and *zillion* (which are on a par with *umpteen*).

The evidence in favour of the rival analysis *mill + ion* is just about as strong. *Mill-* is a well-known productive form occurring in words like *millimeter, milligram, millipede, millisecond, millenium, millesimal, millibar.* In these words the form *mill-* is consistently associated with the meaning 1,000 or (1,000th). There is, furthermore, some phonological evidence for the analysis *mill + ion.* Chomsky and Halle (1968) point out (p. 87) that in order to make their phonological rules work optimally a morpheme boundary must be postulated before the *-ion* in the words *battalion, pavilion, million, rebellion, companion, dominion, union.*

The word *million* clearly cannot be dissected into morphemes in any way that will strike a satisfactory compromise between these two analyses. It would be wrong, for example, to postulate *m + ill + ion.* There is no evidence to suggest that the word has three morphemes. I shall sketch below the outlines of a solution which permits both rival analyses of *million* to be correct simultaneously. Note that the problem with *million* is an unusual one and the solution I suggest can at best only be considered correct in its broad outline. I omit elaboration of many crucial details for lack of proper evidence within the small body of data to which this study is restricted.

Let us begin with American English. In addition to the lexical entries we have already postulated, I propose two more, as in (63) and (64).

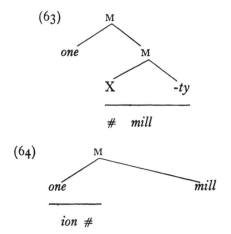

The general constraints we will discuss presently guarantee that the structure specified by the right-hand constituent of the structure given in (63) will be identical to that underlying *thousand*. *Mill-* is thus associated by entry (63) with the number 1,000, which is quite satisfactory. The association made by lexical entry (64) is certainly less satisfactory, since it is not supported by independent evidence, but at least it is not contradicted by evidence of any kind. Rule (63), which lexicalizes *mill-*, must apply before the lexicalization rule for *thousand*, for obvious reasons. This is one of the few statements of extrinsic ordering necessary for lexical entries. All such statements can be subsumed under the following convention:

> Where two lexicalization rules associate different phonological forms with the same structure, and the two rules are not intrinsically ordered, the context-sensitive rule is applicable before the context-free rule.

Entries (63) and (64) will attach the two items *ion #* and *# mill* below the structure underlying American *million*, when this structure is generated by the phrase structure rules. The two items are then reordered by a transformation similar to that involved in the derivation of *fourteen, fifteen*, etc., from *ten + four, ten + five*, etc., to be discussed later. Thus in two steps, lexicalization and a reordering transformation, the structure underlying *million* is associated with the bimorphemic string *# mill + ion #*. This string undergoes the word-level rules of the phonological component of the grammar in the usual way, eventually producing the phonetic representation [mílyən]. In this way three components of the grammar – lexicalization rules, transformational rules, and phonological rules – together provide a correlation between an abstract structure and a phonetic representation, as shown in (65).

(65)

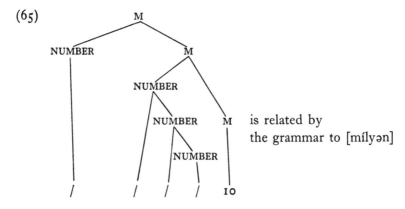

is related by the grammar to [mílyən]

I propose that at this stage the correlation between the abstract structure and its phonetic representation is 'reanalysed' – to use a figure of speech, one might say 'erroneously reanalysed' – the phonetic representation being taken to be two morphs, phonetically [m] and [ilyən], which are in turn taken to correspond to the left- and right-hand immediate constituents respectively of the structure shown in (65). This reanalysis in turn provides the basis for a 'newly created' lexical entry, as given in (66). (Here X and Y are both variables ranging over

(66)

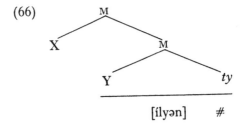

structures which do not need to be fully and explicitly specified in this lexicalization rule.) The 'newly created' lexical entry contains a phonetic, rather than a phonological representation. But this fact does not matter; phonetic and phonological representations are isomorphic in that both are made up of matrices of distinctive features. From looking at a representation one cannot tell whether it is a phonetic or a phonological one unless one knows some of the phonological rules of the language. And in phonological derivations there are many intermediate stages between phonological and phonetic representations. There is thus no theoretical objection to the use of lexical entry (66) to attach the representation [ílyən] # to a phrase marker meeting its structural description. I propose, then, that the lexical entry for *-illion* in American English is (66), an entry which is not explicitly present in the grammar in its full form, but which is generated by the grammar through a process of lexicalization, transformation, phonological interpretation, and ultimate reanalysis. I shall elaborate directly on the mechanism by which lexical entries are 'created'.

Let us illustrate the derivation of the word *trillion* in American English with this treatment. The structure (67), interpreted by the semantic component as 1,000,000,000,000, is generated by the phrase structure rules. The phonological representation of the prefix *tri-* is attached

(67)

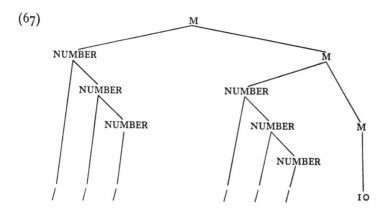

below the left-hand immediate constituent of this structure by the processes described in the last section. The representation [ílyən] is attached below the right-hand constituent by the 'newly created' entry (66). The resulting string is #trī+ílyən#. (Here + is the morpheme boundary separating the two morphemes *trī-* and *-illion*.) A phonological readjustment rule is clearly required to delete the tense high front vowel from the phonological representation of *tri-*, yielding #tr+ ílyən#. If this representation is input to the rules of the phonological component postulated for English by Chomsky and Halle (1968), it remains unaffected, passing through the whole sequence of rules without any modifications. The phonetic representation at the end of the derivation is thus [trílyən], as desired.

For British English something similar, though not identical, takes place. Instead of the entries (63) and (64), which we have postulated for American English, we have in British English (68) and (69). Again,

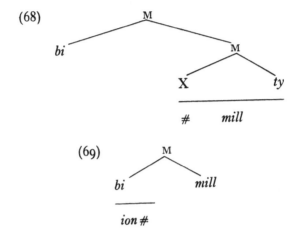

the general constraints we shall soon discuss guarantee that the structure specified by the right-hand constituent of the structure in entry (68) will be that underlying *thousand. Mill-* is thus associated by entry (68) with the value 1,000, as desired. As in the case of American English, the association claimed for the form *-ion* is less well motivated. As in American English, the entry for *mill-* is applicable before that for *thousand*, and this is handled by the same general convention.

When structure (56a), which underlies British *million*, is generated by the phrase structure rules, these two lexical entries will attach the morphemes *ion #* and *# mill* below it. The same reordering transformation applies as in American English, to produce *# mill + ion #*. Again, as in American English, this string is input to the rules of the phonological component, which associates it with the phonetic representation [mílyən]. In the case of British English, then, the grammar makes the association in (70) between an abstract structure and a phonetic representation. This relationship is now reanalysed, with the phonetic representation taken to be a morph [ílyən] preceded by a meaningless adjunct [m]. The morph [ílyən] is taken to correspond to the whole structure specified in (70). This reanalysis provides the basis for the 'newly created' lexical entry (71). I propose this lexical entry for

(70)

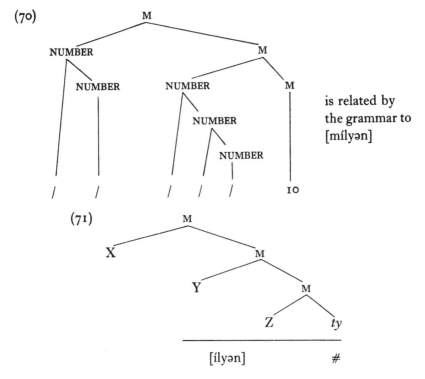

is related by
the grammar to
[mílyən]

(71)

-illion in British English. Derivations of forms containing -illion, e.g.
billion, trillion, will proceed in a way parallel to that outlined above for
American English trillion. In (71) X, Y, and Z are variables over structures which do not need to be specified. The general constraints to be
described directly ensure that the only wellformed structure matching
the right-hand constituent in (71) will be identical with (70), as required.

The treatment I am proposing captures a particular kind of creativity
in language use, the ability of language users to coin new lexical items
on the basis of pre-existing forms and sometimes by 'reanalysing' these
forms. We now examine the restrictions that must be placed on this
extremely powerful mechanism in the grammar. A possible condition
for the creation of a new lexical entry is a need for such an entry. If
American English had words for the cube and fourth power of 1,000,
say *kriss* and *ann*, then there would be no need for the lexical extension
component to synthesize -illion to be used with the prefixes bi- and
tri-. But even without *kriss* and *ann*, it is hard to see why there should
be a particularly pressing need for -illion. Why, for instance, could
three trillion not be expressed as *three million million*? If any systematic

linguistic answer to this question can be given, then it probably will be expressed in terms of the overall economy, in some extremely general sense, of the grammar and the structures, strings, etc., generated by it.

Putting aside the basic question of what creates a need for a particular concept to be expressed in a single word, rather than periphrastically, we can formulate the means by which this need can be represented in a linguistic description. To use a concrete example from American English, once it has been determined, somehow, that the cube and fourth power of 1,000 are to be expressed as single words and moreover by using the prefixes *bi-*, and *tri-*, we can say that there exists a need for some bound form meaning 1,000 to be used with these prefixes. This need can be represented by an 'incomplete' lexical entry, as given in (72).

(72)

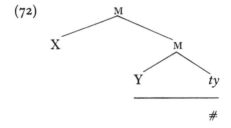

This entry is incomplete because it contains no phonological (or phonetic) information below the line. I postulate that the lexical extension component is sensitive to a need for a lexical item represented in this way and only in cases where such an incomplete lexical entry is present in the lexicon does the lexical extension component operate to 'fill it out' with the necessary phonological information. This explains why we do not have a much larger set of 'newly created' lexical entries ranging over all the possible structures generated by the phrase structure rules. It is, of course, imperative that we avoid unrestricted and unnecessary synthesis of new lexical entries.

The most crucial question concerning this treatment remains, of course, what exactly are the mechanisms provided by the lexical extension component that permit 'reanalyses' to be made? Unfortunately I have only the vaguest notion of what the rules of the lexical extension component might be and what form they might take. I have outlined what the lexical extension component does: it fills out incomplete lexical entries on the basis of information about derivations supplied by several other components of the grammar. But I have little idea *how* it does this. I will show in later chapters that other languages provide evidence for a device of roughly the form I have sketched here, but evidence is still so scant that we cannot yet make anything very explicit about the internal workings of the lexical extension component. Some informal remarks and speculations must at this stage suffice.

Let us remain with our concrete American English example. Given that the lexical extension component has, from the incomplete lexical entry (72), diagnosed the need for a new lexical item, which must be a bound form, capable of taking a prefix, and must mean 1,000, what criteria determine the exact shape of the new lexical item? The answers are far from obvious. A possibility is that a completed derivation is selected involving a structure as similar as possible to that for which the bound form is needed. In our example, this derivation would be the one involving *million* that we have illustrated, so this possibility is in this case quite plausible. But other possibilities are conceivable and there may be examples from other languages that make these seem equally plausible. Why, for example, cannot the initial word boundaries in the already existing entries for *mill-* or *thousand* be made optional? In other words, why don't English speakers say something like *trimill* and *bimill*, or *trithousand* and *bithousand* instead of going to the trouble of concocting the new morpheme *-illion*? We are at present far from being able to answer such a question.

In creating new lexical items, with which to fill out incomplete lexical entries, phonotactic considerations probably play some part. Given, for example, that the lexical extension component has 'decided' to synthesize a new morph out of the phonetic representation [mílyən], then certain possibilities are probably ruled out because they would entail violating otherwise valid phonotactic constraints on the structure of English morphemes. [mily], for example, might be excluded on such grounds. But it also seems that the phonetic distinctiveness of the sequence chosen is an important factor. Thus, though the single segment [n] is a logically possible choice for the new morph, it seems hardly likely that it would be chosen. [yən] is also logically possible, and though preferable to [n], it is still not as distinctive as [ílyən]. Again, on the phonetic and phonological criteria for arriving at new morphemes, we are far from being able to describe them precisely.

In summary, the lexical extension component of the grammar is to a large extent a black box. We postulate that it is responsible for synthesizing new lexical items but can say little precise about the internal mechanisms of the box. Evidence for the need for such a component in a grammar is provided by the problem of the proper morphemic analysis of *million*. We shall see that evidence of rather varied sorts turns up in several languages for a component which functions in some way like that described here.

We have proposed the notion of 'incomplete lexical entry' as a way of making explicit in a grammar the need for the synthesis by the lexical extension component of a new lexical item. In this view the lexicon of a language contains two kinds of lexical entries, which we call 'complete' and 'incomplete'. The function of the lexical extension component is to 'fill out' (72), that is, to convert it to (66). (66), then, is only an entry in the lexicon of American English after the operation of the lexical extension component. For British English, there is the incomplete lexical entry (73). The lexical extension component converts

(73)

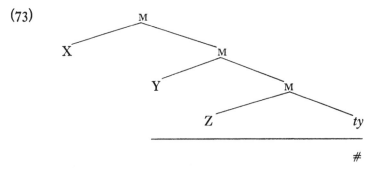

this to (71). (71), then, is only an entry in the lexicon of British English after the operation of the lexical extension component.

In the last section we postponed discussion of the form *-teen*. We postulated a lexical entry (42a) for *ten*, but refrained from postulating a lexical entry such as the hypothetical (45) for the form *-teen*. We did this because postulating two separate lexical entries for phonologically similar forms with identical semantic values misses an obvious generalization. It is clear that the lexical extension component just described in connection with the form *-illion* can be invoked to solve the problem of *-teen* also. We postulate the incomplete lexical entry (74). This rule expresses the need for a bound morpheme, a suffix, with the value 10. The grammar already generates a derivation relating the value 10 to the phonetic form [ten]. On the basis of this connection, the incomplete lexical entry (74) is filled out to become (75). In this treatment the fact that two structures with the same arithmetic value are lexicalized by significantly similar phonological forms is not represented as a matter of

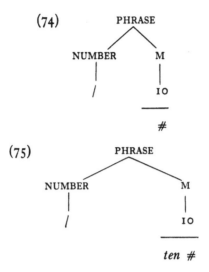

coincidence, but emerges in a natural way from the grammar itself. An idiosyncratic phonological readjustment rule must be postulated to tense the lax vowel in the phonetic representation [ten] just when it is an M, accounting for the difference in pronunciation between *ten* and *-teen.*

Rule (75) is context-sensitive, associating the form [ten] with an M, rather than with the whole PHRASE. In accordance with the convention postulated earlier in this section, the context-sensitive lexicalization rule (75) applies before (34), the context-free lexicalization rule for *-ty.* Justification of the details of (74) as the appropriate formulation of the (incomplete) lexical entry for *-teen* will be given in a later section.

Note that in this case the lexical extension component performs no 'reanalysis' of the phonetic representation, as it does in the case of *-illion.* It appears that in languages generally cases where such a reanalysis takes place are probably less frequent than cases like *-teen,* where there is no reanalysis, but simply an extension of the use of the same form. On the apparently plausible assumption that cases like the lexicalization of *-teen* are more typical instances of the use of the lexical extension component we can hazard a few guesses about the internal workings of this component.

A derivation brings together information of five different sorts: (1) syntactic information in the form of a labelled tree diagram, (2) semantic information associated with the tree diagram by the interpretive semantic component, (3) phonological information, (4) morphological information in the form of word boundary symbols, and (5) phonetic information associated with the phonological information by the phonological component of the grammar. Lexical entries are in a sense the focal points of derivations in that they provide the arbitrary connections between the semantic and syntactic systems on the one hand and the phonetic and phonological systems on the other. In an incomplete lexical entry the phonological information is missing, and since phonetic information is derived from phonological information by phonological rules, an incomplete lexical entry does not make oblique reference, as do complete lexical entries, to phonetic information. I speculate that the lexical extension component supplies incomplete lexical entries with phonetic information in something like the following way.

(76)   Given an incomplete lexical entry associating a structure G with morphological information M, where the semantic interpretation of G is S; and given also a derivation which associates S with a phonetic representation P; the incomplete lexical entry is filled out with the phonetic representation P.

In the case of *-teen*, (74) is the incomplete lexical entry in question, and the semantic information is the representation 10. The grammar provides a derivation, utilizing lexical entry (42a), associating the semantic representation 10 with the phonetic representation [ten]. Therefore (74) is filled out with [ten]. (This [ten] is later converted to [tēn] by an idiosyncratic phonological readjustment rule tensing the vowel.)

I believe that (76) describes the typical working of the lexical extension component. We shall see instances of the use of this component in the numeral systems of other languages and (76) seems in general to be an appropriate condition on its use. The coining of the morpheme *-illion* by a process of reanalysis in conjunction with the use of the lexical extension component remains something of a mystery. It must be emphasized that what is mysterious is not the lexical extension component in general but just the accompanying reanalysis that occurs in the particular case of *-illion*.

Observe that if we had chosen (41a, b, c) as the correct lexical entries for *ten*, *eleven*, and *twelve*, it would not have been necessary to account for the similarity of *ten* and *-teen* by the use of the lexical extension component; the structures underlying *-teen* and *ten* would have been identical. The decision to adopt the lexical entries (42) proceeds necessarily from the assumption that *eleven* and *twelve* are single morphemes, i.e. that there is no significance in the occurrence of *l* and *v* in both these forms and of the sequence *twe-* in *twelve*. In the ancient Germanic history of the forms *eleven* and *twelve* it was certainly possible to analyse the original forms bimorphemically. The transparency of this analysis has been clouded by sweeping phonological changes and now it seems plausible to regard *eleven* and *twelve* as single morphemes attached to phrase markers by their own peculiar lexicalization rules. This historical reanalysis of *eleven* and *twelve* as single morphemes necessitates, as we have seen, the adoption of a different underlying structure for *ten* in order to account for the fact that just the two lowest numbers of the sequences from 11 to 19 are expressed as single morphemes. We should naturally not expect some new word to be substituted for the old form *ten* – language appears to prefer to make use of old forms rather than to put together new ones. The lexical extension component represents the way in which new underlying structures are matched with old phonetic forms in situations such as these.

In French I would judge that there is still enough similarity between the members of the pairs *un/onze*, *deux/douze*, *trois/treize*, *quatre/quatorze*, *cinq/quinze*, *six/seize* to justify the analysis of the forms *onze*, ..., *seize* as bimorphemic, but if phonological change affected them much further, then I think that an analysis of *dix* parallel to that we have proposed for English *ten* would be necessary. For further discussion of French, see ch. 4.

Note that in a diagram attempting to portray the relationships between the separate components of the grammar, as diagram (1) at the beginning of this chapter, the position of the lexical extension component is quite unique. All other components of the grammar are involved in some way, though sometimes vacuously, in the derivation of every numeral expression. But the lexical extension component is not involved at all in the derivations of most expressions and only indirectly in those of the rest. The lexical extension component does not generate abstract tree structures or phonological representations, which are stages in the derivations of expressions: rather, its function is even more abstract. It generates new *rules* for relating abstract tree structures to phonological representations. Thus, where the other components, like the base and the lexicon, can be said to be 'linguistic', the lexical extension component must be said to be 'metalinguistic'. The input to the lexical extension component is in a sense a whole grammar, in which it diagnoses some lack, in the form of an incomplete lexical entry, and the output is another grammar, in which this lack has been rectified, specifically by the filling out of this lexical entry with phonological information.

2.5 General constraints on the wellformedness of numerals

The phrase structure rules we have formulated are extremely powerful. They generate a wide variety of phrase markers which do not correspond to wellformed English numerals. We have seén, however, that these phrase structure rules express a number of significant generalizations about English numerals that apparently cannot be expressed by a less powerful set of rules. Rather than abandon these well justified rules, we therefore seek well-motivated ways of selecting just the wellformed phrase markers from among those generated by the phrase structure rules.

An obvious constraint, to which there are no exceptions, is given in (77).

(77)   Any structure containing an illformed structure is itself illformed.

This constraint entails that the wellformedness of any numeral expression depends, in part at least, on the wellformedness of its constituents. Thus the criteria for the wellformedness of the lower-level constituents form a basis for defining the wellformedness of higher-level constituents. The lowest level category generated by the grammar is M. The phrase structure rules generate an infinite number of distinct Ms, but the lexicon species only a finite, and small, number of Ms. There are, furthermore, no wellformed Ms in English which are not specified by the lexicon. The only Ms are those lexicalized as *-ty, hundred, thousand, million, billion, trillion*. There are no Ms in English formed by the application of context-free lexicalization rules other than those which actually specify particular M structures. An M as in (78), for example, generated by the phrase structure rules, could conceivably be lexicalized by the lexicalization rules for American English as *two million*. But this is undesirable, since we know that *two million* is not an M, but a PHRASE. If we allow *two million* to be an M and to have the structure of (78), we make the false prediction that it can have the meaning 1,000,000,000,000, since the semantic component will interpret this structure by exponentiation. In fact the only structures which the semantic component

(78)

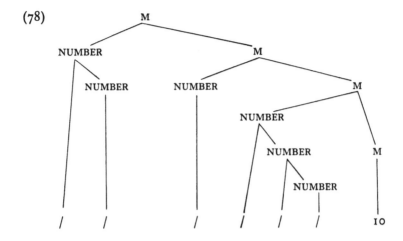

interprets by exponentiation belong to the small class of MS specified explicitly in the lexicon. Compare the case of M with that of the category NUMBER. Some NUMBERS generated by the base component correspond to structures specified in the lexicon, e.g. the items *one*, ..., *twelve*. But other NUMBERS generated by the base are lexicalized by the application of several context-free lexicalization rules, e.g. *seventy five*, lexicalized by the separate and independent attachment of *seven*, *-ty*, and *five*. Both M and NUMBER could be said to be 'lexical categories', since there are MS and NUMBERS specified in the lexicon, but M differs from NUMBER in that it could be called a 'uniquely lexical category', since there are no MS other than those specified in the lexicon. Accordingly, I formulate the following constraint on the wellformedness of MS.

(79)   Any M generated by the phrase structure rules but distinct from all M types characterized in the lexicon is illformed.

The notion of 'M type' used here is to be understood as follows. Sets of structure specifications in lexical entries which are not distinct from each other because they include variables together characterize structure types. Thus the structures specified in lexical entries (46) and (66) characterize an M type, since they are not distinct from each other. Similarly the structures given in the entries (47) and (66) characterize an M type, being also not distinct from each other. But the structures in the entries (46) and (47), which are distinct from each other, do not together characterize an M type.

Constraint (79) rules that structure (78), for example, is illformed since it is distinct from all M types specified in the lexicons of both British and American English. Constraint (79) will not rule out all illformed Ms which may be generated by the phrase structure rules. The structure (80), for example, which is interpreted in British English as 10,000, is not wellformed, since there is no M in the language with this value, but this structure is not rejected by constraint (79), since it is not distinct from the M type characterized in the lexical entries (46) and (68), the

(80)

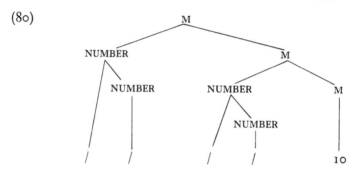

entries for British *bi-* and *mill-*. Another constraint, which is responsible for rejecting this structure, will be formulated directly.

We can now see how constraints (77) and (79) interact to begin to restrict the set of structures generated by the phrase structure rules that might conceivably qualify as not distinct from the specified structures given in some lexical entries. Take (68), the lexical entry for British *mill-*, as an example. The right-hand immediate constituent of the structure given in this entry contains a variable. Constraint (77) tells us that whatever structure this constituent represents must be well-formed, since otherwise the whole structure specified in the entry would be illformed. The basic criterion for wellformedness of Ms is nondistinct-ness from some structure characterized in the lexicon, as stipulated in (79). Therefore the right-hand immediate constituent of the structure in (68) must represent some structure not distinct from it and actually specified somewhere in the lexicon. There are only two structures which fit this description, namely those underlying *hundred* and *thousand*. At present we do not have the means for ruling out the structure underlying *hundred* as a possible candidate here, but we shall provide this directly.

M and NUMBER are, as we have said, both 'lexical categories'. M differs from NUMBER in being a 'uniquely lexical category'. The only wellformed Ms are those characterized in the lexicon. In the case of

NUMBER, on the other hand, the relevant constraint must be formulated as in (81).

(81) Any NUMBER generated by the phrase structure rules and identical to a NUMBER specified in the lexicon is wellformed, and any NUMBER generated by the phrase structure rules which is structurally distinct from, but semantically equivalent to, a NUMBER specified in the lexicon is illformed.

This constraint is in fact only made necessary by our preference for lexical entries (42a, b, c) for *ten, eleven,* and *twelve.* But for constraint (81), the general constraint on the wellformedness of all structures which I shall present directly would characterize the underlying structures we have adopted for *ten, eleven,* and *twelve* as illformed. It must be postulated that constraint (81) overrides this general constraint. The necessity to postulate constraint (81) and to say that it overrides a more general constraint is an unsatisfactory consequence of our adoption of lexical entries (42a, b, c) and may indeed be considered evidence for the correctness of lexical entries such as (41a, b, c). This is not a major issue, however, and I shall not discuss it further here.

We see that the lexicon, in addition to specifying certain pairings of phrase markers and phonological representations, provides a basis for the criteria which select just the wellformed phrase markers from among those generated by the base. The final constraint we shall formulate also depends on this basic constraining function of the lexicon. This constraint, though it appears rather complicated, is in essence quite simple and is very well motivated. It is given in (82), broken up into separate parts to facilitate subsequent illustration of its operation.

(82) PACKING STRATEGY
A structure A generated by the phrase structure rules is illformed if
(a) it is of category X, has value x, and has as immediate constituents a NUMBER and some other structure with value y (not necessarily in that order), where
(b) the phrase structure rules generate a wellformed structure B of category Z with value z, where Z is on the right-hand side of a phrase structure rule expanding X and is not NUMBER, and $y < z \leqslant x$.

The name 'Packing Strategy' is mnemonic. The strategy states, essentially, that the sister constituent of a NUMBER must have the highest possible value, that is, the highest value that a constituent of its category can have less than or equal to the value of the immediately dominating node. Conditions (a) and (b) of (82) are in most instances sufficient to reject an illformed structure. But there are some cases which suggest that a further condition, (c), be stipulated. It is not to be denied, however, that this condition (c) is very *ad hoc* and is motivated by a far smaller class of cases than conditions (a) and (b). I shall begin by illustrating cases of the operation of the Packing Strategy where conditions (a) and (b) are sufficient to reject an illformed structure, and, for simplicity, will not yet mention condition (c) and the exceptional cases which seem to call for it.

Notice first that the Packing Strategy applies to structures of any category which have more than a single immediate constituent. I will illustrate its application to NUMBERs, PHRASES, and Ms. Consider first the structure (83), a NUMBER which is generated by the phrase structure rules, and which corresponds to the illformed expression *two hundred, two thousand*. The left- and right-hand immediate constituents of this

(83)

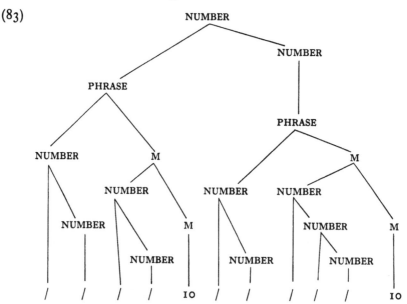

structure, corresponding to *two hundred* and *two thousand* respectively, are wellformed, and so the illformedness of (83) cannot be attributed to its containing some illformed structure. Rather, what is wrong is that the two constituents are 'in the wrong order'. Let us see how the Packing Strategy detects this.

Let structure (83) be the structure A of the Packing Strategy; X is therefore NUMBER, x is 2,200 (the value assigned to A by the semantic component), and y is 200. A wellformed structure B generated by the phrase structure rules is one identical to the right-hand PHRASE in (83); Z is PHRASE, and z is 2,000. 200 is less than 2,000, which is less than 2,200. Structure A, (83), is therefore illformed.

Now consider (84), another illformed NUMBER structure generated by the phrase structure rules. This structure is formed by applying the first phrase structure rule thirteen times, as is, of course, quite

(84)   NUMBER

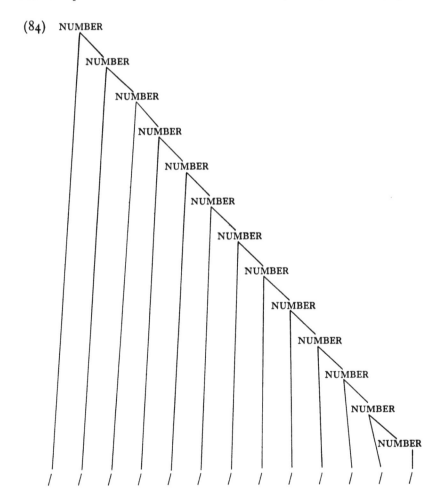

possible. The semantic representation assigned to this structure is 13 and this number is expressed in English as *thirteen*. The general regularity of the processes for forming numerals cannot be captured if we postulate that the underlying structure for *thirteen* is (84). In particular this treatment would leave unexpressed the obvious fact that *thirteen* is formed from variants of *three* and *ten*. These are our grounds for deciding that (84) is illformed. This decision is in accord with the prediction made by the Packing Strategy, as is shown below.

Let structure (84) be structure A of the Packing Strategy; X is therefore NUMBER, x is 13, and y is 1 (the value of the left-hand immediate constituent of (84)). The category symbol PHRASE is on the right-hand side of a phrase structure rule expanding NUMBER and the phrase structure rules generate a wellformed PHRASE which can serve as structure B of the Packing Strategy, namely the structure specified in (74), the (incomplete) lexical entry for *ten*. z is therefore 10, and 1 is less than 10, which is less than 13. Structure A, (84), is therefore illformed.

Note here that the applicability of the Packing Strategy, which is in general well motivated, to structures such as (84) provides further support for such structures in contrast to structures with more than two constituents such as would be generated by the iterative rule schema (10).

(85)

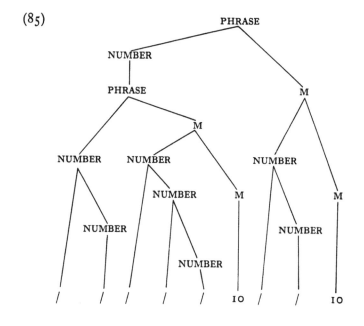

Now consider an illformed PHRASE, (85), which corresponds to *two thousand hundred*. Let this structure be structure A of the Packing Strategy; X is therefore PHRASE, x is 200,000, and y is 100. The category symbol M is on the right-hand side of a phrase structure rule expanding PHRASE, and the phrase structure rules generate a wellformed M which can stand as structure B of the Packing Strategy. This M is that underlying *thousand* (see lexical entry (49) or the M in the left-hand PHRASE in structure (85) above). z is then 1,000. 100 is less than 1,000, which is less than 200,000. Structure A, (85), is therefore illformed.

Take now another illformed PHRASE, (86), corresponding to *twenty hundred*. (*ten hundred*, ..., *ninety hundred* are similarly illformed.)

(86)

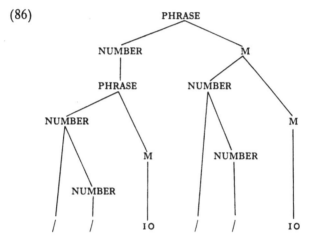

Taking this structure as A, X is PHRASE, x is 2,000, and y is 100. M is on the right-hand side of the rule expanding PHRASE; the structure underlying *thousand* is a wellformed M. We may say, then, that z is 1,000. 100 is less than 1,000, which is less than 2,000. Structure (86) is therefore illformed.

An exactly parallel explanation can be given for the illformedness of *ten hundred*, but in this case both x and z will have the value 1,000. This is a case which motivates the stipulation that z be less than or equal to x.

We see below that the Packing Strategy also accounts for cases such as that of the illformed M (80). With the structure (80) standing for A of the Packing Strategy, X is M, x is 10,000, and y is 100. As we have noted in the last two examples, the structure underlying *thousand* is a wellformed M; let us take it as B of the Packing Strategy, since M is on the right-hand side of the rule expanding M. z is then 1,000; 100 is less than 1,000, which is less than 10,000. Structure (80) is therefore ill-formed.

The illustrations I have given are among the more interesting examples of the operation of the Packing Strategy. The strategy will also reject a wide variety of other illformed structures, such as those listed below.

(87)   *forty forty   vs eighty
        *six hundred, six hundred   vs one thousand, two hundred
        *two thousand, three thousand   vs five thousand
        *nine billion, one billion   vs ten billion
        *five hundred, five thousand   vs five thousand, five hundred
        *five hundred, five trillion   vs five trillion, five hundred
        *five billion, five trillion   vs five trillion, five billion
        *fortyty   vs four hundred
        *six hundred hundred   vs sixty thousand
        *two thousand thousand   vs two million
        *nine billion billion   vs nine million trillion
        *five trillion hundred   vs five hundred trillion
        *eight thousandty   vs eighty thousand

English speakers are more certain of their judgments of the grammaticality of lower-valued numeral expressions. Nevertheless, all of the left-hand examples above would probably be agreed to be peculiar or unacceptable in some way by most English speakers. The judgments on the less clear examples, i.e. the higher-valued expressions, can be said to be generalized from a mass of clearer cases, i.e. the lower-valued expressions. The Packing Strategy is an explicit formulation of the appropriate generalization. Beside the English examples discussed above, there is evidence of different sorts from other languages for constraints similar or even identical to the Packing Strategy. In later chapters we shall review some such evidence.

There is in English one class of counterexamples to the Packing Strategy, which I will now discuss. Although *ten hundred*, *twenty hundred*, ..., *ninety hundred* are illformed, the similar expressions *twenty eight hundred*, *eleven hundred*, *ninety five hundred*, etc., are perfectly acceptable. Yet the Packing Strategy rejects expressions such as these on just the same grounds as *ten hundred*, etc., that is, because of the wellformedness of the M underlying *thousand*. I will illustrate with (88), the structure underlying *twenty two hundred*. Taking this structure as A of the Packing Strategy, X is then PHRASE, x is 2,200, and y is 100. The category symbol M is on the right-hand side of the phrase structure rule expanding PHRASE. The structure underlying *thousand* is a wellformed M which can serve as structure B of the Packing Strategy; z is then 1,000. 100 is less than 1,000, which is less than 2,200. Structure (88) is therefore illformed – obviously an undesirable result.

(88)

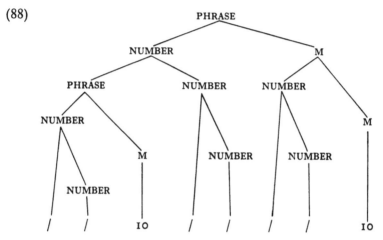

Now we can devise an *ad hoc* modification to the Packing Strategy as formulated in (82) which will result in structures such as (88) being characterized as wellformed. But any such move will automatically lead to a further serious problem, as I will show. Let us say that our *ad hoc* modification to the Packing Strategy is expressed as an extra condition, which we call (ci).

(89) PACKING STRATEGY

   ...

   (a) ...

   (b) ...

   and (c)(i) if X is PHRASE, the phrase structure rules generate a
      structure of value x with B as an immediate constituent.

In the case of (88), X is PHRASE and this extra condition therefore applies. The phrase structure rules do not generate any structure with the value 2,200 which has the underlying structure for *thousand* as an immediate constituent; condition (ci) is thus not met and (88) can therefore be said to be not illformed. But though expressions such as *twenty two hundred* clearly are wellformed, there is another class of wellformed expressions which the Packing Strategy will characterize as wellformed only if one can assume that expressions like *twenty two hundred* are in fact illformed. These are the synonymous expressions *two thousand two hundred*, etc. The structure of *two thousand two hundred* is given in (90). Taking this structure as A of the Packing

(90)

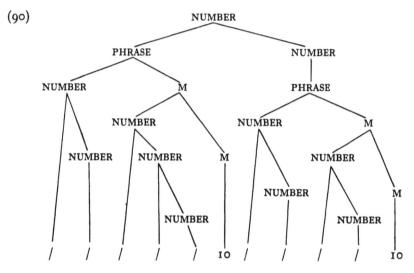

Strategy, X is NUMBER, x is 2,200, and y is 2,000. The category PHRASE is on the right-hand side of the rule expanding NUMBER. The structure underlying *twenty two hundred*, i.e. (88), is a PHRASE, and if we assume that it is wellformed, then it can serve as structure B of the Packing Strategy. z is then 2,200; 2,000 is less than 2,200, which is equal to 2,200. Structure (90) therefore appears to be illformed. We can avoid this undesirable result by formulating another *ad hoc* condition to be appended to the Packing Strategy, as below.

and (c) (ii) if X is NUMBER, the value of the top M in structure B is not
    less than that of the top M in the structure with value y.

Clearly condition (c) is a patchwork quilt that explains nothing about the way numeral expressions are formed. It is of observational adequacy only. Condition (ci) is motivated only by a single class of examples; and condition (cii) merely repairs the damage done by (ci). Furthermore these two conditions appear unrelated, whereas the same phenomenon, namely the wellformedness of expressions such as *twenty two hundred*, etc., motivates them both. I cannot provide here any completely satisfying explanation for the wellformedness of *twenty two hundred*, etc. It is an apparent anomaly that I have been unable to fit into any well-motivated formulation of the constraints applying to English numerals. I can, however, sketch the direction in which I think a solution to this problem might be found.

I do not think that there is anything seriously wrong with the Packing Strategy in its initial formulation (82). It accounts economically for a wide range of examples and the curious situation with regard to expressions such as *twenty two hundred* might actually be construed as evidence in favour of its 'internal coherence'. That is, the Packing Strategy seems to insist in two separate ways that expressions such as *twenty two hundred*, etc., are illformed. Not only does it actually predict that these expressions are illformed, but it also only achieves the correct results in certain other cases when working on the assumption that they are indeed illformed.

Note further that the expressions we are dealing with are the only English numerals that have wellformed synonyms. There are two acceptable ways of expressing 2,200, as we have seen, but this is not true of any other class of cases. The Packing Strategy (82) is formulated in such a manner as to select just one way of expressing a particular number. This formulation is perhaps too strict, too absolute. It might be better to formulate the Packing Strategy in terms of 'optimal' and 'not optimal', rather than 'wellformed' and 'illformed'. Thus expressions such as *twenty two hundred, thirty four hundred, ninety nine hundred*, etc., would be characterized as 'not optimal', but not as 'illformed'; these structures, being 'not optimal' would not be available as candidates for structure B of the Packing Strategy in evaluating other expressions, in particular those of the class *two thousand two hundred, three thousand four hundred, nine thousand nine hundred*, etc. 'Optimal' structures will always be wellformed, but there may be circumstances under which some overriding constraint can characterize certain 'nonoptimal' structures as wellformed also. I have at present only an imprecise notion of how this overriding constraint should be formulated and outline it discursively below.

The effect of the Packing Strategy is often to select structures which are more economic in preference to structures which are less economic. Plausible measures of the economy of phrase markers are: (1) overall number of nodes, (2) number of nodes of a given type, say, branching nodes or nonbranching nodes, (3) maximum depth, i.e. greatest number of nodes intervening between the top of the tree and some terminal node, (4) number of lexical items. By most of these measures, a structure characterized as optimal by the Packing Strategy is very seldom less economic than a semantically equivalent structure characterized as nonoptimal, and is frequently more economic. The expressions in the left-hand column of (87), for example, all have underlying structures which are, in the poorly defined terms we are using here, either less economic or not more economic than those of their wellformed equivalents in the right-hand column. It is rather unusual for a wellformed numeral to have a structure less economic than that of some illformed equivalent, although this situation does occur. An example is given below. The structure underlying *ten thousand* is given in (91), which appears to be marginally less economic than the semantically equivalent

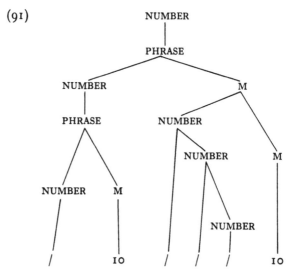

(91)

structure (92). The upper M in structure (92) is rejected by the Packing Strategy, as we have seen.

Despite a few examples such as these, there seems to be some guiding principle of economy which can plausibly be said to be the psychological motivation for the Packing Strategy. The Packing Strategy appears more plausible when we realize that its typical effect is to select more economic structures. Speaking somewhat figuratively, we can say that the Packing Strategy is the instrument by which a general policy of economy is implemented. The strategy can be formulated explicitly, as

(92)

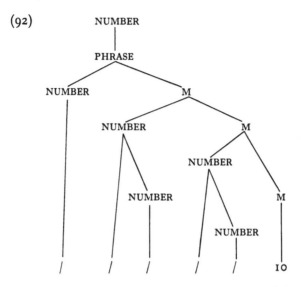

has been shown, but the policy remains vague, because of the difficulty of defining the notion 'economy'. And it appears that the strategy is not always a perfect instrument of the policy which prefers economy. We have already seen one example of this, and expressions such as the problematic *twenty two hundred* provide another. Compare structure (90) underlying *two thousand two hundred* with structure (88) underlying *twenty two hundred*. (For a fairer comparison, since we are treating these expressions as whole isolated numerals, assume a node NUMBER immediately dominating structure (88).) Some possible measures of the relative economy of these two structures are given below.

(93)

	Structure (88) *twenty two hundred*	Structure (90) *two thousand two hundred*
Overall number of nodes	21	28
Terminal nodes	8	11
Nonterminal nodes	13	17
Branching nodes	7	10
Nonbranching nonterminal nodes	6	7
Maximum depth	6	6
Lexical items	4	4

By none of these measures is *two thousand two hundred* more economic than *twenty two hundred*, and by all the node-counting measures the latter is definitely more economic than the former. This seems to be an instance of the failure of the Packing Strategy to implement the policy of economy. I surmise that just in cases such as this structures which are characterized by the Packing Strategy as nonoptimal may yet be wellformed. Until we can make much more explicit what is contained in the notion of 'economy', it will not be possible to give a more satisfactory account of the wellformedness of expressions like *twenty two hundred*. The possibility cannot be ruled out that the correct measure of economy will take into account aspects of surface structure, such as, perhaps, number of stressed syllables. By this measure also, *twenty two hundred* is more economic than *two thousand two hundred*. Even when we have managed to express in some rigorous way what is meant by 'economy', we will probably not be able to dispense with the Packing Strategy, which often discriminates between structures of apparently equal complexity. We will see a particularly good example of this in the chapter on French numerals, where it will be shown that the Packing Strategy can be used to select *soixante-dix* in favour of expressions like **cinquante-vingt*, **quarante-trente*, etc.

There are some other reasons to believe that the Packing Strategy is not the final arbiter of the wellformedness of English numerals, but just a device which labels structures as optimal or nonoptimal, leaving the question of ultimate wellformedness to some other parts of the grammar. There are certain contexts in which otherwise illformed numeral expressions are actually wellformed. In American English, for example, **ten hundred* and **one thousand million* are illformed except in definitions of *one thousand* and *one billion* respectively. Thus (94) are wellformed.

(94) (a) A thousand is ten hundred.
      (b) A billion is a thousand million.

(I assume that the indefinite article is a variant of *one*.) I envisage an explanation of these facts along the following lines.

The grammar of a language characterizes sentences in terms of a distinction roughly corresponding to that between analytic and synthetic, or perhaps between metalinguistic and nonmetalinguistic. That is, the grammar is capable of representing in some way the fact that a given sentence is, or is not, used as a definition. I assume, furthermore, that the grammar (or the metatheory) contains the equivalent of what is probably the cardinal rule of lexicographers, namely 'never define a word in terms of itself'. This restriction results in the *ad hoc* constraint, in (94a), for example, that *thousand* may not be used in the predicate. In other words, *thousand* is in these special circumstances ruled to be illformed, by considerations which override the recommendation of the Packing Strategy. The Packing Strategy is nevertheless employed to select the next best possible expression. If we impose the *ad hoc* constraint on English that *thousand* is illformed and nonoptimal, then the Packing Strategy will automatically select *ten hundred* as the 'correct' expression for 1,000. Other possible candidates, such as **nine hundred one hundred*, **six hundred four hundred*, **nine hundred and ninety ten*, **tentyty*, are rejected by the Packing Strategy. This is quite appropriate, since English speakers do not define *a thousand* with any of these expressions. The 'standard' definition is *ten hundred*.

I envisage, then, that in certain circumstances particular expressions may in an *ad hoc* manner be characterized as illformed. Given a language with a grammar G and an expression X, whose semantic representation is S, characterized in this *ad hoc* manner as illformed, the way to determine the correct expression for S is to assume a hypothetical grammar G' identical to G, but with the *ad hoc* constraint that X is illformed; then the correct expression for S is that characterized as wellformed by G' with the semantic representation S. These remarks can only be brief and programmatic, as a full consideration of phenomena of this sort would take us far beyond the numeral system, which is our main concern.

To summarize the main points in this section, there are some general statements that can be made about the formulation of English numerals that are best expressed as constraints or filters operating on the set of phrase markers generated by the very powerful base component we have postulated. These constraints characterize a subset of the base phrase markers as wellformed. They rely for their correct operation on information contained in or generated by three separate components of the grammar and on certain possibly extralinguistic information. That is, these constraints do not provide any mechanism for distinguishing wellformed structures 'in a vacuum'. Constraint (82), the Packing Strategy, for example, presupposes an analysis of a structure and one of its constituents by the interpretive semantic component, the generation by the base component of a set of other structures, the analysis of these structures by the semantic component, the application to them of the wellformedness constraints we have discussed, and an analysis of the semantic representations assigned to the structures concerned in terms of the notions 'less than' and 'equal to'. Constraints (79) and (81) presuppose the information contained in the lexicon. The constraints we have described cannot, then, be regarded in the same light as the other components of the grammar, e.g. the transformational rule component, the lexicon, or the interpretive semantic component, which are in general fairly straightforward input–output devices, presupposing little or no information other than that which they themselves contain and that which is represented in the input to them. It is thus somewhat misleading to show these constraints in a diagram of the overall shape of the grammar as a box, which tends to imply a relative autonomy of one component in a grammar from the others. It is for this reason that the broken lines are included in the diagram (1) at the beginning of this chapter, attempting to represent the fundamental dependence of the constraints I have discussed on the base component, the interpretive semantic component, and the lexicon.

The 'global' or nonautonomous nature of these constraints means that there is no empirical sense to the question of the relative positions of the lexical attachment box and the general constraint box in diagram (1). The lexicon box could just as well 'precede' the general constraint box as 'follow' it. In either case the facts accounted for would be the same, but the internal workings of the grammar would be slightly different. If we say that lexical attachment precedes the operation of the constraints, then illformed structures will have lexical items attached to them and 'subsequently' be declared illformed; if lexical attachment follows the constraints, then these processes will take place 'in the opposite order', but the empirical adequacy of the grammar is not affected whichever ordering we postulate.

At least one of the constraints proposed here may be overridden by more general considerations of economy and what we may call 'usefulness' in the case of definitions. It is not useful to someone who wants to know the value of *thousand* to be told *a thousand is a thousand*. We are at present rather far away from an exact understanding of these more general considerations, but I see no reason to doubt that they are directly relevant to the description of language.

2.6 Word formation transformations

A lexical item is not necessarily a word, although it may be; and there are lexical items which are sometimes words and sometimes not. In English *hundred* and *thousand* are examples of lexical items which are words. *Hundred* and *thousand* are always words when used in numeral expressions. English *-ty* and *bi-* (as in *billion*) are examples of lexical items that are never words, though they combine with other lexical items to form words. The single digit lexical items *two*, . . ., *nine* are sometimes words, sometimes only parts of words, as in *twenty*, *ninety*, *nineteen*.

What are the criteria for labelling a particular sequence of sounds a 'word'? Conventional orthography is one piece of data that must be accounted for and in the case of the 'lexical categories' (noun, verb, adjective, adverb) other considerations confirm that sequences corresponding roughly to orthographic words have a status different from both shorter and longer stretches of sounds. Some very well-known phonological processes, e.g. assimilation of consonants in certain environments, laxing of vowels in certain environments, operate only within words and not across word boundaries. Other rules, such as those predicting the placement of stress, operate chiefly on strings of word length, not on affixes or phrases. These observations hold true of the English numeral system. The 'lexical categories' of the numeral system, NUMBER and M, behave in the same way as the better known ones, noun, etc. Accordingly, we must provide a set of rules for forming strings of words out of the strings of lexical items attached by the lexicon to phrase markers.

I shall begin by describing two transformational rules that are valid not only for English, but for several other languages as well. The first of these, '1-Deletion', does not actually bring lexical items together to form words and is thus not strictly a word formation transformation, but its prior application is presupposed by the second transformation I shall describe, 'Switch', which does bring together lexical items to form words. In English, the effect of 1-Deletion is to delete the item *one* from in front of the item *-teen* (i.e. the item attached by lexicalization rule (75), whose vowel is tensed by a later rule). Since a rule doing essentially the same thing is found in several languages, we should try to find a formulation of the rule sensitive not to the particular English formatives *one* and *-teen*, but rather to structural elements common to these languages.

The rule of 1-Deletion is more extensive in French, Welsh, German, Russian, Polish, Spanish, Italian, and other languages than in English, applying not only before the item signifying 10, but also before the word for 100 and in some cases before still higher-valued MS. Thus in these languages we find wellformed one-word expressions for 100, whereas the wellformed expression in English is *one hundred* or *a hundred*. **Hundred* by itself is not a wellformed numeral. But in all languages where a deletion rule of this sort applies, the element that is deleted denotes the number 1. We do not find rules for deleting elements denoting 2, or 3, or 6, of course. Thus the formulation of the 1-Deletion rule should refer explicitly to the common underlying structure of the items for 1 in these languages. This is, of course, implied by the name of the rule.

The items in whose environment the 1-Deletion rule applies vary somewhat from language to language. They are all, however, of the category M, so the formulation of the rule may refer explicitly to M, but otherwise the applicability of the rule seems to be conditioned by idiosyncratic properties of individual MS in each particular language. In English, for example, only *-teen* triggers deletion of a preceding *one*. In French, the item *un* is obligatorily deleted before *dix* and *-ze*, its affixal variant, it may optionally be deleted before *cent* and *mille*, but it is never deleted before *million*.

The versions of the 1-Deletion rule for different languages will thus show slight variations. The similarity of rules applying in different languages should not, however, be overlooked, and we can postulate a kind of simplicity criterion operating across languages, capturing the generalization that languages tend to have similar rules. Across languages, one can also make the generalization that MS which are suppletive lexical variants (e.g. *-teen*, the suppletive, environmentally conditioned alternant of *-ty*, which also denotes 10) are more likely to trigger the rule of 1-Deletion than other MS. This generalization can be captured in a description of English and other languages for which it holds by a collapsing into a single rule of the rule of 1-Deletion and the lexicalization rule for the suppletive form. I give in (95) a formulation of the rule of 1-Deletion for English which incorporates the (incomplete) lexical entry (74) already given for *-teen*. The lexical extension component fills this rule out to (96) in just the way described in a previous section. This rule provides that, given a PHRASE analysable into two constituents, of which the first is a NUMBER dominating just /, and the second is an M dominating just 10, the first constituent is to be deleted and the phonetic form [ten], followed by a word boundary, is to be

(95) I-DELETION

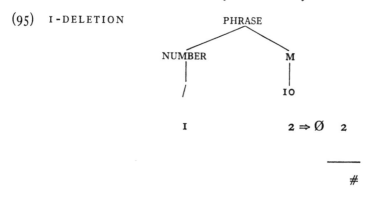

(96) I-DELETION

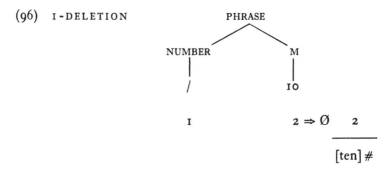

(97)

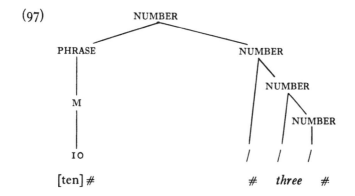

associated with the second constituent. To illustrate the operation of the rule, the structure for *thirteen*, as it stands after the operation of (96) and the lexicalization rule for *three*, is given in (97). Rule (96) is responsible for the shape of the left-hand constituent in this structure. Later rules produce the form *thirteen*.

The fact that I-Deletion and the lexicalization rule for *-teen* are collapsed into a single rule entails that transformational rules that are not lexicalization rules may sometimes apply before lexicalization rules. As far as numeral systems are concerned, there appears to be no reason for stipulating any extrinsic ordering of lexicalization rules and other transformational rules, apart from the convention given in a previous section providing that in the absence of any intrinsic ordering context-sensitive lexicalization rules apply before context-free ones.

We can now discuss the word formation transformation 'Switch'. This is the rule that produces words such as *thirteen, fourteen*, etc., from underlying *ten three, ten four*, etc. Forms such as the English *-teen* words occur in a number of languages and I postulate that a rule like Switch is common to these languages. In decimal systems the rule only involves MS with the value 10 and, as its name implies, moves elements following MS around to a position in front of them. The rule appears to be sensitive to elements of different value in various languages. In Italian, for example, the words for the values 11, ..., 16 are formed by Switch, e.g. *undici, ..., seidici*, but the words for 17, 18, and 19, *diciasette, diciotto*, and *dicianove*, respectively, are not. In English, all NUMBER items occurring after *-teen* are subject to Switch. The rule can thus be expressed in a quite general form for English. The English version of Switch is given in (98). This rule applies to structures to

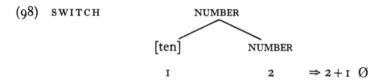

(98) SWITCH

which the 1-Deletion rule has already applied. The Switch rule moves a NUMBER to the position from which a NUMBER dominating / has been deleted by the 1-Deletion rule. Thus the partial derivation of *thirteen*, for example, is as shown in (99). Phonological processes provide the phonetic representation of *thirteen*. Note that the Switch rule gives words such as the English *-teen* words the surface structure of PHRASES. There is no evidence in favour of this treatment in English, but in several other languages in which the Switch transformation applies, there is evidence that the resulting structures are PHRASES, rather than, say, NUMBERS. There is no evidence against this in English and I have assumed that more or less the same rule applies in English as in the other languages that have words like the *-teen* words. The meanings

(99) (a)

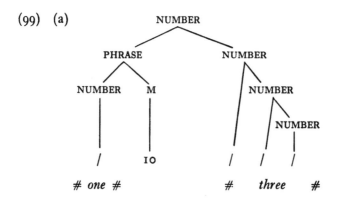

(b)

by 1-Deletion and
⇓ lexicalization of [ten] (96)

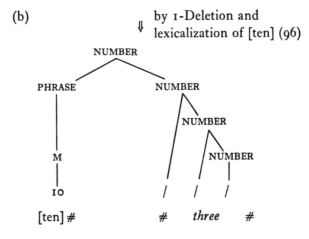

(c)

⇓ by Switch (98)

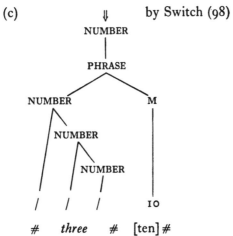

of the English *-teen* words are not evidence against regarding them as PHRASES in surface structure. It is true that the interpretive semantic component we have postulated would interpret structure (99c) as 30, but this is not relevant since the semantic component is designed to interpret structures before the application of any transformations. Structure (99a) is correctly interpreted as 13, and the two transformations we have postulated serve to relate this structure with the English word *thirteen*.

The two transformations we have discussed here are probably adequate in their broad outline, but there is no particularly good evidence in favour of some of their details. Alternative treatments can be envisaged which are equally adequate as far as the data we are considering here are concerned. It remains to provide some means by which the word boundaries are removed from inside words. I propose the following convention, which is of observational adequacy, at least, for English numerals.

(100)   Any word boundary symbol which is not immediately adjacent to another word boundary symbol is deleted.

Convention (100) will convert *# two # ty #* to *# two ty #*, *# three # ty #* to *# three ty #*, etc., as desired. Convention (100) will also convert *# three # teen #*, *# four # teen #*, etc., to *# three teen #*, *# four teen #*, etc., as required.

To summarize, the transformational component of the grammar of English numerals contains lexicalization rules and other transformational rules which perform familiar transformational operations such as deletion and adjunction of elements in phrase markers. The difference between lexicalization rules and other transformations is that the former introduce phonological forms into phrase markers, whereas the latter do not. No general statement appears to be necessary stipulating that lexicalization rules apply before other transformations or vice versa. Indeed we have seen a case where a generalization is captured by collapsing a lexicalization rule and a deletion rule into a single schema, implying simultaneity of application in this case. Lexicalization rules do, however, differ from other transformations in several respects: they play a part in the system of constraints on the wellformedness of base phrase markers, and they may be filled out by the operation of the lexical extension component.

2.7 Overview

With the description of the word formation processes we have completed our description of the syntax and semantics of English numerals. Just the phonology remains. What is most characteristic and interesting in the numeral system, what sets it aside, possibly, from the rest of the language, is the special nature of its semantics and deep syntax. The closer we get to the surface syntax, the less peculiar, probably, is the form of the rules and statements we have to make. Consequently, the closer we get to the surface syntax and the phonology, the more arbitrary and unprofitable is our confinement to just the data of the numeral system. If we are interested in discovering linguistic universals, in discovering what forms of statements must be available for a general and explanatory account of any language, the most powerful light shed by a consideration of just numeral systems is on the semantic and deep syntactic aspects of language. Thus I believe that the study of numeral systems, of which this chapter is an example, shows beyond reasonable doubt that a grammar of a language must contain an interpretive semantic component of the kind I have described, a set of general constraints of the form I have proposed, a set of lexicalization rules of approximately the type I have mentioned, and possibly a lexical extension component after the vague outline I have presented or else some notational equivalent of these devices. Components of a grammar such as these will not necessarily prove useful in all areas of a language outside the numeral system, but since almost all languages have numeral systems, however rudimentary, some of these components will necessarily have a place in any complete description of a language. And the overall economy of descriptions of entire languages will be enhanced to the extent that they make use of components that must be postulated for several independent reasons. Thus it is reasonable to expect that some of the components in the form we have described here will be useful in accounting for parts of languages other than their numeral systems.

General conclusions of any especially interesting kind cannot be drawn from the more superficial aspects of the syntax of numerals. In particular, the transformational components of numeral systems are very meagre. I have presented a description which is adequate for the English numeral system, but which might have to be revised in the light of future research. There are certainly many details of my treatment

remaining unexamined for lack of decisive evidence. The description we
have presented of the more superficial aspects of the syntax of numerals
has value because (a) it has drawn attention to data and raised certain
possible treatments, and (b) it has 'justified' the more interesting
conclusions reached with regard to the semantics and deeper syntax
of numerals by showing that they do not have any obviously unacceptable consequences for the surface syntax.

3 Mixtec numerals

The ancient and modern Mixtec numeral systems, as they are described by Merrifield (1968), provide a pretty example of the operation, within a largely nondecimal system, of the general constraints we have described. Merrifield's informal description of the system is quoted below.

Mixtec number names are sketched below in three sections. Sections A and B taken together is an approximation of the earlier vigesimal system. They account for the positive integers from 1 to 7999. Presumably there was also a morpheme for '8000' which took the system to at least 159999.

Sections A and C taken together illustrate the contemporary forms as used for all aspects of counting. They account for the positive integers from 1 to 9999.

Section A: į̃į '1', ùù '2', ùnì '3', kų̀ų̀ '4', ų̃ʔų̃ '5', ìñù '6', ùhà '7', ùnà '8', į̃į '9', ùšì '10', ùšì į̃į '11', ùšì ùù '12', ùšì ùnì '13', ùšì kų̀ų̀ '14', šìàʔų̃ '15', šìàʔų̃ į̃į '16',...šìàʔų̃ kų̀ų̀ '19', òkò '20', òkò į̃į '21',...òkò į̃į '29',...òkò ùšì ùnì '33',...òkò šìàʔų̃ ùù '37',...ùù šiko šìàʔų̃ ùnì '58',...ùnì šiko ùù '62',...kų̀ų̀ šiko šìàʔų̃ kų̀ų̀ '99'.

Section B: ų̃ʔų̃ šiko '100',...ùšì ùù šiko ùšì '250',...šìàʔų̃ kų̀ų̀ šiko šìàʔų̃ kų̀ų̀ '399',...į̃į tùù ùšì ų̃ '411',...ùù tùù ùšì šiko šìàʔų̃ '1015',...ùnì tùù ùšì ų̃ šiko šìàʔų̃ į̃į '1436',...ùšì tùù ùù šiko ùù '4042',...šìàʔų̃ kų̀ų̀ túù šìàʔų̃ kų̀ų̀ šiko šìàʔų̃ kų̀ų̀ '7999'.

Section C: į̃į sientú '100',...ùù sientú ùù šiko ùšì '250', ...ùšì sientú šìàʔų̃ '1015',...ùšì ų̃ų̃ sientú òkò šìàʔų̃ į̃į '1436', ùù šiko sientú ùù šiko ùù '4042',... kų̀ų̀ šiko šìàʔų̃ kų̀ų̀ sientú kų̀ų̀ šiko šìàʔų̃ kų̀ų̀ '9999'. (Merrifield, 95)

I have left uncorrected the misprints in these data given by Merrifield. The most crucial is that the expression he gives as ùšì ų̃ų̃ sientú òkò šìàʔų̃ į̃į in Section C means 1236, and not 1436, as appears printed in his account. Little sense can be made of the data if it is not assumed that this is a misprint. Since there are at least ten other misprints in this and the next two pages of Merrifield's article (pp. 95–7), my assumption seems likely to be correct.

I present first the phrase structure rules and a sample of the lexicon accounting for the ancient system.

(1)   NUMBER → $\left\{ \begin{matrix} / \\ \text{PHRASE} \end{matrix} \right\}$ (NUMBER)

   PHRASE → NUMBER   M

   M → $\left\{ \begin{matrix} \text{10} \\ \text{15} \\ \text{20} \\ \text{NUMBER M} \end{matrix} \right\}$

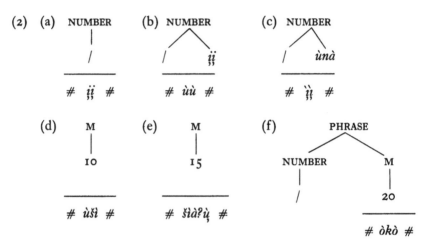

(Lexical entries (2d, e, f) will later be collapsed into a single schema with the rule of 1-Deletion.)

The same semantic component is valid for Mixtec numerals as for (British) English. Thus NUMBERs are interpreted by addition, PHRASEs by multiplication, and Ms by exponentiation, and there is no need for idiosyncratic rules like (31) of ch. 2 accounting for American -*illion*.

In Mixtec, as in other languages, the Packing Strategy is valid and selects the correct underlying structure for any number expressed by the system. The other general constraints, (77) and (79) of ch. 2, are also appropriate for Mixtec numerals. Let us study a few examples of the validity of the Packing Strategy for Mixtec.

Consider first the wellformedness of PHRASES. The phrase structure rules generate two PHRASES with the value 20. These are given, abbreviated with Arabic numeral symbols for convenience, in (3). The M in

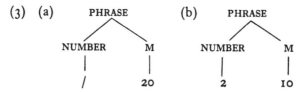

(3a) is the same as that in lexical entries (2f, g) and is thus wellformed; the M in (3b) is the same as that in lexical entry (2d) and is therefore wellformed. The Packing Strategy characterizes structure (3b) as illformed: it has value 20, its right-hand immediate constituent, which is an M, has value 10 and the phrase structure rules generate a well-formed M, namely that in lexical entry (2g), with a value equal to 20 and greater than 10.

The phrase structure rules also generate two distinct PHRASES with value 30. Abbreviated with Arabic notation, these are shown in (4). The

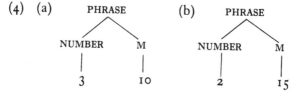

Packing Strategy actually characterizes both of these PHRASES as illformed, because of the wellformedness of the M dominating 20, as in lexical entries (2f, g). It is predicted, then, that there is no wellformed PHRASE in Mixtec with the value 30. This is correct, as the Mixtec expression for 30 is not a PHRASE. The expression is *òkò ùšì*, literally 'twenty ten', which has a structure as in (5).

The phrase structure rules generate three PHRASES with value 60. These are as in (6) (abbreviated). The Packing Strategy characterizes both (6b) and (6c) as illformed, because of the wellformedness of the M dominating (20), as in lexical entries (2f, g). (6a) remains, therefore, as the wellformed PHRASE with value 60. This is correct, as the Mixtec expression for 60 is *ùnì šiko*, literally 'three twenty'. We can see, then, that the Packing Strategy has the effect of restricting the MS *ùšì* and

(5)

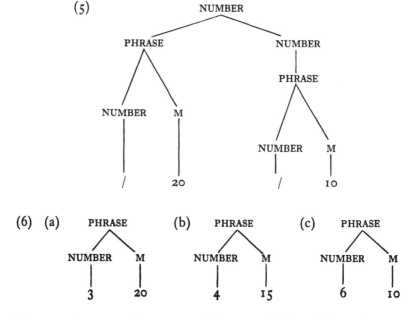

(6) (a) PHRASE   (b) PHRASE   (c) PHRASE

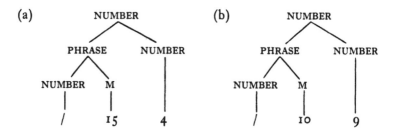

šìáʔụ̀, meaning 10 and 15 respectively, to a single wellformed PHRASE each, in which they are the sister constituents of a NUMBER with value 1.

Now let us consider some NUMBERS. Some of the NUMBER structures generated by the phrase structure rules with value 19 are given in (7).

(7) (abbreviated)

Neither of the PHRASES in these structures, considered in isolation, is illformed. The Packing Strategy characterizes structure (7b) as ill-formed because it has value 19, an immediate constituent, which is a PHRASE, with value 10, and the phrase structure rules generate a well-formed PHRASE, namely that in (7a), with a value less than 19 and greater than 10. The Packing Strategy similarly characterizes all NUMBERS with value 19 except (7a) as illformed. This is correct, as the Mixtec expression for 19 is *šìà?ù̧ kù̧ù̧*, literally 'fifteen four'.

Among the NUMBERs generated by the phrase structure rules with the value 21 are those given in (8), abbreviated. The Packing Strategy

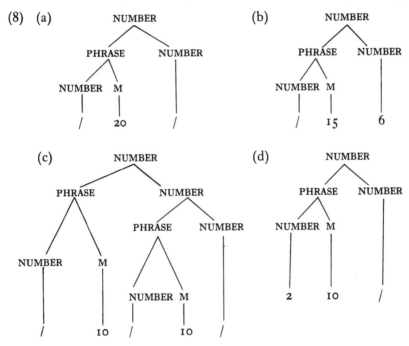

(8) (a) NUMBER (b) NUMBER

(c) NUMBER (d) NUMBER

characterizes structure (8b, c) as illformed because of the wellformedness of the PHRASE in (8a), which has a value greater than those of the PHRASEs which are the immediate constituents of (8b, c). (8d) is illformed because it contains an illformed constituent, its PHRASE. Any other NUMBERs generated by the phrase structure rules with the value 21 are also characterized as illformed by the constraints we have developed. This leaves (8a) as the only structure with value 21. This is correct, as the expression for 21 in Mixtec is *òkò ī̧ī̧*, literally 'twenty one'.

The rule of 1-Deletion is operative in Mixtec. It applies before *ùšì* 'ten', *šìà?ù̧* 'fifteen', and *òkò*, the suppletive variant of *šiko* 'twenty'. The 1-Deletion rule for Mixtec can be collapsed into a single schema with the lexicalization rules for these forms. The schema is as in (9). This rule schema provides that, given a PHRASE whose immediate constituents are a NUMBER dominating just /, and an M dominating either 10 (case i), or 15 (case ii), or 20 (case iii), the left-hand immediate

(9) I-DELETION

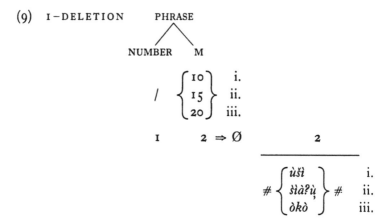

constituent is deleted and the right-hand immediate constituent is associated with either *ùšì* (in case i), or *šìà?ų̀* (in case ii), or *òkò* (in case iii). As noted earlier, the general constraints on wellformedness of phrase markers have the effect of restricting the occurrence of MS with values 10 and 15 to the environment characterized in rule (9).

(10) (abbreviated)

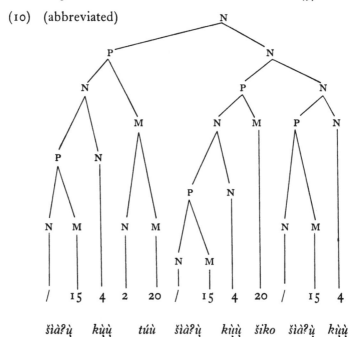

(In this diagram N and P are abbreviations for NUMBER and PHRASE respectively.)

As a final example in this analysis of the ancient Mixtec system, I give in (10) the wellformed structure generated by the phrase structure rules for the highest-valued numeral in the ancient system mentioned by Merrifield, *šàʔù kùù túù šàʔù kùù šiko šàʔù kùù* (15 4 400 15 4 20 15 4). The value assigned to this structure by the semantic component is 7,999, $((15+4) \times 20^2) + ((15+4) \times 20) + 15 + 4$. The reader can check that it is wellformed according to all the constraints we have formulated and also that it is the only wellformed structure with value 7,999.

We turn now to the modern Mixtec system. Merrifield notes, 'The partially decimal system of today for numbers above 99 very likely dates from the introduction of the Spanish loan *sientú* "hundred" into the system' (p. 95). And in fact we can provide a correct grammar of the modern numeral system merely by making the appropriate simple change in the lexicon of the grammar for the ancient system. The grammar for the modern system is exactly the same as that we have presented for the ancient system, except that (2h), the entry for *tùù*, 400, is no longer present, and a new entry for the Spanish loan *sientú* replaces it. The new entry is as in (11).

(11)

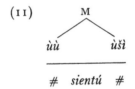

$$\text{\# \quad \textit{sientú} \quad \#}$$

The Packing Strategy, the other general constraints we have described, the semantic component, the phrase structure rules, the formulation (9) of the 1-Deletion rule, and all the entries in the lexicon except that for *tùù* remain valid for the modern system as for the ancient system. Let us consider some examples of how the correct numeral expressions are generated and selected in the modern system.

Obviously the introduction of lexical entry (11) has no effect on expressions for numbers less than 100. These expressions are the same as in the old system. Consider first, then, the expression for 100. Some PHRASES generated by the phrase structure rules with value 100 are as in (12). All the Ms in these PHRASES are wellformed, since each one is identical to some M found in the lexicon. The Packing Strategy characterizes structures (12b, c) as illformed because of the wellformedness of the M in (12a) which has a value greater than those of the Ms which are the immediate constituents of (12b, c). All other structures with value

(12)   (a)

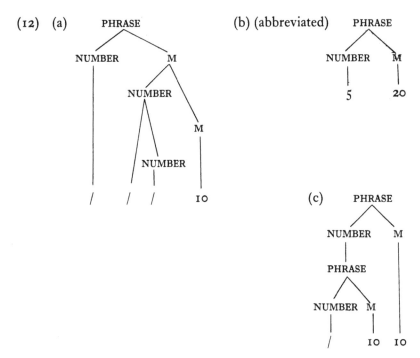

(b) (abbreviated)

(c)

100 are characterized as illformed by our constraints. This leaves (12a) as the only wellformed PHRASE with value 100. Structure (12a) is lexicalized as *ɨɨ sientú*. The 1-Deletion rule (9) is not applicable and does not delete the *ɨɨ* in this expression. This is correct. The modern Mixtec expression for 100 is *ɨɨ sientú*, 'one hundred'.

Now consider expressions for 400. Some of the PHRASES generated by the phrase structure rules with this value are given in (13). The M which is an immediate constituent of (13d) is illformed because it is distinct from all Ms specified in the lexicon of modern Mixtec. (13d) is therefore illformed. The Ms in (13a, b, c) are all wellformed, considered in isolation. The Packing Strategy characterizes (13b, c) as illformed because of the wellformedness of the M in (13a), which has a value greater than those of the Ms which are the immediate constituents of (13b, c). (13a) is the only wellformed PHRASE with value 400. The expression for 400 in modern Mixtec is *kùù sientú*, 'four hundred'.

Some PHRASES generated by the phrase structure rules with value 1,000 are as in (14). Interestingly, modern Mixtec has apparently not borrowed a word for 1,000 from Spanish. The M which is the right-hand immediate constituent of (14b) is therefore illformed, since it is distinct from all Ms

(13) (abbreviated)

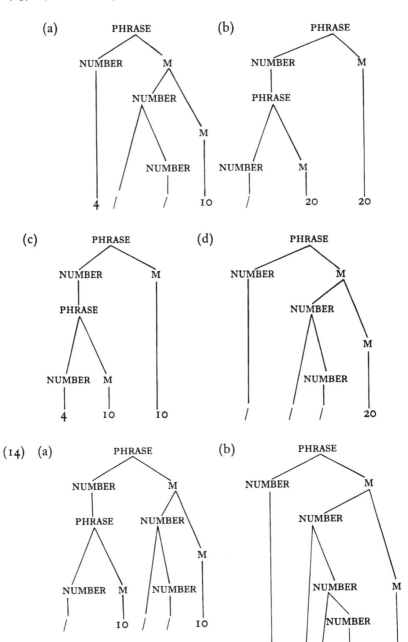

specified in the lexicon. (14b) is therefore itself illformed. All other
structures with value 1,000 are also characterized as illformed by our
constraints. This leaves (14a) as the only wellformed structure with
value 1,000. (14a) is lexicalized as *įį ùšì sientú*. The rule of 1-Deletion
converts this into *ùšì sientú*, 'ten hundred', the modern Mixtec expression for 1,000.

Finally, in (15), I give the structure for the highest-valued numeral
in the modern system mentioned by Merrifield. The value assigned to

(15) (abbreviated)

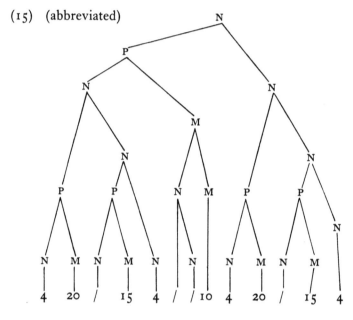

kų̀ų̀   šiko   šìàʔų̀   kų̀ų̀   sientú   kų́ų́   šiko   šìàʔų́   kų́ų́

this structure by the semantic component is 9,999, $(((4 \times 20) + 15 + 4)$
$\times 10^2) + (4 \times 20) + 15 + 4$. The reader can check that this structure is
wellformed according to the constraints we have developed and also
that there are no other wellformed structures in modern Mixtec with
this value.

4   French numerals

4.1 A mixed system

Considered as a single system, French number-names are quite irregular, particularly in the way they express numbers below 100. These irregularities are principally connected with peculiar treatment of the forms for 7, 8, 9, and 20 when these appear, or might be expected to appear, in complex structures. Thus the forms for 17, 18, 19 are formed in a strikingly different way from the forms for 11, ..., 16, which appear to undergo a transformation not undergone by the forms for 17, 18, and 19. Similarly the forms for 70, 80, and 90 are formed in a way even more strikingly different from the forms for 30, ..., 60. As for the form for 20, it, like the form for 10, is morphologically (though not etymologically) simple, while the forms for 30, ..., 90 are morphologically (or syntactically) complex. The form for 20 is used, in a single idiosyncratic instance, in a multiplicational relationship in the expression for 80, 4 × 20. Though there are forms for higher powers of 10, such as *cent* and *mille* (100 and 1,000 respectively), there are not single forms for higher powers of 20, despite its use in a multiplicational relationship in the expression for 80. The conjunction *et* is found before the names for 1 and 11 when these follow a multiple of 10 except when they follow the form for 20 used in a multiplicational relationship in the expression for 80 (e.g. *vingt et un* = 21, *soixante et un* = 61, *soixante et onze* = 71, but *quatre-vingt-un* = 81, and *quatre-vingt-onze* = 91). The form *vingt*, 20, is pronounced slightly differently when used in a multiplicational relationship.

It seems plausible to regard the French numerals not as a single system, but as two separate interacting systems. I shall refer to these systems as Romance and Celtic. I postulate that the Romance system has exactly the same set of phrase structure rules as English (see ch. 2). The Celtic system, of which only fragments of the historical original are deducible and synchronically relevant, uses 20 in a multiplicational relationship, but has no special way of forming structures for powers of 20, so there is in this system a rule (1).

(1)   M → 20

I postulate further that the Celtic system, as it survives in modern French, forms structures for the numbers from 1 to 19 in the same way as the Romance system. Thus the value 10 is also used as an M and it is possible for both 10 and 20 to occur as Ms in the same structure, as, for example, in the structure (see below) which I postulate to underlie *quatre-vingt-dix*, 90. Thus the base components of the Romance and Celtic systems, merged in modern French, have some basic semantic concepts in common, namely 1 and 10, but direct reference to the concept of 20 is peculiar to the Celtic system. French tends to avoid structures containing 20 wherever possible. Before this can be shown, it must first be explained why modern French cannot avoid structures containing 20 altogether by simply abandoning this vigesimal relic and adopting a purely decimal system. The reason appears to be that in French, as in other Romance languages, certain other number concepts namely 7, 8, and 9, are singled out for special treatment, and in French these concepts appear to be highly marked, to be avoided even at the cost of sometimes using the Celtic remnant 20. I will give examples of this below. I propose the following 'merged' set of phrase structure rules as the rules of modern French.

(2)

$$\text{NUMBER} \rightarrow \left\{ \begin{array}{c} / \\ \text{PHRASE} \end{array} \right\} \quad (\text{NUMBER})$$

$$\text{PHRASE} \rightarrow \text{NUMBER} \quad \text{M}$$

$$\text{M} \rightarrow \left\{ \begin{array}{c} 10 \\ 20 \\ \text{NUMBER M} \end{array} \right\}$$

The semantic component of the French numeral system is identical to that of the American English numeral system (see ch. 2).

4.2 Wellformedness constraints

The phrase structure rules (2) actually generate several phrase markers corresponding to a single number: i.e. in many cases they generate sets of semantically equivalent phrase markers. Some of these phrase markers are wellformed; others are not. Many phrase markers can be naturally rejected by the same constraints as I have proposed for English, which appear to be appropriate for French. The phrase structure rules are actually more powerful than the English ones and generate larger sets of phrase markers for most numbers up to 99. Nevertheless French, like English, has only one wellformed number-name corresponding to each number below 100. There is an additional process in French for 'weeding out' phrase markers which are not wellformed. It turns out that this can be defined quite easily in terms of what can be called the 'highly marked' semantic values 7, 8, and 9, and the 'peculiarly Celtic' value 20. We will now formulate the additional constraint that is needed specifically in French for selecting wellformed base phrase markers. This is given in (3).

(3) A PHRASE generated by the phrase structure rules is illformed if:
  (a) it contains no more than one M node and contains a NUMBER with value greater than 6, or
  (b) it contains the terminal symbol 20 and is not semantically equivalent to some structure meeting condition (a) above.

Application of constraint (3) precedes application of the Packing Strategy, which is the same for French as for English (see (82), ch. 2). The other general constraints proposed for English, namely (77) and (79) in ch. 2, are also appropriate to French. Thus any structure containing an illformed structure is itself illformed, and any M distinct from all M types characterized in the lexicon is also illformed. We will mention the relevant parts of the French numeral lexicon directly. I illustrate below the way in which the constraints I have described select just the set of wellformed numeral expressions in French.

First consider the set of PHRASEs generated by the phrase structure rules with the value 20. There are just two members of this set, (4a) and

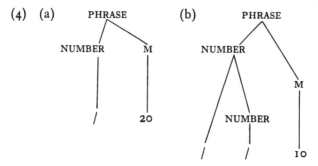

(4b). Condition (3a) does not apply to either of these PHRASES, since no NUMBER with value greater than 6 occurs in them. Condition (3b) applies and characterizes (4a) as illformed. All other structures but (4b) (and, irrelevantly here, the M in (4a)) generated by the phrase structure rules with the value 20 are characterized as illformed by the Packing Strategy, just as in the case of their English counterparts.

Now consider how the correct structure for the expression for 60 is selected by constraint (3) from the two possibilities in (5). (For convenience, I abbreviate with Arabic notation here and in the following passages the tree structures of NUMBERs with a value less than 10.)

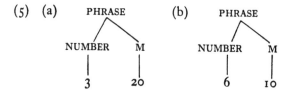

Condition (a) of (3) is not applicable; condition (b) is and characterizes structure (5a) as illformed. All other structures generated by the phrase structure rules with the value 60 are characterized as illformed by the Packing Strategy. This result is correct, since (5b) is an appropriate structure for *soixante*, 'sixty'.

The only PHRASE generated by the phrase structure rules with the value 70 is (6). This structure is characterized as illformed by condition

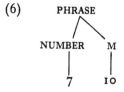

(a) of constraint (3). There is thus no wellformed PHRASE in French with the value 70. The only remaining structures generated by the phrase structure rules with the value 70 are all NUMBERs. I give some of the more obvious candidates for wellformedness from among these in (7). Of these structures (7b) and (7d) are characterized as illformed by the Packing Strategy because the phrase structure rules generate a well-formed PHRASE with a value greater than 50 and less than 70, namely (5b). (7c) and (7d) are illformed because they contain illformed constituents, the left-hand PHRASE in (7c) and the right-hand PHRASE in (7d). ((7d) is thus actually characterized as illformed by two separate

(7) (a)   (b)

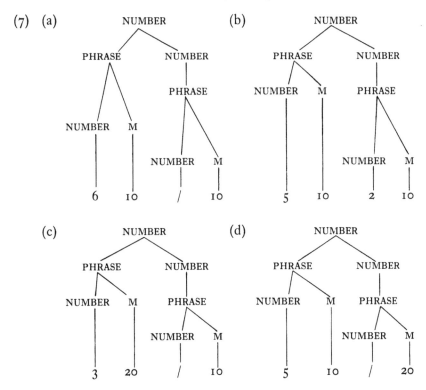

constraints.) The remaining structure, which is not eliminated by any constraint, is (7a). This structure is thus the correct underlying form for the French expression for 70. The result is again appropriate, as the French for 70 is *soixante-dix*, literally 'sixty ten'.

Let us watch the same processes at work in the selection of the correct French deep structure for 80. The two PHRASES generated by the phrase structure rules with this value are given in (8). Condition (a) of constraint

(8) (a)   PHRASE   (b)   PHRASE

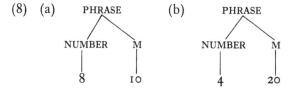

(3) applies to characterize (8a) as illformed. Condition (b) does not eliminate (8b) because of the existence of the semantically equivalent (8a) just excluded by condition (a). This leaves (8b) as the only well-formed PHRASE with the value 80. All other structures with value 80

are characterized as illformed by the Packing Strategy. This is right, as the French for 80 is *quatre-vingts*, literally 'four-twenties'.

Finally the only PHRASE generated by the phrase structure rules with the value 90 is (9). This structure is characterized as illformed by

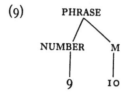

condition (a) of constraint (3). The only remaining structures with value 90 are thus all NUMBERS. In (10) I give some of those which come to mind as the more likely candidates for wellformedness. Structures

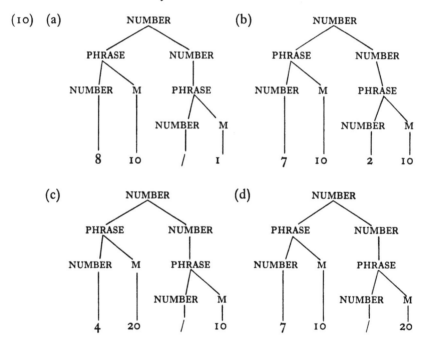

(10a, b, d) all contain illformed PHRASES – (10d) in fact contains two. They are therefore themselves illformed. (10b, d) are also characterized as illformed by the Packing Strategy. (10c) is the only remaining structure and this is in fact the correct underlying structure for the French expression for 90, *quatre-vingt-dix*, literally 'four-twenty-ten'.

The reader may check for himself that one can go through this

exercise in selecting the correct French deep structure corresponding to any numerical value. I should note here that condition (a) of (3) stipulates that the PHRASE contain 'no more than one M node' because the irregularities connected with 'highly marked' values 7, 8, and 9 occur only in the numerals with values lower than 100. *Sept cent, huit cent*, and *neuf cent*, literally 'seven hundred', 'eight hundred', and 'nine hundred' respectively are all, for example, wellformed. The structure underlying *cent* is the same as that underlying English *hundred*, which contains two M nodes (one dominating the other). Constraint (3a) therefore does not apply to PHRASES with *cent* or any of the higher-valued MS.

In summary, the numeral system of a given language may have certain constraints in common with other numeral systems. The Packing Strategy is an example of such a constraint. In addition, a given numeral system may have constraints which are peculiar to it alone. Constraint (3) is a language-specific constraint of this sort. The order of application of the constraints in a numeral system may sometimes have to be stated explicitly, as here in the case of French, where we must explicitly state that constraint (3) operates before the Packing Strategy.

In connection with the constraints I have proposed I must disclaim any equation of these theoretical devices with 'psychological reality'. There is little, if any, reason to suppose that French speakers today are actually aware, at any level, of an aversion to the concepts 7, 8, and 9. And it is most implausible that French speakers actually produce number-names by first generating large sets of semantically equivalent deep structures and then systematically weeding out the unacceptable ones. It seems, on the other hand, that the constraints I have postulated correspond in some way to the statistical sociological mean of the implicit preferences of French speakers during the whole evolution of the modern language. This is borne out by evidence that the numeral system of French has been in the past much more fluid than it is now, with a number of rival expressions vying for recognition as standard. Brunot writes thus of the state of the language in the sixteenth century.

La lutte continue entre les nombres hérités du latin pour les dizaines, et les formes faites par addition: *soixante dix, quatre vingt dix*. Presque tous les grammairiens donnent encore *septante* et *nonante*. Cependant Palsgrave reconnaissait que si cette manière de compter était celle des gens instruits, le peuple tenait pour *soixante dix*, et Meigret dit formellement que la manière nouvelle est plus reçue est plus approuvée. Ces témoignages sont confirmés par celui de Fabri, qui se plaint 'de cet erreur incorrigible de dire *quatre vingt douze* pour *nonante deux*'.

. . .

En second lieu, il faut signaler la continuation de la lutte entre le système latin de numération par dix et le système rival de numération par *vingt*.

Quatre vingts s'impose peu à peu au depens de *octante* ou *huitante*. Non que *octante* soit proscrit; il est au contraire recommandé par plusieurs grammairiens et donné par tous. Il se rencontre de même chez les auteurs.

Mais Meigret considère déjà *qatre vins* comme plus reçu.

En revanche, les autres multiples de *vingt*, quoïqu'usités jusqu'à 400, ne sont pas également en usage. *Sis vins* l'emporte sur *cent vins*, mais *cent soessante* est aussi bien dit que *huyt vins*, et *quinze vins*, sauf dans le nom de l'hospice, est à peu pres abandonné. (Brunot, 309–10)

A grammar of sixteenth-century French numerals would not contain the language-specific constraint which is appropriate for the modern language and the variation described by Brunot would be predicted. This is interesting in that it leads to the conclusion that the language has become standardized at the expense of complicating the grammar. Such need not have been the case; the numeral system could also have been standardized by a simplification of the phrase structure rules, i.e. by omitting 20 from the rule expanding M.

4.3 The lexicon and word formation

The French words for *one*, . . . , *nine* are *un, deux, trois, quatre, cinq, six, sept, huit, neuf*. The lexicalization rules for these words look just like their English counterparts. The lexical entries for *cent* and *mille* look like the entries for their English counterparts *hundred* and *thousand*. In French the *-illions* follow the American, rather than the British model. Thus in a British English–French dictionary French *trillion* is found in the entry for English *billion*. If we look up French *billion*, we find *thousand million*. The lexical extension component postulated to account for the English *-illions* is also necessary for the French *-illions*. The form *milliard* occurs in French dictionaries, with an English translation of *thousand million*, but forms like **billiard, *trilliard* do not occur, at least as numerals. I have not investigated the use of *milliard*.

Of more interest are the various lexicalizations of the semantic value

10. The most straightforward of these is the suffix *-ante*, which corresponds roughly to English *-ty*. The lexical entry for *-ante* is as in (11).

(11)

I assume that this suffix is present in all the forms *trente, quarante, cinquante, soixante*. The underlying structure of *trente*, for example, is as in (12). The left-hand immediate constituent of this structure is

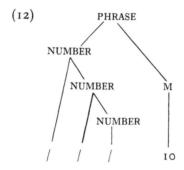

lexicalized as *trois*; the right-hand immediate constituent is lexicalized as *-ante* by rule (11). Later rules, mainly phonological, convert the resulting #*trois*# *ante*# to #*trente*#.

The form for 10 used in isolation and also in the forms for 17, 18, and 19, is *dix*. As with English *-teen*, the lexical entry for this form can be collapsed with the rule of 1-Deletion (see rules (95)–(96) of ch. 2), but in French there is a complication in that the rule of 1-Deletion is also applicable, optionally, before the forms *cent* and *mille*. That is, both *cent* and *un cent* are acceptable expressions for 100, and both *mille* and *un mille* are acceptable expressions for 1,000. Before *dix*, however, 1-Deletion applies obligatorily, since **un dix* is not an acceptable expression for 10. The rule of 1-Deletion in French, collapsed with the lexical entry for *dix*, is given in (13). This rule schema specifies certain operations to be performed on a PHRASE whose immediate constituents are a NUMBER dominating just /, and either an M dominating just 10 (case i), or an M with two immediate constituents, of which the right-hand one is an M dominating just 10 (case ii). In case i the left-hand immediate

(13) 1-DELETION

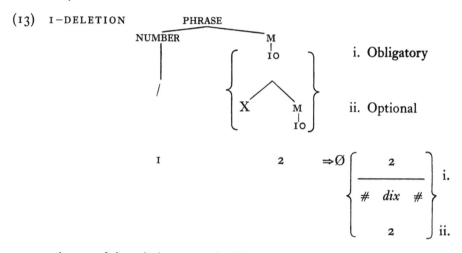

i. Obligatory

ii. Optional

constituent of the whole PHRASE is obligatorily deleted and the phonological form *dix* is associated with the right-hand immediate constituent. In case ii, the left-hand immediate constituent of the PHRASE is optionally deleted. The formulation of case ii here takes advantage of the fact that *cent* and *mille* are the only two forms whose underlying structures contain just two MS, one dominating the other. Examples of the operation of rule (13) are given below.

The underlying structure of *dix-sept*, 17, is as in (14). The right-hand

(14) (abbreviated)

(15) (abbreviated)

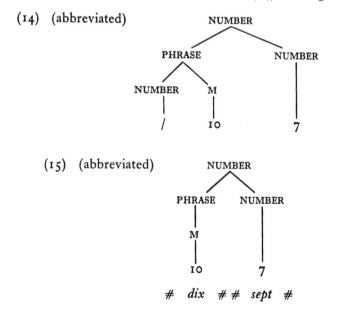

immediate constituent of this structure is lexicalized as *sept*. After this lexicalization and the operation of case i of rule (13), (14) becomes (15). I have not investigated the matter of whether *dix-sept* should be considered a word or not. If it is a word, then some mechanism must remove the internal word boundary symbols. Apart from this no further processes of any interest apply to the terminal string of (15). The forms *dix-huit*, 18, and *dix-neuf*, 19, are, of course, generated in a similar way, as is the simple form *dix*, 10.

The underlying structure for *mille*, after lexicalization rules have applied to it, is as in (16). Case ii of rule (13) may optionally apply to

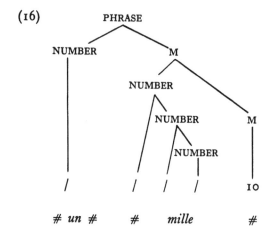

(16)

this structure. If it does, the left-hand immediate constituent is deleted and the result is simply *mille*. If it does not apply, the result is the synonymous *un mille*.

The suffix *-ze* is a form for 10 just in the expressions *onze, douze, treize, quatorze, quinze, seize*, 11, ..., 16. And it is just in these expressions that the form for 10 follows, rather than precedes, as in *dix-sept, dix-huit, dix-neuf*, the form for the value to which 10 is added. The French forms with *-ze* are, then, like the English *-teen* forms. We generate them by a French version of the Switch rule. This version, given below as (17), incorporates the lexicalization rule for *-ze*, thus capturing the significant generalization that the forms to which Switch applies are just those that also contain *-ze*. This rule provides that, given a NUMBER whose left-hand immediate constituent is a structure lexicalized as *dix*, and whose right-hand immediate constituent is a NUMBER with value less than 7, then the right-hand constituent must be moved

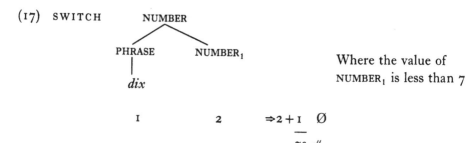

(17) SWITCH

Where the value of NUMBER₁ is less than 7

to become a sister constituent of *dix*; the phonological form *-ze* is now associated with the structure previously associated with the form *dix*, which is now suppressed. The condition in rule (17) that the NUMBER to be moved must have a value less than 7 expresses the significant generalization that the *-ze* forms denote a semantically natural class of values, i.e. all and only the values from 11 to 16, rather than some random set of values. To illustrate the operation of this rule, consider the derivation of the form *onze*, whose underlying structure is given in (18).

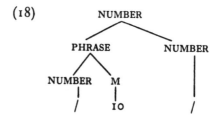

(18)

Lexicalization of *un* and 1-Deletion (13) convert this to (19). Applying

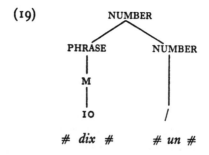

(19)

Switch (17) to this, we get (20). Similar derivations are also provided for the forms *douze*, ..., *seize*. As in the case of the forms with *-ante*, some fairly idiosyncratic phonological processes must be postulated to yield the final phonetic forms in some cases. The French *-ze* forms are here

(20)

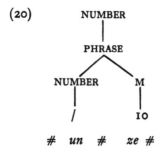

assigned the surface structure of PHRASES. As in English, there is no compelling evidence for this treatment, but it is adopted in order to allow a fairly universal formulation of the Switch rule. In other languages there is evidence that forms produced by a process like Switch are PHRASES (see, for example, ch. 6, on Welsh).

At this point we can mention that convention (100) of ch. 2, which deletes isolated internal word boundaries, is also appropriate for French. It will delete the internal word boundary symbol from the terminal string of (20), for example, yielding #*un ze*# (converted later by phonological processes to *onze*). Clearly this mechanism will apply to all the -*ze* forms and also to all the -*ante* forms. #*Cinq*# *ante*#, for example, becomes #*cinq ante*#.

The phrase structure rules (2) allow for generation of structures with recursion of the node M whatever value, 10 or 20, the last, nonrecursive application of the rule selects. But structures of the form (21) are ill-formed in French because they are distinct from all M types character-

(21)

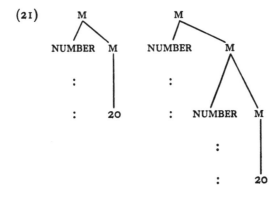

ized in the lexicon (see (79) of ch. 2). The only M in the lexicon that contains the terminal symbol 20 has the structure in (22).

(22)   M
|
20

Structure (22) is lexicalized as *vingt*. I take up the subject of the lexicalization of *vingt* in the next section.

4.4 The lexical extension component

The constraints described earlier in this chapter operate to select distinct underlying structures for the formative *vingt*, depending on how it is used. In the expression *quatre-vingts*, as we have seen (see structure (8b)), the postulated underlying structure for *vingt* is as in (22). But the constraints I have proposed select structure (4b) as that underlying *vingt* when this morpheme is used in the expressions for 20, ..., 29. This structure is preferred to (4a), which contains the peculiarly Celtic element 20. At first blush it might seem quite unnatural to derive *vingt* thus in two different ways, but further consideration of French numerals provides some support for this analysis.

In general the conjunction *et* must be inserted between an M dominating 10 and a NUMBER with value 1. Thus we find *trente et un*, 'thirty and one', *quarante et un*, 'forty and one', *cinquante et un*, 'fifty and one', *soixante et un*, 'sixty and one'. Conforming to this general pattern we find *vingt et un*, 'twenty and one'. But we do not find the conjunction *et* before *un* in *quatre-vingt-un*, literally 'four-twenty-one', 81. This is a small piece of evidence that *vingt* in *vingt et un* is in some way different from *vingt* in *quatre-vingt-un* and furthermore that the latter does not contain an M dominating 10 in its underlying structure. The general success of the other descriptive devices we have postulated, especially constraint (3), lends more credence to this conclusion. There is also a phonetic difference between *vingt* in *vingt et un*, ..., *vingt-neuf* and *vingt* in *quatre-vingts*, ..., *quatre-vingt-dix-neuf*. This difference, as I shall argue directly, also lends credence to the treatment of *vingt* being developed here.

Let us assume, then, that the structure of *vingt* in the expressions for 20, ..., 29 is as in (4b), while the structure of *vingt* in the expressions for 80, 81, ..., 99 is as in (22). If we postulate two separate, and apparently unrelated lexical entries for *vingt*, one specifying structure (4b) and the other specifying structure (22), we shall miss capturing the important generalization that, whatever its structure, *vingt* is always associated with the same semantic representation, 20.

This generalization can be captured by making one of the lexical entries for *vingt* incomplete, to be filled out with the appropriate phonological form by the lexical extension component. I envisage the two lexical entries in (23). The incomplete lexical entry (23b) represents

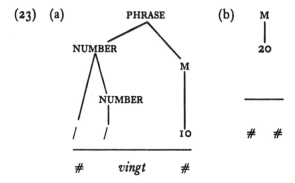

a need for a word, to be used as an M, i.e. in a multiplicational relationship with another numeral, and with the value 20. The grammar already, by means of a derivation utilizing lexical entry (23a), expresses an association between the semantic representation 20 and the phonetic form [vɛ̃] or [vɛ̃t]. On the basis of this association, the lexical extension component fills out the incomplete entry (23b) according to principle (76) of ch. 2, converting it to (24).

(24)   M
          |
          20
       ―――――――
       #[vɛ̃]#

We can now mention the phonetic difference that exists between the *vingt* of *vingt et un*, etc., and that of *quatre-vingts*, etc. Bullock (1949, p. 208) puts the matter very succinctly: 'La consonne finale de *vingt* se prononce de 21 à 29 inclusivement, mais elle est muette de 80 à 99 inclusivement.' She gives the following transcriptions which bear out this observation.

20. vingt [vɛ̃]
21. vingt et un [vɛ̃t e œ̃]
22. vingt-deux [vɛ̃tdø] [vɛ̃ddø]

23. vingt-trois [vɛ̃ttrwa]

    ...

80. quatre-vingts [katrə vɛ̃]
81. quatre-vingt-un [katrə vɛ̃ œ̃]
90. quatre-vingt-dix [katrə vɛ̃ dis]
91. quatre-vingt-onze [katrə vɛ̃ ɔ̃ːz]

                                        (Bullock, 207–8)

I presume that the phonological representation of *vingt* as in *vingt et un*, etc., is /vinte/. That is, the actual phonological representation specified in lexical entry (23a) is /vinte/. The regular phonological rules proposed for French by Schane (1968) will convert this to the phonetic form [vɛ̃t], the form of *vingt* that occurs in the numerals from 21 through 29.

In isolation and before MS and nouns beginning with a consonant, the phonetic form of *vingt*, 20, is [vɛ̃]. Before nouns beginning with a vowel, the phonetic form of *vingt*, 20, is [vɛ̃t]. Thus we find:

(25)   numéro vingt 'number twenty' [nymero vɛ̃]
       vingt mille 'twenty thousand' [vɛ̃ mil]
       vingt jours 'twenty days' [vɛ̃ ʒur]
       vingt ans 'twenty years' [vɛ̃t ɑ̃]

This seems to indicate that the final /e/ in the phonological representation of *vingt*, 20, is dropped in these environments. Schane's rules will convert /vint/ into [vɛ̃t] before a vowel and into [vɛ̃] elsewhere. Presumably there is an early idiosyncratic rule deleting the final /e/ of /vinte/ when this is the sole constituent of a NUMBER, as it is in the examples of (25) but not in the numeral expressions *vingt et un*, ..., *vingt-neuf*. To illustrate this point, the structure of *vingt mille* is as in (26a) below, while that of *vingt et un* is as in (26b). In (26a), but not in (26b), *vingt* is the sole constituent of a NUMBER.

Postulating an early rule changing /vinte/ to /vint/ in certain environments accounts for an irregularity of a type that is met in connection with other French numerals. Bullock writes, 'La consonne finale de *cent* se prononce seulement pour faire la liaison devant un nom multiplié par le nombre:

cent officiers [sɑ̃t ɔfisje]
cent voitures [sɑ̃ vwatyːr]' (Bullock, 209)

(26)   (a) (abbreviated)   (b)

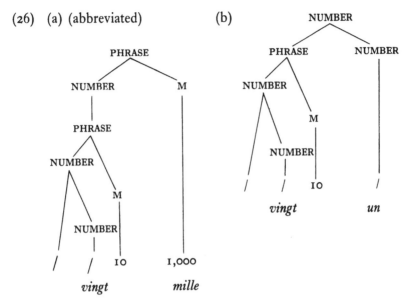

In *cent un*, [sɑ̃ œ̃], and *cent onze*, [sɑ̃ ɔ̃ːz], 101 and 111 respectively, the final consonant of *cent* is not pronounced, even though it occurs before a vowel. These facts can be accounted for by postulating the phonological form of *cent* to be /sent/, which is converted to /sen/ just when *cent* is not the sole constituent of a NUMBER, e.g. in *cent un* and *cent onze*.

Thus it appears that the phonological form of *vingt*, 20, is /vinte/, which is related by phonological rules to two phonetic representations [vɛ̃t] and [vɛ̃]. Note now that if we were to postulate the phonological form in *quatre-vingts*, *quatre-vingt-un*, ..., *quatre-vingt-dix-neuf*, to be /vinte/, we would make the false predictions that these expressions are pronounced *[katrə vɛ̃t], *[katrə vɛ̃t œ̃], ..., *[katrə vɛ̃t diz nøf]. But if we postulate that the lexical extension component fills out the incomplete lexical entry (23b) with the *phonetic* form [vɛ̃], then all is well: the form of *quatre-vingt-un* input to the phonological rules will be the 'mixed' representation /katre vɛ̃ un/ and the phonetic output will be [katrə vɛ̃ œ̃], as required.

An obvious question remains, to which we can give no certain answer. The grammar actually provides two derivations associating the value 20 with two separate phonetic representations [vɛ̃] and [vɛ̃t], as we have seen. On what basis does the lexical extension component choose to fill out the incomplete lexical entry (23b) with [vɛ̃], rather than with [vɛ̃t]?

A possibility is that the lexical extension component chooses, where possible, a derivation involving a phonetic representation that may occur in isolation, as [vɛ̃], but not [vɛ̃t], may. There is obviously not enough evidence available at present to enable us to make a judgment on this matter. Nevertheless it can be claimed that French numerals provide evidence of an interesting sort in favour of a lexical extension component as described in this book. Some peculiar properties of the form *vingt* can be accounted for by postulating two distinct underlying structures for it and hence two lexical entries, and relating these lexical entries to each other via the lexical extension component.

5 Danish numerals

We shall only be concerned here with the Danish numerals from *en*, 'one' to *nioghalvfems*, the expression for 99. The names for the values 100 and greater are not especially remarkable and we shall not say much about them here. Below 100, however, the Danish numeral system displays several odd features and we shall be concerned with describing these within the framework we are developing. An illustrative sample of the expressions for the numbers from 1 to 99 is given below.

(1)

1 en	11 elleve	20 tyve	21 enogtyve
2 to	12 tolv	30 tredive	37 syvogtredive
3 tre	13 tretten	40 fyrre	42 toogfyrre
4 fire	14 fjorten	50 halvtreds	59 nioghalvtres
5 fem	15 femten	60 tres	67 syvogtres
6 seks	16 seksten	70 halvfjerds	86 seksogfirs
7 syv	17 sytten	80 firs	
8 otte	18 atten	90 halvfems	
9 ni	19 nitten		

(These examples are taken from Norlev and Koefoed, 1959.) The numerals in the first and second columns above follow a familiar Germanic pattern and resemble the numerals from *one* to *nineteen* in English. They can be accounted for by a set of rules (including 1-Deletion and Switch) essentially similar to those accounting for English *one*, ..., *nineteen*, and I shall not repeat such rules here.

5.1 Wellformedness constraints

The numerals in the third column of (1) are intriguing, even baffling, at first sight, especially the forms for 50, 60, 70, 80, and 90 and it is to these forms that we shall turn our attention first. The following facts clarify the formation of the expressions *halvtreds*, *halvfjerds*, and *halvfems*. Corresponding to these forms, there are fuller, but now some-

117

what archaic forms *halvtredsindstyve, halvjerdsindstyve,* and *halvfemsindstyve. Halvtredie* and *halvfjerde* are forms, also now somewhat archaic, meaning respectively 2½ and 3½. *Halvtredsindstyve* is, then, literally '2½ times 20', and *halvtreds* is a truncation of this form. Similar explanations can be given for the forms *halvfjerds* and *halvfems. Tres* and *firs* are also truncations, of *tresindstyve* and *firsindstyve* respectively, literally 'two times twenty' and 'four times twenty'. In order to assign appropriate semantic representations to *halvtreds,* etc., in as general way as possible we postulate underlying structures that closely resemble the longer forms and derive the more current forms by a process of truncation. For a similar reason we postulate that *fyrre* 'forty' is a truncation of an underlying form resembling the somewhat archaic form *fyrretyve,* 'four tens'. Strong independent motivation for postulating the long forms as the underlying structures is found in the fact that all ordinal numerals are still formed on the basis of the long forms. Thus we have: *fyrretyvende,* 40th, *halvtredsindstyvende,* 50th, *tresindstyvende,* 60th, etc. Represented in underlying structure, then, we have formulas like the following.

(2) 3 × 10
     4 × 10
     2½ × 20
     3 × 20
     3½ × 20
     4 × 20
     4½ × 20

There is a clear pattern here: up to 40, multiples of 10 are expressed as such; after 40, they are expressed as multiples of 20, even though this sometimes necessitates the use of fractions. Danish is not the only language that uses fractions to form some higher numeral expressions, though the use of fractions is nevertheless rare. Let us leave aside for a moment the question of the proper structure for numerals containing *halv,* simply assuming that they are NUMBERS. I now give two of the phrase structure rules of the Danish numeral system which will allow structures corresponding to the formulas of (2) to be generated.

(3) PHRASE →   NUMBER   M

           ⎧   20   ⎫
     M → ⎨   10   ⎬
           ⎩ NUMBER   M ⎭

These rules are the same as two that we postulated for French. Like the French rules, the Danish rules of (3) actually generate several PHRASES with the same value and as in the French case, the correct structure in each instance can be selected by means of a language-specific constraint. I give below the appropriate formulation of the constraint for Danish, followed by examples of its application.

(4)   A PHRASE generated by the phrase structure rules is illformed if:
    (a) it contains no more than one M node and contains a NUMBER with value greater than or equal to 5, or
    (b) it contains the terminal symbol 20 and is not semantically equivalent to some structure meeting condition (a) above.

This constraint applies in exactly the same way as its French counter-part, (3) of ch. 4. In the following examples, remember that we assume nonwhole numbers such as 2½, 3½, 4½ to be represented in deep structure as NUMBERs. With this assumption, the rules of (3) generate two phrases with the value 30. These, abbreviated for convenience, are as in (5).

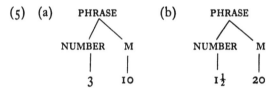

Constraint (4a) is not applicable to either of these structures; constraint (4b) applies and characterizes structure (5b) as illformed. In just the same way, constraint (4) characterizes structure (6b) below as illformed, leaving (6a) as the only wellformed PHRASE with value 40.

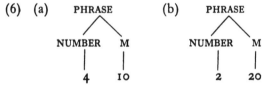

The two alternative PHRASES generated by the rules of (3) with value 50 are as in (7). Constraint (4a) characterizes (7a) as illformed. Constraint

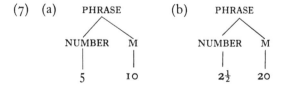

(4b) is not applicable to (7b), because (7b) is semantically equivalent to (7a), characterized as illformed by condition (4a). (7b) therefore remains as the wellformed PHRASE with value 50 in Danish. The correct structures for 60, 70, 80, and 90 are selected in just the same way as that for 50. The two possible structures for 80, for example, are as in (8): (8b) is, of course, the wellformed one. As in the French case, the irregularities

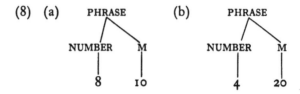

(8)   (a)   PHRASE   (b)   PHRASE

accounted for by the language-specific constraint occur only in PHRASES with a value of less than 100. That is why constraint (4a) includes the condition '...contains no more than one M node'. The general constraints discussed in connection with English are also applicable in Danish (i.e. (77), (79), (82) of ch. 2).

5.2 Some idiosyncratic word formation processes

The constraints just discussed select (9) as the structure underlying

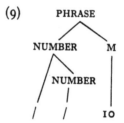

(9)

tyve in the expressions for 20, 21, ..., 29. This structure is motivated on other grounds, as *tyve* is in fact the (irregular) plural form of *ti*. *Tyve* is then literally 'tens'. *Tyve* is found in just this sense in the form *fyrretyve*, 'four tens', of which the more current form for 40, *fyrre*, is a truncation. The form *-dive* in *tredive*, 'thirty' is also recognizable as a phonologically modified version of *tyve*. The derivations of the forms *tyve*, *tredive*, and *fyrre*, require, then, a rule pluralizing the form for 10, followed by some fairly idiosyncratic processes of deletion and phonological modification. Let us formulate the 'Pluralization' rule as (10).

(10) PLURALIZATION

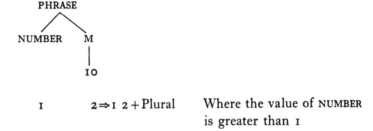

I   2 ⇒ 1 2 + Plural   Where the value of NUMBER
is greater than 1

This rule appends the marker Plural to the right of the form for 10 when it is a constituent of a PHRASE and its sister constituent has a value greater than 1. The rule is a special case of the more general processes of pluralization in Danish, which I do not investigate here. For some more discussion of pluralization in connection with numerals, see the chapter on Welsh (ch. 6). The marker Plural is lexicalized as the irregular suffix *-ve* after *ti*, the form for 10. I give the lexicalization rules for *ti*, *to*, *tre*, and *fire* in (11).

(11)

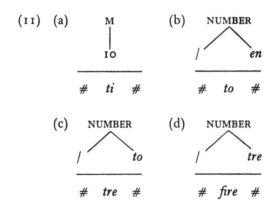

Structure (9) is lexicalized as # *to* # # *ti* #. Rule (10) applies, giving # *to* # # *ti* # + Plural. Lexicalization of the Plural marker and convention (100) of ch. 2 give # *to* # # *ti* + *ve* #. Phonological processes associate the correct phonetic form of *tyve* [ty:və] with # *ti* + *ve* #. There must be an idiosyncratic rule deleting # *to* # when it occurs before *tyve*. By these processes the grammar expresses the association between the semantic representation 20, assigned by the semantic component to structure (9) and the phonetic form [ty:və].

(12)

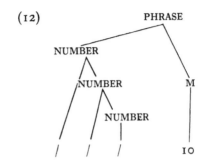

The structure underlying *tredive* is as in (12). This structure is lexicalized as #*tre*# #*ti*#. Rule (10), lexicalization of the Plural marker, and convention 100 of ch. 2 convert this to #*tre*# #*ti+ve*#. After deletion of the internal word boundaries by a rule we shall discuss directly, phonological processes associate this with the appropriate phonetic form [trɛðvə].

The structure underlying *fyrre* is as in (13). Lexicalization, applica-

(13)

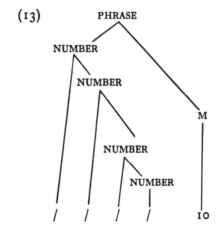

tion of rule (10), lexicalization of the Plural marker, and application of convention (100) of ch. 2 relate this structure to the morphophonological representation #*fire*# #*ti+ve*#. Phonological processes convert this to the phonetic representation [fœr:əty:və]. There must be a rule deleting [ty:vð] as a special case of a somewhat more general process of truncation to be discussed directly, leaving [fœr:ə], the phonetic representation of *fyrre*.

We now consider the structure of the expressions for 2½, 3½, 4½, *halvtredie, halvfjerde, and halvfemte.* The treatment I propose cannot be considered particularly well motivated, since there are so few numeral systems that make use of fractions in constructing their expressions for whole numbers. To my knowledge, the only fraction that is used in this way is $\frac{1}{2}$, as used, for example, in the Danish expressions we are considering here and in Welsh *hanner cant*, 'half hundred', 50. I know of no languages that express whole numbers by means of any other fractions, such as $\frac{1}{4}$ or $\frac{3}{4}$. Although many languages have expressions for fractions, I am not concerned in this study with fractions except where they are used, as in Danish and Welsh, in the formation of expressions for whole numbers.

I introduce here the category FRACTION, of which *halv* is a member. The category FRACTION occurs in the Danish phrase structure rule expanding NUMBER, which I give below.

(14)
$$\text{NUMBER} \rightarrow \left\{ \begin{array}{c} \text{FRACTION} \\ / \\ \text{PHRASE} \end{array} \right\} \quad (\text{NUMBER})$$

This rule differs from its counterpart in English and French only in its inclusion of the category FRACTION. FRACTION has constituents as in rule (15).

(15)   FRACTION → NUMBER   NUMBER

The semantic interpretation of structures generated by these rules will be discussed in a later section. All we need to say here is that the value of a FRACTION is arrived at by dividing the value of the first constituent by that of the second; and in the case where a FRACTION is an immediate constituent of a NUMBER, the value of the NUMBER is the arithmetic difference of the value of the FRACTION and the value of the second immediate constituent. In a theory of numerals which accounted fully for fractions, the semantic rule for interpreting FRACTIONs might turn up quite frequently, but I imagine that the Danish method of subtracting fractions from the NUMBER following them is rather unusual. I postulate rule (15) because it is quite likely to be appropriate for the formation of expressions for fractions in a large number of languages, including Danish. It would be appropriate, for example, in generating English forms such as *two thirds, eight ninths, five hundred and seven one thousandths,* and Danish forms such as *tre ottendele,* $\frac{3}{8}$, and *en fyrretyvendedel,* $\frac{1}{40}$. (These examples are from Bredsdorff, 1956.) I assume the plural and ordinal suffixes in these forms to be appended to them by transformational processes sensitive to the fact that they occur in FRACTIONs. But I do not go into the detailed theory of expressions for fractions in this study. For our purposes, all we need to know is the structure for Danish *halv*. In (16) I give what I envisage to be the

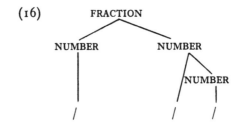

underlying structure for *halv*. The structure in (16) would probably also be appropriate for English *half*. To account for the fact that *halv* is the only FRACTION occurring in Danish expressions for whole numbers I postulate the following *ad hoc* constraint.

(17)   A NUMBER containing any FRACTION other than *halv* is illformed.

We must also formulate some statement characterizing structures such as (18), generated by the phrase structure rules we have postulated, as

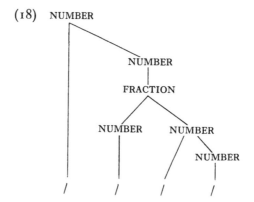

illformed. To eliminate structures such as this, we postulate the *ad hoc* constraint (19).

(19)   A NUMBER is illformed if it has value x, where x is not a whole number, and its left-hand immediate constituent is not a FRAC-TION.

A more detailed study of fractions in various languages would presumably discover more general statements that would account for the facts covered by our *ad hoc* constraints (17) and (19), but these constraints are adequate for our purposes. With the rules and constraints we have postulated, the structure in (20) is generated corresponding to *halvtredie*.

(20)

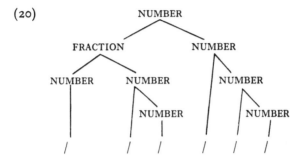

The ordinals of *tre*, *fire*, and *fem* are formed irregularly as *tredie*, *fjerde*, and *femte* respectively. I envisage a rule assigning the marker Ordinal to the structures underlying *halvtredie*, etc. This marker is lexicalized as *-die*, *-de*, or *-te* depending on which particular NUMBER precedes it. The rule assigning the marker Ordinal is as in (21). This

(21) ORDINALIZATION

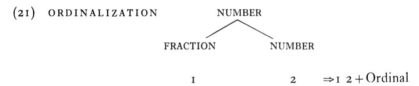

rule appends the marker Ordinal at the right-hand end of a structure matching that specified. With lexicalization of *tre* and *halv* and the appropriate lexicalization rule for the marker Ordinal, structure (20) is lexicalized to # *halv* # # *tre* # *die* #. A rule we shall discuss directly deletes the internal word boundary symbols, yielding # *halvtredie* #. The forms *halvfjerde* and *halvfemte* can be derived by parallel processes.

Now consider the archaic forms *halvtredsindstyve*, *tresindstyve*, *halvfjerdsindstyve*, *firsindstyve*, and *halvfemsindstyve*. The underlying structure for the first of these is as in (22). The processes we have just discussed associate the left-hand immediate constituent of this structure with # *halv* # # *tre* # *die* #. The form *sinds* translates into English as 'times' and is thus the lexical realization of the relationship of multiplication obtaining between the two constituents of a PHRASE. I postulate

(22)

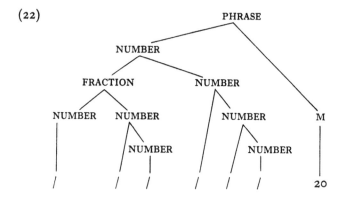

the following lexical entry for *sinds*. This rule attaches *sinds* between the

(23)

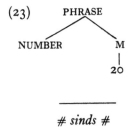

sinds

constituents of a PHRASE when the M of the PHRASE is 20. Finally, to account for *tyve* in expressions such as *halvtredsindstyve* I postulate the incomplete lexical entry (24). We have seen that the grammar provides

(24)   M
         |
         20

         ─────────

         #   #

a derivation associating the phonetic form [ty:və], which is morphologically a word, with the semantic representation 20. The conditions described in (76) of ch. 2 are met in this case and the lexical extension component therefore fills in the incomplete lexical entry (24) with the phonetic representation [ty:və]. The case of Danish *tyve* is a close parallel to that of French *vingt* in that well motivated constraints select two distinct deep structures for various occurrences of the same surface morpheme.

With these lexicalization rules, structure (22) is lexicalized as

 # half # # tre # die # # sinds # # tyve #. There must be an idiosyncratic phonological rule deleting *ie* from *die* just before *sinds*. Finally we have to provide some device for deleting the internal word boundaries. It is a characteristic common to several Germanic languages that even rather lengthy numeral expressions are treated as single words. This characteristic of Danish is adequately described by rule (25).

(25) Within a NUMBER containing no more than one M node, all internal word boundaries are deleted.

After deletion of *ie* and internal word boundaries, we have *# halvtredsindstyve #*, as desired. In a parallel way, the expressions *tresindstyve, halvfjerdsindstyve, firsindstyve*, and *halvfemsindstyve* can also be derived. (Danish grammars actually disagree on whether higher numeral expressions are treated as words or not. Thus Norlev and Koefoed give *enogtyve* for 21, but Bredsdorff gives *en og tyve*. I arbitrarily follow Norlev and Koefoed here, but rule (25) may easily be modified to fit other data.)

The modern Danish expressions for 40, 50, 60, 70, 80, and 90 are derived from the archaic expressions ending in *-tyve* by a process of truncation. I believe this process to take place at a very late stage in derivations, after internal word boundaries have been deleted by rule (25), since the truncation removes part of the word *sinds* but leaves behind its initial consonant. It seems likely that a study of a range of truncation processes of this sort would discover that considerations such as phonetic distinctiveness play some part in determining the extent of the truncation. If, for example, *tresindstyve* were truncated to *tre*, it would become homophonous with the word for 3, obviously undesirable from the point of view of a language user. Phonotactic considerations probably also play a part in determining the extent of the truncation. We would not expect *halvtredsindstyve* to be truncated to *halvtr*, for example, since *vtr* is not a permissible final consonant cluster in Danish. The same sort of considerations are probably involved in processes of truncation of the sort we are discussing as are relevant to the 'reanalysis' of the English phonetic form [milyən] into [m + ilyən]. Serious theories on the nature of such processes cannot be put forward until much more data than we consider here is studied. The best we can do in the case of the truncation in Danish is state *ad hoc* rules as in (26).

(26) TRUNCATION
   (a) *tyve* is deleted after *fyrre*
   (b) *indstyve* is deleted

With these rules we derive *fyrre*, *halvtreds*, *tres*, *halvfjerds*, *firs*, and *halvfems*, as required, for modern Danish.

5.3 Inversion and conjunction-insertion

I now discuss the derivation of the expressions in the fourth column of (1). The underlying structure for *enogtyve*, 'one and twenty', is as in (27).

(27)

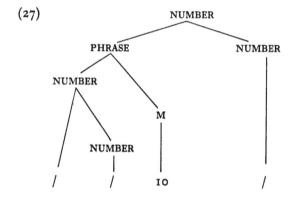

The right-hand immediate constituent of this structure is lexicalized as #*en*#. The left-hand immediate constituent is related, by the processes we have already discussed, to *tyve*. What is needed is a rule to reverse the order of the two constituents and another to insert the conjunction *og* between them. I give these rules in (28) and (29).

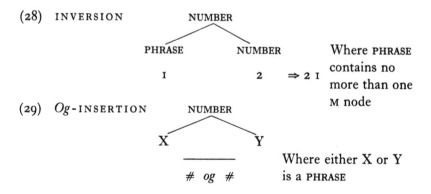

(28) INVERSION ... Where PHRASE contains no more than one M node

(29) *Og*-INSERTION ... Where either X or Y is a PHRASE

Rule (29) actually inserts *og* between a PHRASE and a NUMBER whether they have been reordered by Inversion rule (28) or not. I will give examples of the operation of these two rules.

Structure (27), after lexicalization and assuming the various idiosyncratic processes involved in the derivation of *tyve*, is converted by Inversion to (30). Rule (29) converts this to *# en # # og # # tyve #*,

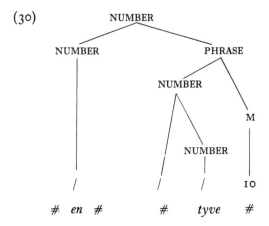

and rule (25) removes the internal word boundaries to produce *# enog-tyve #* .

The expression for 213 is *to hundrede og tretten* (example from Bredsdorff). The underlying structure of this expression is as in (31).

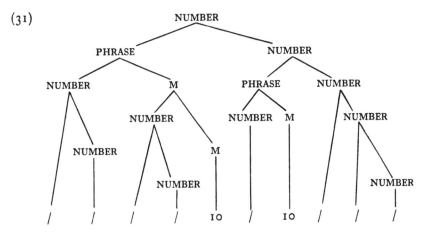

After lexicalization of *to, hundrede* and derivation of *tretten*, we have *to hundrede tretten*. Inversion is not applicable since the first PHRASE in (31) contains more than one M node; rule (29) inserts *og*, giving to *hundrede og tretten*.

We shall see that the rule of Inversion and a rule inserting a conjunction between the constituents of a NUMBER occur in a variety of languages, like the rules 1-Deletion and Switch.

5.4 The semantics of subtraction and division

Recall that in our discussion of the semantic component of a grammar of English numerals we defined an operation CALCULATE taking four arguments, and, depending on the value of the second argument, equivalent to the mathematical operation of addition, multiplication, or exponentiation. Thus (CALCULATE + 1 x y) is equivalent to $x+y$; (CALCULATE + 2 x y) is equivalent to xy; and (CALCULATE + 3 x y) is equivalent to y^x. Obviously Danish calls for an extension of this theory to deal with subtraction and division. We say that subtraction and division are the converse operations of addition and multiplication respectively, and we represent these converse operations by making the first argument of operation CALCULATE a 'minus' sign rather than a 'plus' sign. Thus (CALCULATE − 1 x y) is equivalent to $x−y$; and (CALCULATE − 2 x y) is equivalent to x/y. We can define these converse operations as in (32).

(32)   If and only if (CALCULATE + d x y) = z, then (CALCULATE − d z y) = x.

This definition subsumes the specific definition (25) in ch. 2 of the operation we previously called DECREMENT and which we defined there as the converse of what we had previously called INCREMENT. Definition (32) also subsumes the following definitions of subtraction and division, given in a normal mathematical notation.

(33)   (a) If and only if $x+y = z$, then $z−y = x$.

(b) If and only if $xy = z$, then $\dfrac{z}{y} = x$.

Definition (32) also subsumes the following definition of 'logarithm', but this operation will not concern us here.

(34)   If and only if $y^x = z$, then $\log_y z = x$.

Not surprisingly, natural languages do not make use of the notion 'logarithm' in constructing their numeral expressions.

The interpretation of numeral structures in Danish, just as in English, depends on the 'depth' of the constituent being interpreted and the same depth-assigning algorithm is valid for Danish as for English. For convenience, I repeat this algorithm here.

(35) (= (28) of ch. 2)
Where there exists a phrase structure rule X → Y Z and X is a constituent at depth n, all Ys and Zs in the phrase structure rules are marked as constituents at depth $n+1$ unless they have already been assigned a depth by a previous application of this convention. All NUMBERs in phrase structure rules are assigned depth 1.

Applied to the phrase structure rules we have postulated for Danish, this algorithm assigns depth 1 to NUMBERs, depth 2 to PHRASEs and FRACTIONs, and depth 3 to MS. In general the interpretation of numeral structures in Danish can be predicted by the same general projection rule as is valid for English. I repeat this rule in (36). For Danish, two

(36) (= (29) of ch. 2)

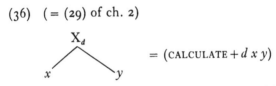

$$= (\text{CALCULATE} + d\ x\ y)$$

extra conditional statements must be postulated, applicable after rule (36). These are:

(37) (a) If $d = 2$ and $y = 2$, change + to −
     (b) If $x < 1$, change + to − and interchange the values of x and y

(37a) provides that FRACTIONs are interpreted by the converse of multiplication, i.e. by division; and (37b) provides that in expressions with *halv*, it is the value of *halv* that is to be subtracted from that of its sister constituent, rather than vice versa.

As an example of the application of these statements, consider how structure (20), underlying *halvtredie*, is interpreted by them. All NUMBERs are assigned depth 1 and the FRACTION is assigned depth 2 by algorithm (35). Consider first the interpretation of the FRACTION. Projection rule (36) first states that its value is (CALCULATE + 2 1 2); but since here $d = 2$ and $y = 2$, rule (37a) is applicable and + is changed to −. The value, then, of the FRACTION in structure (20) is (CALCULATE − 2 1 2), or in standard mathematical notation ½.

Now consider the interpretation of the whole of structure (20), i.e. the value assigned to the top NUMBER. The right-hand constituent is assigned the value 3 in a straightforward way by addition. Rule (36) now states that the value of the top NUMBER in (20) is (CALCULATE + 1 $\frac{1}{2}$ 3); and since here *x* has a value less than 1, rule (37b) is applicable and + is changed to −, and the values of *x* and *y* are interchanged. The value, then of structure (20) is (CALCULATE − 1 3 $\frac{1}{2}$), or in standard mathematical notation 3 − $\frac{1}{2}$.

In operation CALCULATE we have developed a mathematical notation that seems to be particularly appropriate to the interpretation of deep structures of numerals in natural languages. It should be borne carefully in mind that the statements and rules we present in this section are of two kinds. One kind consists of statements about mathematics, e.g. (32): the truth of such statements is independent of the facts of any particular language. The other kind of statement consists of statements that are true only in relation to some particular languages, e.g. (35), (36), and (37). In determining the semantic representation of a given structure, all language-specific rules apply to the structure before the universal mathematical statements become relevant.

Observe now that although our definition of the operation (CALCULATE + *d x y*), i.e. (26) of ch. 2, actually described a procedure to be followed in determining the output of the operation, our definition (32) of the converse operation (CALCULATE − *d x y*) does not describe any such procedure. Given the definition and some arguments for the converse operation, say (CALCULATE − 1 5 3), the only conceivable procedure one could follow in trying to determine the 'output' of this particular operation would be to search, by some process of trial and error, for a number *x* such that (CALCULATE + 1 *x* 3) = 5. And, unless one directed one's search in some intelligent way, reflecting that one already had some inkling of the 'right answer', one might never come to the end of it, since the numbers that can be tried are infinite. We are not necessarily concerned in this study with describing procedures by which the output of mathematical operations can be determined. We are only concerned with defining in a precise manner the operations themselves and the relationships between them and only in a case where a procedure is actually the best form of definition, as in the case of (CALCULATE + *d x y*), do we describe a procedure. (32) does not describe a method for determining the output of the operation (CALCULATE − *d x y*), but it does give us a criterion for determining whether some given number *z* is or is not the output of this operation. Definition (32), in other words, allows us to 'prove theorems' involving subtraction and division. Given, for example, the theorem (CALCULATE − 1 5 3) = 2, we can verify that this is a true theorem by seeing that its implication, namely that (CALCULATE + 1 2 3) = 5, is true. From this point of view (32) is a perfectly adequate definition of the operations of subtraction and division.

We have offered no special type of semantic representation for fractions. What is the correct semantic representation, for example, of Danish *halv*? The form of semantic representations that we assume throughout this study, i.e. series of marks as /, //, ///, etc., is appropriate only to whole numbers. Since we have insisted that the particular shape, size, or colour of these marks is arbitrary and irrelevant, we cannot define some special type of mark to be the semantic representation of some fraction. Any mark we devise will already, in the scheme we have defined, be a semantic representation for the number concept 1. We have in fact made assumptions about semantic representations that preclude our assigning distinct semantic representations to nonnatural numbers. But this need cause us no embarrassment at all, since we are only concerned with fractions in so far as they are used by languages to form expressions for natural numbers. We are concerned, that is, with *halv* in Danish only as a constituent of the expressions *halvtredsindstyve*, *halvfjerdsindstyve*, and *halvfemsindstyve*. We want to relate these expressions to their semantic representations 50, 70, and 90 respectively and it is possible to do this without making reference to any semantic representations other than those of whole numbers. As an example, consider (22), the underlying structure of *halvtredsindstyve*.

As we have seen, the language-specific statements we have postulated for Danish tell us that the value of the FRACTION in (22) is (CALCULATE − 2 1 2). This is written in normal mathematical notation as '1 over 2', $\frac{1}{2}$. Note that '$\frac{1}{2}$' is not a semantic representation any more than (CALCULATE − 2 1 2) is a semantic representation. These are both notations representing operations. The statements we have postulated also tell us that the value of the left-hand immediate constituent of structure (22) is (CALCULATE − 1 3 (CALCULATE − 2 1 2)), in standard mathematical notation $3 - \frac{1}{2}$. Finally the interpretation rules for Danish tell us that the value of the whole structure in (22), i.e. the value of the top NUMBER is (CALCULATE + 2 (CALCULATE − 1 3 (CALCULATE − 2 1 2))20) or in standard mathematical notation $(3 - \frac{1}{2}) \times 20$. Now our task is to relate this formula to the semantic representation 50, to 'prove the theorem' that

$(3 - \frac{1}{2}) \times 20 = 50$. This can be done by the laws of mathematics, as I will show.

For simplicity and clarity in what follows, I will use standard mathematical notation, rather than the special notation we have developed in terms of the operation CALCULATE. The two notations are, of course, completely equivalent (at least as far as our notation with CALCULATE is developed) and everything that follows may be 'translated' into terms of operation CALCULATE without any change in the significance of the claims being made. The only point that may need explanation involves the representation of negative numbers and zero. Standard mathematical notation allows for the use of 'negative numbers', e.g. -3. -3 is in fact the difference between zero and 3, and can be written as $\emptyset - 3$. This can be translated into our notation in terms of operation CALCULATE only if we allow ourselves some method of representing zero. In our scheme of semantic representations the representation of zero is the complete absence of marks. In theory there is nothing wrong with this, but it presents a difficulty when it is desired to express the concept of zero in a particular place on a sheet of paper. The difficulty could be overcome by postulating for each of the four arguments of operation CALCULATE a 'slot', represented perhaps by a space between commas. In this way we could translate -3 into our notation as (CALCULATE, $-$, 1, ,3,). The absence of a symbol in the third slot here represents that the third argument is zero. The use of standard mathematical notation in the following 'proof' is purely a matter of expository convenience in the same way as the use of Arabic numeral symbols rather than representations like $/$, $//$, $///$, etc., is a convenience. No theoretical significance attaches to the actual notation used.

We have so far in this study made certain statements about mathematical operations, e.g. the definitions of addition, multiplication, exponentiation, subtraction, and division represented in (26) of ch. 2 and (32) of this chapter (translated into ordinary mathematical notation in (33) and (34)). But our knowledge of mathematical operations does not end there, of course. There are many other statements that can be made about the relationships between the operations we have defined. Some of these statements follow in an obvious way from the definitions we have given; others are not obvious corollaries of the definitions we have given, but are universally true nevertheless. I give below a sample of such statements which will prove relevant to our purposes here. Some of these may be called 'Laws' of mathematics in that their truth is axiomatic; others are theorems in that their truth can be deduced from the truth of the axioms. Whether actually axiomatic or not, they are all so obviously true that the reader will not question them, at least within the framework of 'natural mathematics', i.e. that relevant to 'ordinary language' that we are considering here.

(38) (a) $xy = yx$ ('Law of Commutativity of Multiplication')
      (b) $(x+y)z = (xz)+(yz)$ ('Law of Distribution')
      (c) $\dfrac{x}{y} = x\left(\dfrac{1}{y}\right)$
      (d) $x-y = x+(-y)$
      (e) $-(xy) = (-x)y$

Now remember that what we are setting out to establish is the truth of the theorem that $(3-\frac{1}{2})\times 20 = 50$. We assume the truth of the statements in (38) and also of the following three statements, which can be verified by reference to the definitions already given, in (26) of ch. 2 and (32) of this chapter.

(39) (a) $3\times 20 = 60$
      (b) $60-10 = 50$
      (c) $\dfrac{20}{2} = 10$

From (39c) it follows by (38c), that $20\times\frac{1}{2} = 10$;
from this it follows, by (38a), that $\frac{1}{2}\times 20 = 10$;
therefore it follows that $-(\frac{1}{2}\times 20) = -10$;
from this it follows, by (38e), that $(-\frac{1}{2})\times 20 = -10$; call this conclusion A.
From (39b) it follows, by (38d), that $60+(-10) = 50$;
from this and conclusion A it follows that $60+((-\frac{1}{2})\times 20) = 50$;
From this and (39a) it follows that $(3\times 20)+((-\frac{1}{2})\times 20) = 50$;
from this it follows, by (38b), that $(3+(-\frac{1}{2}))\times 20 = 50$;
and from this it follows, by (38d), that $(3-\frac{1}{2})\times 20 = 50$.

We have established what we set out to establish, and we have done it without making reference to semantic representations of nonwhole numbers. Thus, by applying the language-specific interpretation rules (35), (36), and (37) and by assuming certain universally true statements from mathematics we have succeeded in relating structure (22) underlying *halvtredsindstyve* to the semantic representation 50. By essentially similar processes *halvfjerdsindstyve* and *halvfemsindstyve* can be related to the semantic representations 70 and 90 respectively.

6   Biblical Welsh numerals

The variety of Welsh with which we shall be concerned in this chapter is the language of the Welsh Bible, rather than the modern spoken variety. The numeral system of modern Welsh, as spoken by most speakers, is either a recently created and very straightforward decimal system or else is nonexistent in that many Welsh speakers actually use the English numerals as systematic loans when speaking Welsh. The variety of Welsh described in most Welsh grammars (e.g. Morris-Jones, 1922, 1931; Saunderson, 1833; Jones, 1897; Evans, 1946; Bowen and Rhys Jones, 1960; Smith ('Caradar'), 1925) might aptly be called 'Classical Welsh'. The numerals of Classical Welsh are more interesting than those of modern spoken Welsh, but not so interesting as the numerals found in the Welsh Bible. Almost the same base component, semantic component, general constraints, and lexicon account for the numerals of Classical Welsh as for those of the Biblical system, but, in addition, the Biblical numerals illustrate a number of interesting transformational processes not referred to (or at least not adequately described) in the grammars of Classical Welsh. It is for this reason that I have chosen to deal with the numeral system of Biblical Welsh.

Some justification should be given for using the Bible as a corpus to illustrate a systematic aspect of the Welsh language, such as the numeral system, since it is not, of course, a document conceived and originally composed in Welsh, but a translation. I quote below some of the pertinent facts about the version of the Welsh Bible I have used.

In 1567 the New Testament first appeared in Welsh, translated from the Greek mainly by William Salesbury (c. 1529–95). It served as the basis for the complete Bible published in 1588 by William Morgan (c. 1547–1604), Bp. of St. Asaph. This was revised by Richard Parry (1560–1623; Morgan's successor in the see of St. Asaph), probably with the help of John Davies (1570–1644), his chaplain, and published in 1620. This Bible, which used the language of the bards, was an important formative influence on the Welsh prose language. It is the Welsh Bible in general use today. (F. L. Cross (ed.) 1957, pp. 1444–5)

W. Morgan...was a good Hebrew and Greek scholar...In his task [of preparing the 1588 version] W. Morgan was encouraged and assisted by many eminent Welshmen...The translation was undoubtedly made from the Hebrew and Greek. W. Morgan seems also to have used the Latin Vulgate, the Latin version of Sanctes Pagninus and the English Geneva Bible. (Darlow and Moule, 1905–11, pp. 1660–1)

The issue of King James's English Bible in 1611 prepared the way for a revision of the Welsh Bible, which was undertaken by R. Parry...The Hebraisms of the earlier translator were rejected by R. Parry, whose endeavour seems to have been to conform the version to the English A.V.

This revised Bible [1620]...became, and still remains, the standard edition of the Welsh Bible, though changes have been made in the orthography. (Darlow and Moule, 1905–11, p. 1663)

The version I have used in this study is that of 1620, which 'used the language of the bards' and whose translator seems to have endeavoured 'to conform the version to the English A.V.'. These two quoted phrases are not contradictory. I take them to indicate that the translation is always good Welsh, but that where equally good Welsh alternative renderings are possible, that which more closely resembles the rendering of the English Authorized Version tends to be chosen.

If we compare the numerals of the Welsh Bible with those of the English Authorized Version, we do see some possible evidence of imitation in that a Welsh numeral can sometimes be seen as almost a word-by-word gloss of its English counterpart (or vice versa). But this is not necessarily evidence of imitation, since close equivalences in numerals can be found in almost any pair of languages, which may have had no influence on each other at all. Up to 9,999, for example, the Welsh numeral system is remarkably similar to the modern Mixtec system (see ch. 3), yet there is obviously no question of either of these two languages having had an influence on the other. The similarity is a mere coincidence. And the similarity between the numerals of the Welsh Bible and those of the English Authorized Version is certainly no greater than that between the Biblical Welsh numerals and the modern Mixtec numerals.

It is more important to note the very common dissimilarities between Biblical Welsh numerals and their counterparts in the English Authorized Version. Only a small minority of numerals in the Welsh Bible, and these usually the very short expressions, can be seen as word-by-word glosses of their counterparts in the Authorized Version. In all other cases rules which are clearly non-English, non-Hebrew, and non-Greek systematically determine the form of the numeral expressions. I naturally assume that these are rules of Welsh, more specifically of a variety of the language that I call 'Biblical Welsh'. We shall see that the rules accounting for Biblical Welsh numerals can be presented as a whole, integrated system, without any of the anomalies or inconsistencies we might expect if there were interference from another system, such as Early Modern English. The numerals of the Welsh Bible are constructed according to a system of rules which is sufficiently independent of and distinct from any other system of rules to give Biblical Welsh, at least as far as the numerals are concerned, a status as a natural language as likely to shed light on the problems in which we are interested as any of the other languages we have investigated. In this chapter I have cited, giving chapter and verse, an ample enough quantity of examples to demonstrate convincingly the systematic nature of the facts noted. Where fewer data are cited, and where chapter and verse are not given, this is normally because examples are extremely common and need little seeking out. Where data to demonstrate a particular point sufficiently are not available, this is indicated.

To the question, 'Why the Bible?', there are two answers. Firstly, the data are easily accessible by means of a concordance. I used *Nelson's Concordance to the Standard Revised Version* to help me to find numerals in the Welsh Bible. Secondly, the data are, as I hope the following pages will demonstrate, quite interesting.

The highest-valued word in the Biblical Welsh numeral system is *mil*, 1,000. There is a word *myrdd*, which occasionally has the exact meaning of 10,000, but the status of this word in Biblical Welsh numerals is marginal. I have found only one numeral formed with *myrdd*:

(1)   deuddeng myrdd (12 10,000) (= 120,000) (Jonah 4.11)

There are, on the other hand, many numerals with values equal to or greater than 10,000 that are not formed with *myrdd*. Some examples follow.

(2)   ddengmil (10 1,000) (= 10,000) (Judges 1.4; Deuteronomy 32.30)
       pymtheng mil (15 1,000) (= 15,000) (Judges 8.10)
       cant ac ugain mil (100 + 20 1,000) (= 120,000) (Judges 8.10)

The plural of *myrdd* occurs in the sense of 'ten thousands', where this indicates simply some very large number, not necessarily exactly 10,000, e.g. *Dychwel, ARGLWYDD, at fyrddiwn miloedd Israel,* 'Return, o LORD, unto the ten thousands of the thousands of Israel' (Revised Version), or 'Return o LORD, unto the many thousands of Israel' (Authorized Version). I shall assume, from this point on, that *myrdd* plays no part in the Biblical Welsh numeral system.

The words used in Biblical Welsh numerals are as follows:

1	un	9	naw
2	dau	10	deg
3	tri	12	deuddeg
4	pedwar	15	pymtheg
5	pump	20	ugain
6	chwech	100	cant
7	saith	1000	mil
8	wyth		

(The reader is warned that these words may frequently vary in shape at their beginnings and ends because of the characteristic Welsh phenomenon of consonantal mutation. Among the alternations to be expected are *dau/ddau, tri/thri/dri, pedwar/phedwar/bedwar, pump/phump/bump, deg/ddeg/deng/ddeng, pymtheg/phymtheg/bymtheg/pymtheng/bymtheng/phymtheng, ugain/hugain, cant/chant/gant, mil/fil.* Consonantal mutation pervades the whole language, not just the numeral system, and I shall not describe the mutation rules here.)

In (3) I give the phrase structure rules accounting for all numerals in Biblical Welsh.

(3)

$$\text{NUMBER} \rightarrow \left\{ \begin{array}{c} / \\ \text{PHRASE} \end{array} \right\} \text{(NUMBER)}$$

$$\text{PHRASE} \rightarrow \text{NUMBER} \quad \text{M}$$

$$\text{M} \rightarrow \left\{ \begin{array}{c} \text{10} \\ \text{15} \\ \text{20} \\ \text{NUMBER} \quad \text{M} \end{array} \right\}$$

The Packing Strategy and the other general constraints, (77) and (79) of ch. 2, are valid for Welsh. I give an illustrative sample of the lexicon in (4). (The incomplete lexical entry (4d) is filled out by the lexical

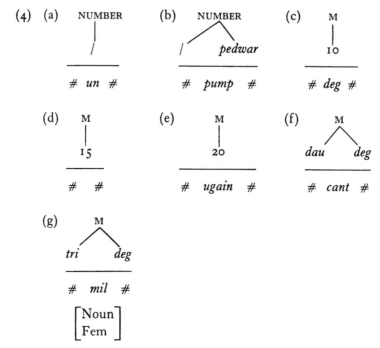

extension component with the phonetic form of *pymtheg*, as we will see directly. The specifications [Noun, Fem] in the entry for *mil* will also be explained later.)

6.1 Subtraction

(In following the examples of this section, the reader must assume the operation of several transformations we have not yet described, in particular, transformations inverting the constituents of NUMBERs and inserting the forms *ar*, 'on', *ac*, 'and', *onid* and *namyn*, 'minus'. These rules, which are quite similar to those of Danish described in ch. 5, will be described in detail later on and it will be seen that their postulation is justified.) Biblical Welsh makes a limited use of subtraction. The interpretation of a numeral by subtraction is signalled by the forms *onid* and *namyn*, which are in free variation. Some examples are given below.

(5)   onid un pum ugain (minus 1 5 20) (= 99) (Luke 15.7)
       onid pedwar pum ugain (minus 4 5 20) (= 96) (Ezra 8.35)
       namyn tri pedwar ugain (minus 3 4 20) (= 77) (Ezra 8.35)
       onid pedwar, cant (minus 4 100) (= 96) (Jeremiah 52.23)

(I ignore the rare instances of commas in Biblical Welsh numerals as in the last example above.)

I propose that the structure generated by the phrase structure rules underlying the last expression of (5) is (6). This structure is identical

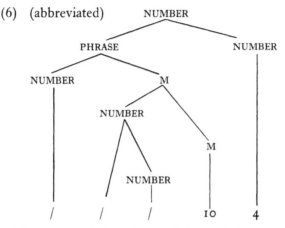

(6) (abbreviated)

to that underlying *cant a phedwar* (100 + 4) (= 104). Structure (6) can, in other words, be interpreted in two ways, either by subtraction or by addition. We express this in the grammar in the following way. The general projection rule postulated for the other languages we have investigated, repeated below as (7), is also valid for Welsh. The depth-assigning algorithm ((28) of ch. 2, or (35) of ch. 5) is valid for Welsh,

(7) $\quad$ X_d
$$\underset{x \quad\quad y}{\diagdown} = (\text{CALCULATE} + d\ x\ y)$$

as for the other languages we have studied. There is one semantic rule peculiar to Biblical Welsh, which applies after the operation of the general projection rule (7) and before the actual operation of operation CALCULATE. This Biblical Welsh-specific rule is given in (8).

(8) $\quad$ If $x > 20$ and $y < 5$, optionally change + to −

Note that this rule is optional. The grammar allows two possibilities concerning this rule: it may apply, or it may not. If rule (8) applies in the interpretation of structure (6), this structure is interpreted as (CALCULATE − 1 100 4), i.e. as 96. If, on the other hand, rule (8) does not apply to structure (6), then the structure is interpreted as (CALCULATE + 1 100 4), i.e. as 104.

I propose that certain syntactic transformations affecting structures such as (6), including the rules inserting *onid* and *namyn*, are sensitive to information on whether the semantic rule (8) has or has not applied to these structures. Note that if rule (8) applies in the interpretation of structure (6), the value of the PHRASE is greater than that of the whole structure, whereas if rule (8) does not apply, the reverse is true. The rule inserting *onid*, then, will specify a condition like 'where the value of PHRASE is greater than that of $NUMBER_1$'. We will discuss the precise formulations of these transformations in detail later.

The treatment outlined here correctly associates the expression *onid pedwar cant* with its semantic representation, 96, and the expression *cant a phedwar* with its semantic representation, 104. The method by which this association is expressed involves an optional semantic rule (8) and a semantic condition on the applicability of certain transformations. These mechanisms seem to me to be maximally simple in accounting for the facts. In particular they involve less loss of generality than another conceivable approach to the problem. In this approach a 'subtraction morpheme' is introduced by the phrase structure rules, interpreted as a subtraction operator by the semantic component, and lexicalized as either *onid* or *namyn*. This approach would incur difficulties in the disruption of the Packing Strategy and the general semantic projection rule (7), both of which assume nodes in deep structure to dominate at most two immediate constituents.

Some comments are necessary on the details of the formulation of rule (8). Numbers below 20 are never expressed by subtraction in Biblical Welsh. Thus one does not find, for example, **onid un ugain* (minus 1 20) (= 19) or **namyn tri pymtheg* (minus 3 15) (= 12). Numbers greater than 4 are never subtracted. Thus one does not find **onid pump tri ugain* (minus 5 3 20) (= 55) or **namyn saith cant* (minus 7 100) (= 93). The lowest number expressible by subtraction is 36, which can be expressed as *onid pedwar deugain* (minus 4 2 20) (Ezra 2.66). With the condition $y < 5$, it is not necessary to stipulate that $d = 1$, since only a NUMBER can possibly have a right-hand immediate constituent with a value less than 5.

6.2 Wellformedness constraints

In general the Packing Strategy and the other general constraints on wellformedness (77) and (79) of ch. 2 are valid for Biblical Welsh in that they generally select the correct deep structure corresponding to any given number. Biblical Welsh does, however, provide a class of counterexamples to the universality of the Packing Strategy. We will see that this class of expressions presents a problem similar to that of English expressions such as *eleven hundred, twenty one hundred, ninety nine hundred*, whose wellformedness is also a counterexample to the universal validity of the Packing Strategy. But first let us examine the evidence in favour of the Packing Strategy and the other general constraints in Biblical Welsh.

Consider first the wellformedness of PHRASES. As a first example, we choose PHRASES with value 20. The phrase structure rules generate two PHRASES with value 20. These are (abbreviated) as in (9). Both MS

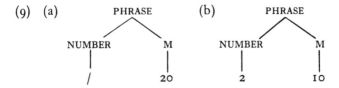

in these structures are wellformed, since they are identical to MS specified in the lexicon. The Packing Strategy characterizes (9b) as illformed because the M in it has a value less than that of the M in (9a). (9a) is in fact the appropriate structure for the Welsh expression for 20, which is *ugain*. (The rule of 1-Deletion is operative before *ugain*.)

The PHRASES generated by the phrase structure rules with the value 60 are as in (10) (abbreviated). All the MS in these structures are wellformed, since they are identical to MS specified in the lexicon. The

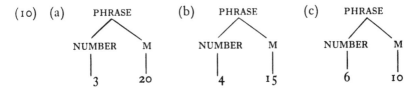

Packing Strategy characterizes (10b, c) as illformed because of the wellformedness of the M in (10a), which has a higher value than the MS which are the immediate constituents of (10b, c). This leaves (10a) as the predicted underlying structure for the Biblical Welsh expression for 60. This is correct, since the expression is *tri ugain* (3 20).

The phrase structure rules generate two PHRASES with the value 90. These are as in (11) (abbreviated). Neither of these structures is well-

(11) (a)

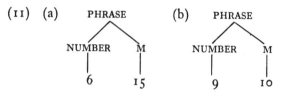

formed, because the phrase structure rules generate a wellformed M, namely that in lexical entry (4e), with a value greater than those of the MS which are the immediate constituents of (11a, b) and less than 90. It is predicted, then, that the wellformed expression for 90 in Biblical Welsh is not a PHRASE. This is correct, since the expression is *deg a phedwar ugain* (10 + 4 20), which is a transform of a deep structure as in (12).

(12) (abbreviated)

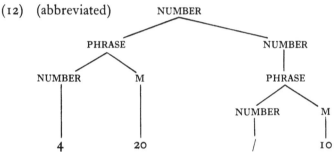

PHRASES like the problematic English *eleven hundred, twenty one hundred, ninety nine hundred*, etc., are not found in the Welsh Bible and thus this particular class of counterexamples to the Packing Strategy does not exist in Biblical Welsh. Forms such as **un ar ddeg cant* (1 on 10 100) (= 1,100), **dau ar bymtheg cant* (2 on 15 100) (= 1,700), and **saith ar hugain cant* (7 on 20 100) (= 2,700) do not occur and I assume that they are ungrammatical. Instead we find:

(13)   un fil a chant (1 1,000 + 100) (Judges 16.5)
        mil a saith gant (1,000 + 7 100) (I Chronicles 26.30)
        ddwy fil a saith gant (2 1,000 + 7 100) (I Chronicles 26.32)

(Note that corresponding to the first of these examples the English Authorized Version has *eleven hundred*, rather than *one thousand one hundred*.) The Packing Strategy correctly predicts that the wellformed expressions for 1,100, 1,700, and 2,700, for example, are as in (13), rather than the ungrammatical forms mentioned above, because of the wellformedness of the M underlying *mil* (see lexical entry (4g)).

Among the NUMBERS generated by the phrase structure rules with value 33 are those shown in (14). The PHRASES in (14b, c) are illformed

(14) (abbreviated)

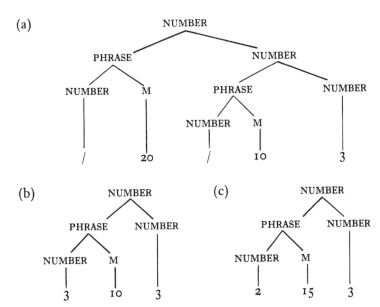

because of the wellformedness of the M in lexical entry (4e), which has a value greater than those of the MS which are the immediate constituents of the PHRASES in (14b, c) and less than 30, the value of the PHRASES. (14b, c) are thus themselves illformed. All other NUMBERS with value 33, except (14a), can similarly be shown to be illformed. This is correct, since the Biblical Welsh expression for 33 is *tri ar ddeg ar hugain* (3 on 10 on 20), which is a transform of structure (14a).

NUMBERS with value 19 generated by the phrase structure rules include those of (15). Here the Packing Strategy characterizes (15b) as

(15) (abbreviated)

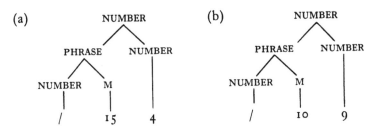

illformed because of the wellformedness of the PHRASE in (15a), which
has a value greater than that of the PHRASE which is the immediate
constituent of (15b). All other NUMBERs with value 19 are likewise
characterized as illformed by the Packing Strategy. This leaves (15a)
as the only wellformed structure with value 19. This is correct: the
expression for 19 in Biblical Welsh is *pedwar ar bymtheg* (4 on 15),
which is a transform of structure (15a).

Structures interpreted, by means of the semantic rule (8), by subtraction are all wellformed according to the Packing Strategy. As an
example, consider the following structure underlying the expression
onid pedwar tri ugain (minus 4 3 20) (= 56) (Ezra 2.14). If the semantic

(16)   (abbreviated)

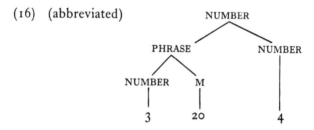

rule (8) applies, as it must if the structure is to be related to *onid pedwar
tri ugain*, the value of the whole structure, and therefore of the variable x
in the Packing Strategy, is 56; the value of the PHRASE which is the
immediate constituent of this structure, and thus of the variable y in
the Packing Strategy, is 60. Hence there can be no PHRASE with value z
where $y < z < x$, and structure (16) cannot be characterized as illformed
by the Packing Strategy. For similar reasons, no structure interpreted
by subtraction can be characterized as illformed by the Packing Strategy.

There are in the Welsh Bible some instances of vigesimal numeration
for numbers between 100 and 199. These expressions constitute exceptions to the Packing Strategy. Out of over sixty numerals expressing
numbers within the range 100–199, about one fourth do not use *cant*.
Some examples are given below.

(17)   chwech ugain (6 20) (= 120) (Numbers 7.87)
       tair ar ddeg a saith ugain (3 on 10 + 7 20) (= 153) (II Chronicles
       2.17)
       deuddeg ac wyth ugain (12 + 8 20) (= 172) (Ezra 2.3)

The deep structure of the first of these examples is as in (18). The Packing Strategy characterizes the PHRASE in this structure as illformed

(18) (abbreviated)

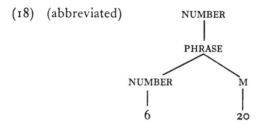

because of the wellformedness of the M underlying *cant* (see lexical entry (4f)), which has a value greater than that of the M and less than that of the PHRASE in (18). The expression selected by the Packing Strategy with value 120 is *cant ac ugain*, which has a deep structure as in (19). *Cant ac ugain* occurs in the Welsh Bible (Judges 8.10), as do

(19)

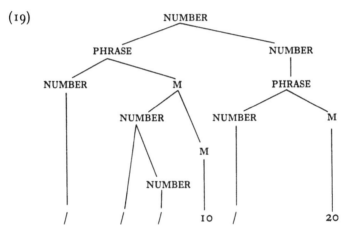

several transforms of it. The Packing Strategy is correct in so far as it selects these expressions, but wrong in that it rejects structures such as (18). As in the case of English *eleven hundred*, etc., I have nothing very satisfactory to say on this failure of the Packing Strategy. The best we can do, apparently, is to say that the Packing Strategy does not characterize structures as illformed, but rather as 'not optimal' and then to formulate an *ad hoc* statement as in (20) below accounting for the wellformedness of expressions such as those of (17). This accounts for, though it hardly explains, the fact that numbers between 100 and 199 may be expressed in two different ways. As in the case of English *eleven hundred*, etc., some very general, though still imprecisely understood policy of economy, of which the Packing Strategy is in this instance an imperfect implement, seems to be involved here.

(20)   Structures of the form

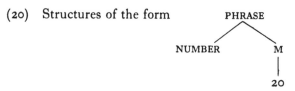

where the value of NUMBER is greater than 4 and less than 10 are wellformed, even though they are not 'optimal'.

6.3 Word formation

The rule of 1-Deletion is operative in Welsh and the relevant formulation of it is given in (21). As an example of the application of this rule,

(21) 1-DELETION

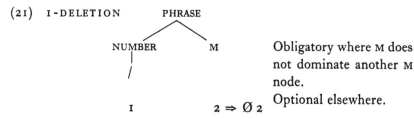

Obligatory where M does not dominate another M node.

Optional elsewhere.

the structure underlying *deg*, 10, is (22). This is lexicalized as *un deg*.

(22)

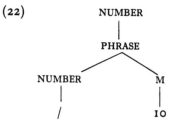

The *un* is deleted obligatorily, leaving *deg* with a structure as in (23).

(23)

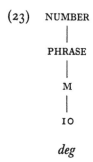

deg

In a similar way underlying *un pymtheg* and *un ugain* are obligatorily

converted to *pymtheg* and *ugain*. Underlying *un cant* and *un mil* optionally become *cant* and *mil*.

The Switch transformation is applicable in Welsh in just two cases,
those of the expressions for 12 and 15, *deuddeg* and *pymtheg*. The formulation of Switch, then, is as in (24) for Welsh. The structures of *deuddeg*

(24) SWITCH

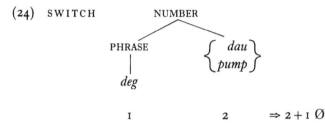

and *pymtheg* after the application of Switch are PHRASES, as in (25)
(abbreviated). There is evidence that *deuddeg* and *pymtheg* are surface

(25) (a)   (b)

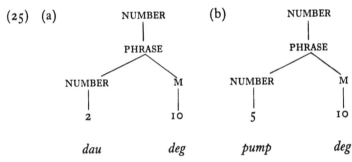

structure PHRASES. Phonological changes from *dau* to *deu* and from
pump to *pum* occur regularly in PHRASES. *Dau* becomes *deu* not only in
deuddeg, but also in *deugain* (2 20) (= 40) and *deucant* (2 100) (= 200),
a variant form of *dau cant*, as in, e.g., *chwe mil a deucant* (6 1,000 + 2
100) (= 6,200) (Numbers 3.34). In some varieties of Classical Welsh
the expression for 18 is *deunaw* (2 9). Note the change from *dau* to *deu*
here too. *Pump* changes to *pum* in *pum cant* (5 100) (= 500) and *pum
mil* (5 1,000) (= 5,000). *Pum ugain* (5 20) (= 100) occurs in the Welsh
Bible (Ezra 8.35, Luke 15.7), but is rare, the preferred form being
cant, but note again the change from *pump* to *pum*.

Biblical Welsh PHRASES are also subject to a rule deleting internal
word boundaries, sometimes optionally, sometimes obligatorily. Thus
we find the PHRASES *deugain* (2 20) (= 40), *chweugain* (6 20) (= 120),
deucant (2 100) (= 200), *dengmil* (10 1,000) (= 10,000), and *saithugain-
mil* (7 20 1,000) (= 140,000) all occurring as single words. In the case of

deugain, this is the only possible form and the rule deleting internal word boundaries is obligatory here, as it must be in the case of *deuddeg* and *pymtheg*. The vowel change between *pum* and *pymtheg* is idiosyncratic only as far as orthography is concerned. In modern Welsh pronunciation these words are [pIm] and [pəmθɛg] respectively. There is a regular alternation between [I] and [ə] which depends, partly, on whether the word concerned is monosyllabic or polysyllabic. Thus we have *llyn* [ɬIn] 'lake' vs *llynnoedd* [ɬɛnɔɪð] 'lakes' and *llifr* [ɬIvr] 'book' vs *llyfrau* [ɬəvrɛI] 'books'.

There must be a rule mutating the plosive [d] of *deg* in these forms to the fricative [ð] represented orthographically as 'dd'. And in the case of *pymtheg* this fricative must subsequently undergo devoicing to become the voiceless sound represented in orthography as 'th'.

6.4 The lexical extension component

The phrase structure rules generate a structure as in (26). The semantic

(26)

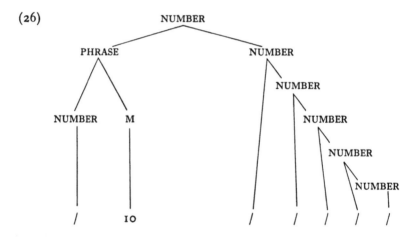

component interprets this structure as 15; the Packing Strategy characterizes it as illformed because of the wellformedness of a PHRASE with value 15 containing the M in lexical entry (4d). Notwithstanding its illformedness, structure (26) is related by the grammar through the rules of 1-Deletion and Switch and the morphophonological processes we have just described to the phonetic form [pəmθɛg]. Note that there is nothing in the general constraints on the wellformedness of numerals that causes illformed structures to disappear; they are simply branded 'illformed', and are still available as input to other processes in the grammar, such as lexicalization, word formation transformations, and phonological rules. It is obvious that this is the case, since we are able to speak meaningfully about the illformedness, for example, of *twenty thirteen*, a form whose constituents have undergone in a regular way the rules of 1-Deletion and Switch and various morphophonological processes, even though the form's underlying structure, and hence the form itself, is illformed. Given the relationship established by the Welsh grammar between the semantic representation 15 and the phonetic representation [pəmθɛg], the conditions set out in (76) of ch. 2 permit the incomplete lexical entry (4d) to be filled out with [pəmθɛg] by the lexical extension component.

The treatment I have proposed for *pymtheg* expresses a number of facts about this form. In deriving it from structure (26), we express the fact that it is interpreted as a NUMBER, i.e. by the addition of the values of its constituents. By making structure (26) subject to the Switch rule, we express the fact that *pymtheg* has the morphophonological properties of a PHRASE. And by means of the lexical extension component we express the fact that *pymtheg* functions in the larger constructions in which it is embedded as an M, particularly with regard to the general constraints on the wellformedness of numerals and the rules of 1-Deletion, Inversion, and *ar*-Insertion. We will discuss the latter two rules directly.

Note that the initial and final consonants of *pymtheg* are susceptible to the same mutations and in the same environments as the initial consonant of *pump* and the final consonant of *deg* respectively. This is not remarkable since it means that the mutation rules apply in a quite general way. As an example, the conjunction *a* generally causes a following consonant to undergo the 'Aspirate' mutation, e.g. from *p* to *ph*. We see this both in *pump* and in *pymtheg* in the following examples.

(27) fil a phump (1,000 + 5) (I Kings 4.32)
      mil a saith gant a phymtheg a thri ugain (1,000 + 7 100 + 15 + 3 20)
      (= 1,775) (Exodus 38.25,28)

Similarly we find a change from *g* to *ng* in both *deg* and *pymtheg* before *mil*.

(28) ddengmil (10 1,000) (Judges 1.4, Deuteronomy 32.30)
      pymtheng mil (15 1,000) (Judges 8.10)

I am not sure whether the assimilation here is part of a general process or due to some idiosyncratic property of the items involved, but there definitely are other cases of a change from *g* to *ng* which must be accounted for by postulating some idiosyncratic property of lexical items. And it is interesting that both *deg* and *pymtheg* possess this peculiar property. Both *deg* and *pymtheg* (and actually *deuddeg* as well) belong to a group of numeral words which trigger the 'Nasal' mutation in a handful of lexical items when these follow them. Thus *blynedd*, 'years' becomes *mlynedd* after words in this group. 'Ten years', for example, is *deng mlynedd*, and 'fifteen years' is *pymtheng mlynedd*. The changes from *deg* to *deng* and from *pymtheg* to *pymtheng* here are assimilations like those in (28). But the fact that *blynedd* undergoes the nasal mutation to *mlynedd* can only be accounted for in terms of some idiosyncratic property of the words preceding, in particular of *deg* and *pymtheg*. *Blynedd* does not change to *mlynedd* after every numeral word, but only after a subset of these. 'Three years', for example, is *tair blynedd* (*tair* is the feminine form of *tri*); 'two years' is *dwy flynedd* (*dwy* is the feminine form of *dau*), which triggers not the nasal, but the 'Soft' mutation, changing *b* to *f* among other things.

The idiosyncratic property of *deg* that it triggers the nasal mutation in some words must be recorded in its lexical entry. And these facts about Welsh mutation seem to indicate that when the lexical extension component fills out the incomplete lexical entry (4d) with [pəmθɛg], this new lexical item assumes the idiosyncratic properties of the items *pump* and *deg*, to which it is related by the lexical extension component. That is, since *deg* has the idiosyncratic property that it triggers the nasal mutation in certain words, *pymtheg*, which is synthesized on the basis of a derivation involving *pump* and *deg*, takes on this idiosyncratic property of *deg*. We thus have a small piece of evidence contributing to our detailed understanding of the operation of the lexical extension component.

6.5 Agreement

The forms *dau*, *tri*, and *pedwar* have feminine forms *dwy*, *tair*, and *pedair* respectively. These forms are used before any feminine noun. The most common feminine noun used with numerals in the Welsh Bible is *blynedd*, 'years'. Thus we find *dwy flynedd*, *tair blynedd*, *pedair blynedd*. This agreement in gender also takes place before *mil*. Thus we have *dwy fil* (2 1,000), *tair mil* (3 1,000), and *pedair mil* (4 1,000). Whether or not a noun is feminine is a quite idiosyncratic property,

generally independent of semantics, syntax or phonology. Items which
trigger feminine agreement must be marked idiosyncratically in the
lexicon. It is for this reason that (4g), the lexical entry for *mil* contains
the specification [Fem]. The specification is referred to by the agreement

(29) AGREEMENT   Obligatory.

   NUMBER [Fem]   Applies after Switch.

      I   2   ⇒ [Fem] 2   Where NUMBER has a
                              I   value greater than I and
                                         less than 5.

rule, which I formulate in (29). The effect of this rule is illustrated
below. Immediately after lexicalization, the terminal string of the
structure corresponding to 4,000 is as in (30). Rule (29) converts this to

(30) *pedwar* $\begin{bmatrix} \text{Noun} \\ \text{Fem} \end{bmatrix}$

               mil

(31)   *mil*

     pedwar $\begin{bmatrix} \text{Noun} \\ \text{Fem} \end{bmatrix}$
     [Fem]

(31). Processes of a phonological nature later convert $\frac{pedwar}{[\text{Fem}]}$ to *pedair*.

In this way *pedair mil* is derived. *Dwy fil* and *tair mil* are derived by a
similar process. The condition of rule (29) expresses the fact that the
class of NUMBERS affected by it is a semantically natural class, i.e. with
the values 2, 3, 4, rather than some more random set of values. The
specification Noun in the lexical entry for *mil* has yet to be explained.

   The Agreement rule (29) must apply after the Switch rule (24). The
evidence for this is that the expression for 12,000 is *deuddeng mil*,
rather than **dwyddeng mil*. After lexicalization and I-Deletion and
before the application of Switch, the structure of *deuddeng mil* looks
like (32). If Agreement applies to this structure, *dau* will receive the
specification [Fem], ultimately becoming *dwy*. Switch will move this
form to the left of *deg*, producing eventually the incorrect **dwyddeg*.
If, however, Switch applies to structure (32), it will move *dau* away from
the environment of *mil* and Agreement will not be able to apply. This
will generate the correct form *deuddeng mil*.

   An Agreement rule must also affect certain adjectives with feminine
(singular) nouns in Welsh, but I make no attempt here to formulate it

(32) (abbreviated)

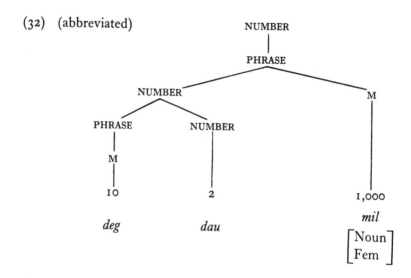

and conflate it with the Agreement rule (29), which is concerned solely with NUMBERs.

6.6 Cyclic transformations: Inversion

There is a transformation in Biblical Welsh that permutes the constituents of NUMBERs under certain conditions. I give the formulation of this rule in (33) and will now explain and illustrate all its details. The phrase structure rules generate structure (34) with value 45. This structure is lexicalized as *dau ugain pump*; the correct expression for 45 is *pump a deugain*. The Inversion rule converts *dau ugain pump* to *pump dau ugain*. Later rules render this as *pump a deugain*. In the case of

(33) INVERSION

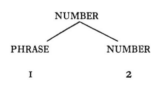

⇒ 2 1

Applies after Agreement.
Cyclic on NUMBER.
Obligatory where PHRASE contains a NUMBER with value less than 3 and no more than one M node. Obligatory where the value of PHRASE is greater than that of the NUMBER dominating it.
Optional elsewhere: may not apply it if has not applied on the previous cycle.

structure (34), since the PHRASE contains a NUMBER with value less than 3 and a single M node, the Inversion rule is obligatory. This condition

(34) (abbreviated)

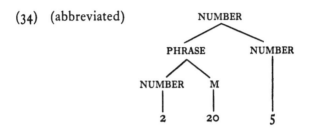

expresses the fact that numbers up to 60 are always expressed with the lower-valued constituent first. We find hundreds of examples with the constituents in this order, but no examples like *deugain a phump* (2 20 + 5), or *ugain ac un* (20 + 1).

In the case of numbers over 60, Inversion is optional. Thus along with *un a thri ugain* (1 + 3 20) (= 61) (Numbers 31.39) we find *dri ugain a dau* (3 20 + 2) (= 62) (I Chronicles 26.8). In the derivation of the former, Inversion applies; in the derivation of the latter, Inversion does not apply. I give below some more examples illustrating the optionality of Inversion in expressing numbers over 60.

(35) (a) Inversion applies:
bum...a chan (5... + 100) (= 105) (Genesis 5.6)
saith...ac wyth gan (7... + 8 100) (= 807) (Genesis 5.7)
ddeuddeng...a naw can (12... + 9 100) (= 912) (Genesis 5.8)
bymtheng...ac wyth gan (15... + 8 100) (= 815) (Genesis 5.10)
ddeugain...ac wyth gan (2 20... + 8 100) (= 840) (Genesis 5.13)

(The ellipses in these examples may be ignored; they will be explained later.)

(b) Inversion does not apply
dri chant a thri ugain (3 100 + 3 20) (= 360) (II Samuel 2.31)
bedwar cant ac ugain (4 100 + 20) (= 420) (I Kings 9.28)
tair mil a thri chant (3 1,000 + 3 100) (= 3,300) (I Kings 5.16)

ugain mil a dau cant (20 1,000 + 2 100) (20,200) (I Chronicles
7.9)
fil a phump (1,000 + 5) (= 1,005) (I Kings 4.32)

As these examples tend to suggest, Inversion applies less frequently in
expressions for higher numbers. To exemplify once more the operation
of this transformation, the structure of the third example in (35a)
ddeuddeng a naw can before Inversion (and after Switch) is as in 36.

(36) (abbreviated)

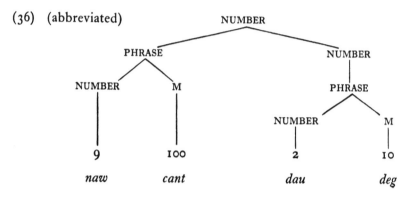

Inversion converts this structure into one whose terminal string is
dau deg naw cant. Other rules convert this to *ddeuddeng a naw can*.
    The next-mentioned condition on rule (33) expresses the fact that all
structures interpreted by subtraction must undergo Inversion. We have
seen some examples of this in (5); some more examples follow.

(37) onid dwy...deugain (minus 2...2 20) (= 38) (Deuteronomy
2.14)
namyn dwy...deugain (minus 2...2 20) (= 38) (John 5.5)
onid un tri ugain (minus 1 3 20) (= 59) (Numbers 2.13)
onid un...chwech ugain (minus 1...6 20) (= 119) (Genesis
11.25)

(Again, ignore the ellipses; they will be explained later.) The structure,
before Inversion, of the first example here is as in (38). Here the value
of the PHRASE is 40, greater than that of the NUMBER dominating it,
38 and Inversion must therefore apply. Inversion permutes the
immediate constituents of this structure, yielding eventually *onid dwy
deugain*.

(38) (abbreviated)

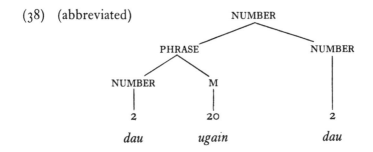

All the examples we have mentioned so far involve just a single application of Inversion. There are numerals in which it is clear that Inversion applies more than once. Some examples follow.

(39) (a) Inversion applies three times
pump a thri ugain a thri chant a mil (5 + 3 20 + 3 100 + 1,000)
(= 1,365) (Numbers 3.50)
tri ar ddeg a thri ugain a deucant (3 on 10 + 3 20 + 2 100)
(= 273) (Numbers 3.46)
(b) Inversion applies twice
thri ar bymtheg ar hugain (3 on 15 on 20) (= 38) (Nehemiah
7.45)
ddeg ar hugain a chant (10 on 20 + 100) (= 130) (Numbers
7.13)
ddeng...ar hugain ac wyth gan (10...on 20 + 8 100) (= 830)
(Genesis 5.16)
tair...ar hugain a chant (3...on 20 + 100) (= 123) (Numbers
33.39)

(Ignore the ellipses.) The structure, before Inversion (and after I-Deletion) of the first example in (39a) is as in (40).

The subscript integers on some NUMBERs here are for convenience of reference only; they have no theoretical significance. If we invert the constituents of NUMBER$_1$, we obtain a structure with the terminal string *mil tri cant pump tri ugain*; if we now invert the constituents of NUMBER$_2$, we get *mil pump tri ugain tri cant*; and if we now apply Inversion to the constituents of NUMBER$_3$, we get *pump tri ugain tri cant mil*. This is converted by later rules to *pump a thri ugain a thri chant a mil*. All the other examples of (39) can be generated by multiple application

(40)   (abbreviated)

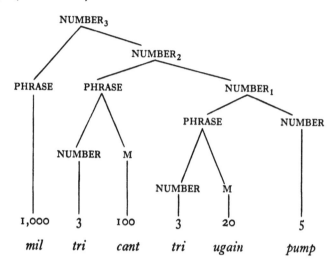

of Inversion in this way. For the purposes of these examples it does not matter to which NUMBER in the structure the Inversion rule applies first or next. To derive *pump a thri ugain a thri chant a mil*, for example, we could just as well have applied Inversion first to the constituents of NUMBER$_2$, then to those of NUMBER$_1$, and finally to those of NUMBER$_3$. But we shall see that there is reason to postulate that Inversion must apply to innermost NUMBERs first, working upwards through a structure towards the top NUMBER.

There are examples in the Welsh Bible of numerals in which Inversion has applied once or twice, but not as many times as it could have done. Some of these examples are given below.

(41)   naw can...a deng...ar hugain (9 100... + 10...on 20) (= 930)
(Genesis 5.15)
dau cant a deg a deugain (2 100 + 10 + 2 20) (= 250) (Numbers 16.2, 17)
dwy fil ac onid pedwar tri ugain (2 1,000 + minus 4 3 20) (= 2,056) (Ezra 2.14)
dwy fil a deuddeg ac wyth ugain (2 1,000 + 12 + 8 20) (= 2,172) (Ezra 2.3)
cant a deuddeg a thri ugain (100 + 12 + 3 20) (= 172) (Nehemiah 7.8)

Note that in all these examples Inversion has applied to the constituents of the inner NUMBER, but not to those of the outer, 'top' NUMBER. To illustrate, (42) is the structure of the first example of (41) before Inversion. (Again, the subscripts on NUMBERs are for convenience of reference only.) To generate the first example in (41), Inversion applies to NUMBER$_1$, but not to NUMBER$_2$. This produces *naw cant deg ugain*, which later becomes *naw can...a deng...ar hugain*. There are many cases like this where Inversion applies to an inner NUMBER, but not to an outer or 'top' one.

(42) (abbreviated)

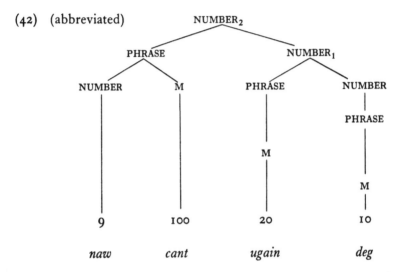

But there are no instances in the Welsh Bible in which Inversion applies to an outer NUMBER, but not to an inner one. That is, we never find examples like those of (43).

(43) *wyth ugain a deuddeg a dwy fil (8 20 + 12 + 2 1,000) (= 2,172)
      *tri ugain a deuddeg a chant (3 20 + 12 + 100) (= 172)

In general, then, Inversion cannot apply to an outer NUMBER unless it also applies to an inner NUMBER. To account for this fact I postulate that the Inversion rule (33) applies in a cyclic manner, first to the most deeply embedded NUMBER, then to the next most deeply embedded NUMBER, then to the next, and so on; furthermore, if on any cycle Inversion does not apply, then it may not apply on any subsequent cycle. In terms of the subscripted NUMBERs in diagrams (40) and (42), if Inversion does not apply to permute the constituents of NUMBER$_n$, then it may not apply to permute the constituents of NUMBER$_{n+1}$. In support of this treatment, we have examples such as the following.

(44)   THREE OR FOUR CYCLES POSSIBLE
(a) Inversion applies on cycles 1, 2, and 3.
(See examples (39a))
(b) Inversion applies on cycles 1 and 2, but not 3 and 4
   mil dau cant a phedwar ar ddeg a deugain (1,000 2 100 + 4 on
      10 + 2 20) (= 1,254) (Nehemiah 7.12, 34, Ezra 2.7)
   saith mil tri chant a dau ar bymtheg ar hugain (7 1,000 3
      100 + 2 on 15 on 20) (= 7,337) (Ezra 2.65, Nehemiah 7.67)
   ddwy...ar hugain [mil] a dau cant a thri ar ddeg a thri ugain
      (2...on 20 [1,000] + 2 100 + 3 on 10 + 3 20) (= 22,273)
      (Numbers 3.43)
(c) Inversion applies on cycle 1, but not 2 and 3.
   tair mil a chwe chant a deg ar hugain (3 1,000 + 6 100 + 10 on
      20) (= 3,630) (Ezra 2.35)
   tair mil naw cant a deg ar hugain (3 1,000 9 100 + 10 on 20)
      (= 3,930) (Nehemiah 7.38)
   dwy fil tri chant a dau ar hugain (2 1,000 3 100 + 2 on 20)
      (= 2,322) (Nehemiah 7.17)
   mil a saith gant a phymtheg...a thri ugain (1,000 + 7 100 + 15
      ... + 3 20) (= 1,775) (Exodus 38.25, 28)
   mil dau cant a saith a deugain (1,000 2 100 + 7 + 2 20) (=
      1,247) (Ezra 2.38, 7.41)
   dwy fil cant a deuddeg a thri ugain (2 1,000 100 + 12 + 3 20)
      (= 2,172) (Nehemiah 7.8)
   dwy fil ac wyth gant a thri ar bymtheg (2 1,000 + 8 100 + 3 on
      15) (= 2,818) (Nehemiah 7.11)
   dwy fil saith gant a deg a deugain (2 1,000 7 100 + 10 + 2 20)
      (= 2,750) (Numbers 4.36)
   mil dau cant a deg a phedwar ugain (1,000 2 100 + 10 + 4 20)
      (= 1,290) (Daniel 12.11)
   ddwy fil a chwe chant a deg ar hugain (2 1,000 + 6 100 + 10 on
      20) (= 2,630) (Numbers 4.40)

   TWO CYCLES POSSIBLE
(d) Inversion applies on cycle 1 and 2
   bymtheng...a phedwar ugain ac wyth gan (15... + 4 20 + 8
      100) (= 895) (Genesis 5.17)
   ddwy...a thri ugain a naw can (2... + 3 20 + 9 100) (= 962)
      (Genesis 5.20)

bymtheng...a phedwar ugain a phum can (15... +4 20 + 5
100) (= 595) (Genesis 5.30)

bum...a thri ugain a thri chant (5... +3 20 + 3 100) (= 365)
(Genesis 5.23)

naw...a thri ugain a naw can (9... +3 20 + 9 100) (= 969)
(Genesis 5.27)

ddwy...a thri ugain a chan (2... +3 20 + 100) (= 162)
(Genesis 5.18)

ddwy...a phedwar ugain a saith gan (2... +4 20 + 7 100)
(= 782) (Genesis 5.26)

ddwy...a phedwar ugain a chan (2... +4 20 + 100) (= 182)
(Genesis 5.28)

bump a phedwar ugain a chant (5 + 4 20 + 100) (= 185) (II
Kings 19.35)

saith...a phedwar ugain a chant (7... +4 20 + 100) (= 187)
(Genesis 5.25)

(e) Inversion applies on cycle 1, but not 2

cant ac wyth a phedwar ugain (100 + 8 + 4 20) (= 188)
(Nehemiah 7.26)

ddau cant a phedwar a phedwar ugain (2 100 + 4 + 4 20)
(= 284) (Nehemiah 11.18)

bedwar cant ac wyth a thri ugain (4 100 + 8 + 3 20) (= 468)
(Nehemiah 11.6)

chwe chant a saith a thri ugain (6 100 + 7 + 3 20) (= 667)
(Nehemiah 7.18)

chwe chant a chwech a thri ugain (6 100 + 6 + 3 20) (= 666)
(Ezra 2.13)

dwy fil a saith a thri ugain (2 1,000 + 7 + 3 20) (= 2,067)
(Nehemiah 7.19)

chwe chan...a phymtheg a thri ugain (6 100... + 15 + 3 20)
(= 675) (Numbers 31.32)

can...a phymtheng...a thri ugain (100... + 15... + 3 20)
(= 175) (Genesis 25.7)

(See also examples (41))

(f) Inversion applies on neither cycle

wyth mil pum cant a phedwar ugain (8 1,000 5 10 + 4 20)
(= 8,580) (Numbers 4.48)

fil a saith gant a thri ugain (1,000 + 7 100 + 3 20) (= 1,760)
(I Chronicles 9.13)

chwe mil saith gant ac ugain (6 1,000 7 100 + 20) (= 6,720)
(Ezra 2.67, Nehemiah 7.69)

fil a deucant a thri ugain (1,000 + 2 100 + 3 20) (= 1,260)
(Revelations 11.3, 12.6)

chwe chant a thri ugain a chwech (6 100 + 3 20 + 6) (= 666)
(I Kings 10.4, II Chronicles 9.13, Revelations 13.18)

gant a phedwar ugain a phump (100 + 4 20 + 5) (= 185)
(Isaiah 37.36)

gan...a phedwar ugain...a chwe (100...+ 4 20...+ 6)
(= 186) (Numbers 2.9)

ddau cant phedwar ugain ac wyth (2 100 4 20 + 8) (= 288)
(I Chronicles 25.7)

(Ignore, once more, the ellipses in these examples; they will be explained later. The square-bracketed *mil* in the last example of (44b) is not actually present in the text, but I postulate that the word *mil* has been deleted from this position by a transformation that I will discuss later.)

The examples in (44), which are not exhaustive, are all consistent with the hypothesis that the Inversion rule (33) applies cyclically, beginning with the innermost NUMBER in a structure and progressing to the outermost NUMBER, and that if on any cycle Inversion does not apply, then it may not apply on any subsequent cycle. There are no counterexamples to this claim in the numerals of the Welsh Bible.

Inversion must apply after the Agreement rule (29). Agreement assigns the specification [Fem] to *dau*, *tri*, and *pedwar*, causing them later to become *dwy*, *tair*, and *pedair*, just when these forms immediately precede a feminine noun. The only instances of *dau*, *tri*, and *pedwar* that undergo Agreement are those at the extreme right-hand end of a NUMBER in deep structure. The Inversion rule may move a *dau*, *tri*, or *pedwar* away from this position. When this happens, the form still undergoes Agreement as we see from the following examples.

(45)   onid tair deugain a chan mlynedd (minus 3 2 20 + 100 years)
        (= 137 years) (Exodus 6.20)

pedair a phedwar ugain mlynedd (4 + 4 20 years) (= 84 years)
(Luke 2.37)

gant a phedair a deugain o filoedd (100 + 4 + 2 20 of 1,000s)
(= 144,000) (Revelations 7.4)

dri chan...a dwy ar bymtheg ar hugain o filoedd (3 100...+ 2
on 15 on 20 of 1,000s) (= 337,000) (Numbers 31.36, 43)

tair ar ddeg a saith ugain o filoedd (3 on 10+7 20 of 1,000s)
(= 153,000) (II Chronicles 2.17)

In the last three examples here the plural form *o filoedd* of *mil* is used.
The Pluralization rule converting *mil* to *o filoedd* applies after Agreement
and Inversion, so the difference between the two forms does not affect
the formulation of the Agreement rule. We will discuss Pluralization
later.

To illustrate the interaction of Agreement and Inversion, we can use
the last example of (45). The structure, before Agreement, of this
expression is as in (46). Agreement assigns the specification [Fem] to

(46) (abbreviated)

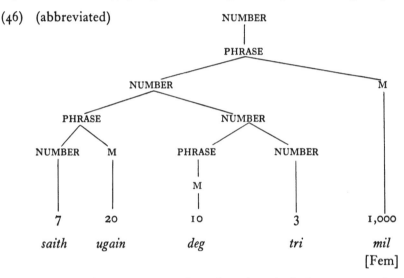

tri. For convenience, assume that the phonological processes that
change $\begin{bmatrix} tri \\ Fem \end{bmatrix}$ to *tair* take place at this stage. This renders *saith ugain*
deg tair mil. Inversion applies on a first cycle, giving *saith ugain tair deg*
mil. Inversion applies again on a second cycle, yielding *tair deg saith*
ugain mil. Later rules convert this to *tair ar ddeg a saith ugain o filoedd*.

6.7 Insertion of *ar*

Expressions for numbers up to 40 formed by Inversion always have the
preposition *ar* between the inverted constituents. Thus we find:

(47) un ar ddeg (1 on 10) (= 11)
      pedwar ar ddeg (4 on 10) (= 14)

un ar bymtheg (1 on 15) (= 16)
pedwar ar bymtheg (4 on 15) (= 19)
un ar hugain (1 on 20) (= 21)
naw ar hugain (9 on 20) (= 29)
deg ar hugain (10 on 20) (= 30)
tri ar ddeg ar hugain (3 on 10 on 20) (= 33)
pymtheg ar hugain (15 on 20) (= 35)
pedwar ar bymtheg ar hugain (4 on 15 on 20) (= 39)

To account for these facts we postulate the following lexicalization rule for *ar*. To illustrate the application of this rule, the structure, after

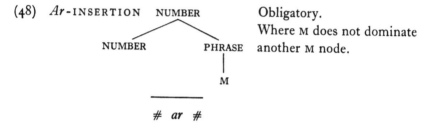

(48) *Ar*-INSERTION   NUMBER   Obligatory.
                                        Where M does not dominate
                                        another M node.

Inversion, of *un ar bymtheg* is as in (49). Rule (48) converts this to (50).

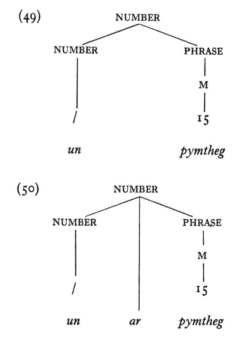

The consonantal mutation rules alter the terminal string of this structure to *un ar bymtheg*.

Clearly rule (48) must sometimes apply twice to the same structure, as in the derivations of *un ar ddeg ar hugain* or *dau ar bymtheg ar hugain*, for example. We simply postulate that rule (48) applies as often as its structural description is met. There is no need to postulate cyclic application of this rule. The condition of rule (48) ensures that *ar* is not inserted before *cant* or *mil*. **Un ar gant*, for example, is ungrammatical, as is **un ar fil*. The specific formulation we have given to rule (48) implies that it applies after Inversion, and therefore after Switch. Other formulations are conceivable, implying other orderings of the rules, but the formulation we have given in (48) is the most economic formulation possible.

6.8 Insertion of *onid* or *namyn*

As we have seen, either *onid* or *namyn* must be inserted before a NUMBER which is interpreted by subtraction. I give the appropriate lexicalization rules in (51). Rule (51) attaches either *onid* or *namyn*, the choice being

(51)   *Onid/namyn*-INSERTION

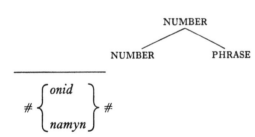

Obligatory.
Where the value of PHRASE is greater than that of the NUMBER dominating it.

apparently a matter of style, immediately to the left of a NUMBER interpreted by subtraction. It converts (52) into (53), for example. *Onid*

(52) (abbreviated)

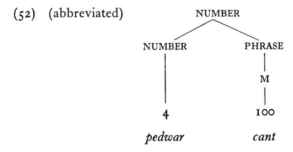

(53) (abbreviated)

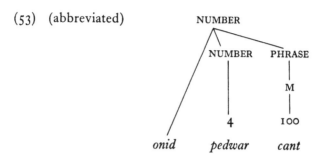

pedwar, cant is an expression for 96 found at Jeremiah 52.23. See (5) for some other examples.

The specific formulation in (51) implies that *onid* or *namyn* is inserted after Inversion. Other formulations are possible, implying different ordering of the rules, but the one we have given is the most economic.

6.9 Cyclic transformations: Insertion of *ac*

As we have seen, the conjunction *ac* occurs frequently in Biblical Welsh numerals. The variant of *ac* occurring before words beginning with a consonant is *a*. I formulate in (54) the rule for inserting *ac*. In this

(54) *Ac*-INSERTION

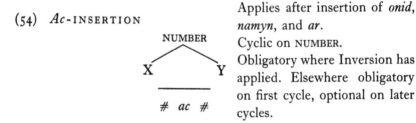

Applies after insertion of *onid*, *namyn*, and *ar*.
Cyclic on NUMBER.
Obligatory where Inversion has applied. Elsewhere obligatory on first cycle, optional on later cycles.

rule, X and Y are variables ranging over syntactic categories, which in this context, of course, can only be PHRASE and NUMBER. Rule (54) applies to some structures to which Inversion has applied and to others where Inversion has not applied. If Inversion has applied, the variable X in rule (54) will stand for NUMBER and Y for PHRASE; if Inversion has not applied, X is PHRASE and Y is NUMBER. Whenever Inversion takes place, we always find *ac* between the inverted constituents, unless *ar*, *onid*, or *namyn* are inserted by the rules just discussed. To ensure that we do not get both *ar* and *ac* in the same NUMBER, or *onid* and *ac* or *namyn* and *ac*, rule (54) specifies that the NUMBER involved has just two immediate constituents. If *ar*, *onid*, or *namyn* are inserted, the resulting NUMBER has three immediate constituents and rule (54) is not applicable.

It follows that the grammar must explicitly state that the rules inserting *ar, onid,* or *namyn* are applicable before the rule inserting *ac.* As examples of structures which have undergone Inversion and which contain *ac,* consider those of (39a) and (44d), already given. There are no examples in the Welsh Bible of NUMBERs which have undergone Inversion which do not also contain *ac* (or *ar, onid,* or *namyn*).

In NUMBERs which have not undergone Inversion, insertion of *ac* is obligatory if the right-hand immediate constituent (which in this case is a NUMBER), (a) has had its constituents permuted by Inversion, or (b) dominates just a PHRASE, or (c) is a lexical item NUMBER, e.g. *un, dau, tri,* etc. Examples of *ac* in these positions are given below. Since some of the examples contain more than one *ac,* the *ac* which is under discussion here is capitalized in these examples.

(55) (a) *ac* inserted before a NUMBER whose constituents have been inverted

ddwy fil saith gant A deg a deugain (2 1,000 7 100 + 10 + 2 20) (= 2,750) (Numbers 4.36)

mil dau cant A deg a phedwar ugain (1,000 2 100 + 10 + 4 20) (= 1,290) (Daniel 12.11)

saith mil tri chant A dau ar bymtheg ar hugain (7 1,000 3 100 + 2 on 15 on 20) (= 7,337) (Ezra 2.65, Nehemiah 7.67)

mil dau cant A phedwar ar ddeg a deugain (1,000 2 100 + 4 on 10 + 2 20) (= 1,254) (Nehemiah 7.12, 34)

tri chan…A deg a phedwar ugain (3 100… + 10 + 4 20) (= 390) (Ezekiel 4.5, 9)

pedwar cant A deng…a deugain (4 100 + 10… + 2 20) (= 450) (Acts 13.20)

cant A thri ar bymtheg ar hugain (100 + 3 on 15 on 20) (= 138) (Nehemiah 7.45)

pum cant A deg a deugain (5 100 + 10 + 2 20) (= 550) (I Kings 9.23)

dwy fil AC onid pedwar tri ugain (2 1,000 + minus 4 3 20) (= 2,056) (Ezra 2.14)

saith cant AC onid pedwar deugain (7 100 + minus 4 2 20) (= 736) (Ezra 2.66)

   (b) *ac* inserted before a NUMBER dominating just a PHRASE

chwe mil saith cant AC ugain (6 1,000 7 100 + 20) (= 6,720) (Ezra 2.67, Nehemiah 7.69)

wyth mil pum cant A phedwar ugain (8 1,000 5 100+4 20)
   (= 8,580) (Numbers 4.48)
chwe mil AC wyth cant (6 1,000+8 100) (= 6,800) (I
   Chronicles 12.24)
onid un tri ugain mil A thri chant (minus 1 3 20 1,000 + 3 100)
   (=59,300) (Numbers 2.13)
dri chant A thri ugain (3 100 + 3 20) (= 360) (II Samuel
   2.31)
bedwar cant AC ugain (4 100+20) (= 420) (I Kings 9.28)
fil A phedwar cant (1,000 +4 100) (= 1,400) (I Kings 10.26)
tair ar ddeg a saith ugain o filoedd A chwe chant (3 on 10+7
   20 of 1,000s +6 100) (= 153,600) (II Chronicles 2.17)
ugain mil AC wyth cant (20 1,000+8 100) (= 20,800) (I
   Chronicles 12.30)
tri ugain mil A phum cant (3 20 1,000+5 100) (= 60,500)
   (Numbers 26.27)

(c) *ac* inserted before a NUMBER which is a lexical item
   ddau cant pedwar ugain AC wyth (2 100 4 20+8) (= 288)
      (I Chronicles 25.7)
   fil A phump (1,000 + 5) (= 1,005) (I Kings 4.32)
   dri ugain A dau (3 20+2) (= 62) (I Chronicles 26.8)
   pedwar ugain...A chwech (4 20...+6) (= 86) (Genesis
      16.16)
   chwe chant a thri ugain A chwech (6 100+3 20+6) (= 666)
      (Revelations 13.18)
   gant a phedwar ugain A phump (100+4 20+5) (= 185)
      (Isaiah 37.36)
   gan...a phedwar ugain...A chwe (100...+4 20 ...+6)
      (= 186) (Numbers 2.9)

What do the environments illustrated in (55a, b, c) have in common?
The examples of (55) all illustrate insertion of *ac* between the constituents
of a NUMBER which have not been permuted by Inversion and in each
case this NUMBER is the lowest NUMBER in its structure whose constituents
could have been, but were not, permuted by Inversion. The structure,
after Inversion, for instance, of the first example of (55a) is as in (56).
(As before, the subscript integers on NUMBERs here are for convenience
of reference only.) The constituents of NUMBER$_1$ in this structure have
undergone Inversion. The constituents of NUMBER$_2$ could have under-

gone Inversion but in fact they have not, the rule being optional in this environment. *Ac* is inserted obligatorily between the constituents of NUMBER₂.

(56) (abbreviated)

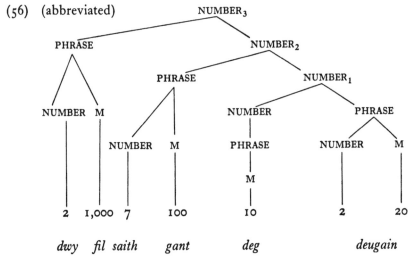

dwy	*fil*	*saith*	*gant*	*deg*	*deugain*

Parallel remarks can be made about the examples of (55b). The structure, after Inversion, of the first example in (55b) is as in (57). Here, although Inversion could have applied to the constituents of NUMBER₂,

(57) (abbreviated)

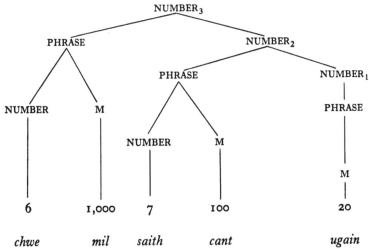

chwe	*mil*	*saith*	*cant*	*ugain*

and subsequently to the constituents of NUMBER₃, Inversion has in fact not applied anywhere. The lowest NUMBER to which Inversion might have applied is NUMBER$_2$, since NUMBER$_1$ only has a single constituent. *Ac* is inserted obligatorily between the constituents of NUMBER$_2$.

Similar remarks can obviously be made in the case of the examples of (55c). I conclude, then, that *ac* must be inserted between the constituents of the lowest NUMBER in a structure whose constituents have not been permuted by Inversion. To account for these facts I postulate that application of rule (54) inserting *ac* is cyclic, applying first to the lowest NUMBER in a structure, then to the next NUMBER up in the structure, and so forth; on the first cycle where the NUMBER being considered has not undergone Inversion, rule (54) applies obligatorily. All the examples of (55) support this treatment. There are no counterexamples in the Welsh Bible, i.e. there are no expressions like *ddwy fil saith gant deg a deugain*, or *fil pump*, or *chwe mil saith cant ugain*.

On cycles after the first one on which Inversion has not applied rule (54) inserting *ac* applies optionally. For cases where *ac* is not inserted on such subsequent cycles see the first four examples of (55a), the first two of (55b), and the first one of (55c). For cases where *ac* is inserted on such subsequent cycles see the last three examples of (55c) and those given below.

(57)   tair mil a chwe chant a deg ar hugain (3 1,000 + 6 100 + 10 on 20)
    (= 3,630) (Ezra 2.35)
    dwy fil ac wyth gant a thri ar bymtheg (2 1,000 + 8 100 + 3 on 15)
    (= 2,818) (Nehemiah 7.11)
    fil a deucant a thri ugain (1,000 + 2 100 + 3 20) (= 1,260) (Revelations 11.3, 12.6)
    mil a saith gant a phymtheg...a thri ugain (1,000 + 7 100 + 15...
    + 3 20) (= 1,775) (Exodus 38.25, 28)

Although we have considered facts that lead us to postulate two rules that apply cyclically, namely Inversion and *ac*-Insertion, we have seen no evidence that these two rules share (or do not share) the same cycle. That is, as far as the data in the Welsh Bible are concerned, it does not matter whether all the cyclic applications of Inversion are gone through before a single *ac* is inserted or whether Inversion is applicable first to the innermost NUMBER, then *ac*-Insertion is applicable to that same NUMBER, then Inversion is applicable to the next highest NUMBER, with *ac*-Insertion being applicable to that NUMBER after it, and so on. All that we can say is that both these rules apply cyclically, with certain restrictions formulated in terms of their cyclic application, as we have seen, and that, for any given NUMBER, Inversion must be applicable before *ac*-Insertion.

6.10 Categories in derived structure

There are, as we shall see in the next sections, at least three processes for the purposes of which *mil* is, in effect, a noun, i.e. behaves exactly like one. It is for this reason that the lexical entry (4g) for *mil* includes the specification [Noun]. This specification expresses the fact that *mil* is a noun, which is not to deny, of course, that it is also an M. With this device of introducing categorial specifications into phrase markers through the lexicalization process, we make it possible to formulate a set of rules referring simply to the category noun, rather than having to repeat several times a formula such as 'nouns and *mil*'.

Lexical entry (4g) associates a phonological specification *mil* and the syntactic specifications [Noun] and [Fem] with a particular tree structure generated by the phrase structure rules. The phrase structure rules themselves associate this structure with the category M. Now although these associations with a particular structure are stated by different components of the grammar, i.e. by the lexicon in the cases of *mil*, [Noun], and [Fem], and by the phrase structure rules in the case of M, the nature of the association expressed in each case is the same in so far as it affects the whole structure. That is, just as the label M can be said to represent some property of the structure dominated by a node so labelled, so also do the specifications *mil*, [Noun], and [Fem] represent properties of the structure associated with them by a lexical entry such as (4g). The diagrammatic notation we are using may possibly be misleading on this point. To clarify the matter, consider the following two diagrams, which should be seen as exact notational equivalents. Both diagrams represent the association of a given structure with the properties represented by the terms M, Noun, Fem, and *mil*. The nature of the associations expressed are the same in each diagram. These diagrams, furthermore, do not express any hierarchy or relationships of priority between the associations they represent. We have not, for example, implied that the category M is in any sense 'more essential' to the given structure than the specification [Fem]. Both terms are indispensable and necessarily associated with this structure in a full account of the facts of Biblical Welsh. The structure shown in diagrams (58) is a noun in just the same sense as it is an M and when we formulate

(58)   (a)

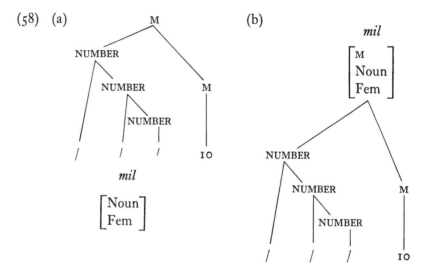

(b)

rules affecting nouns in the next few sections, it is to be understood that *mil* and the structure underlying it, being a noun, is affected.

The rules affecting *mil* as a noun, which we shall discuss in the next three sections, also affect the PHRASES immediately dominating *mil* as if they were noun phrases (NPS). That is, in just the sense in which *mil* is both an M and a noun, *un ar hugain mil*, for example, is both a PHRASE and an NP. There are a number of processes affecting PHRASES which immediately dominate some NUMBER and *mil*; and these processes affect in precisely the same way NPS which immediately dominate some NUMBER and a noun. I propose below, tentatively, a convention which will have the desired effect of associating the category label NP with any PHRASE that immediately dominates *mil*.

(59)   If there exists a phrase structure rule X → Y Z and if during the course of a derivation a node comes to immediately dominate a Y and a Z, in that order, then that node receives the specification X.

The formulation of convention (59) in such a general way captures the significance of the connection between *mil* behaving as a noun and expressions like *un ar hugain mil* behaving as NPS. A basic connection between nouns and NPS is established in the phrase structure rules and by referring to these rules, convention (59) expresses the fact that, given that *mil* behaves as a noun, it is in some sense natural for expressions like *un ar hugain mil* to behave as NPS, rather than, say, as verb phrases, or adverbials. This convention manages to express some facts about the numeral system of Biblical Welsh, as we shall see, but can only be proposed tentatively here as its formulation is extremely general and further research may show it to be misconceived. But some way must be found to express the facts which convention (59) allows us to express and for the purposes of this study I assume this convention to be appropriate. I illustrate the operation of this convention below.

The phrase structure rules generate a structure as in (60). Lexicaliza-

(60) (abbreviated)

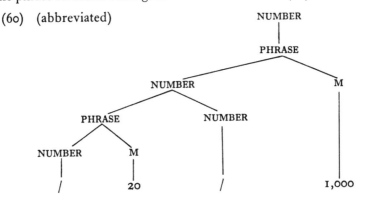

tion rule (4g) associates the right-hand M in this structure with the specifications *mil*, [Noun], and [Fem]. I assume that the phrase structure rules of Biblical Welsh include (61).

(61) NP → NUMBER noun

This is a quite natural assumption, since NUMBERs and nouns regularly occur as constituents of NPs in that order in the surface structure of

(61) (abbreviated)

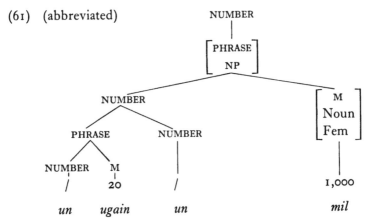

Biblical Welsh. Assuming this phrase structure rule, the top PHRASE in structure (60), now lexicalized, receives the specification NP by convention (59). That is, after lexicalization and the operation of convention (59), structure (60) appears as in structure (61). For convenience, I write phonological specifications below the structure diagram, as usual, while writing all syntactic specifications at the appropriate node in the diagram. No theoretical significance attaches to this usage. Structure (61) becomes, through 1-Deletion, Inversion, and *ar*-Insertion, a structure specified phonologically as *un ar hugain mil*. In so far as *un ar hugain mil* (= 21,000) behaves in the same way, as we shall see, as *un ar hugain mlynedd* (= 21 years), the former expression is an NP, and this is what is expressed by convention (59). In the next section we shall see that there is some further justification for a convention with the effect of (59).

It is convenient at this point, while on the topic of derived structure, to mention a type of transformational operation not encountered so far in this study. The transformations we have discussed so far involve simple operations such as deletion (e.g. 1-Deletion), substitution (e.g. Switch), permutation (e.g. Inversion), and simple adjunction (e.g. the rules inserting *ac*, *ar*, *onid*, and *namyn*). In the next section we shall make use of another operation that appears to be useful in writing transformational grammars, namely the operation called 'Chomsky-adjunction'. Imagine that we have a tree structure as in (62a) below, and wish to convert it by a transformation to (62b). The instruction necessary

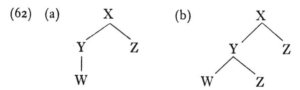

(62)   (a)   X   (b)   X

for converting (62a) to (62b) is simply 'adjoin Z as right daughter of Y'. But imagine that we wish to convert (62a) to 62c). Cases of this nature

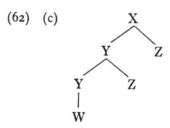

(62)   (c)   X

have been found with sufficient frequency in studies in transformational grammar to warrant the invention of a special operation for converting structures like (62a) to structures like (62c). In this case the relevant instruction is 'Chomsky-adjoin Z as right daughter of Y'. The difference between Chomsky-adjunction and simple adjunction is that the former builds extra structure by a copying downward of the node to which something is being adjoined. In our example, an extra Y node appears between X and W and Z is adjoined to the higher of the resulting two Ys. In the next section we shall have occasion to use Chomsky-adjunction, in interaction with convention (59).

6.11 Distribution

In this section we come to an explanation of the ellipses found in examples of previous sections. Each ellipsis stands for a noun that is 'distributed' into the interior of a numeral expression from a position on the right of it. I give below some examples of the distribution of the noun *blynedd* 'years'.

(63)   saith mlynedd ac wyth gan mlynedd (7 years + 8 100 years) (= 807 years) (Genesis 5.7)

deugain mlynedd ac wyth gan mlynedd (2 20 years + 8 100 years) (= 840 years) (Genesis 5.13)

bum mlynedd a chan mlynedd (5 years + 100 years) (= 105 years) (Genesis 5.6)

ddeuddeng mlynedd a naw can mlynedd (12 years + 9 100 years) (= 912 years) (Genesis 5.8)

bymtheng mlynedd ac wyth gan mlynedd (15 years + 8 100 years) (= 815 years) (Genesis 5.10)

bum mlynedd a naw can mlynedd (5 years + 9 100 years) (= 905 years) (Genesis 5.11)

ddeng mlynedd ar hugain ac wyth gan mlynedd (10 years on 20 + 8 100 years) (= 830 years) (Genesis 5.16)

bymtheng mlynedd a phedwar ugain ac wyth gan mlynedd (15 years + 4 20 + 8 100 years) (= 895 years) (Genesis 5.17)

ddwy flynedd a thri ugain a chan mlynedd (2 years + 3 20 + 100 years) (= 162 years) (Genesis 5.18)

ddwy flynedd a thri ugain a naw can mlynedd (2 years + 3 20 + 9 100 years) (= 962 years) (Genesis 5.20)

With respect to this phenomenon of Distribution, *mil* behaves exactly as a noun. Thus we find instances of *mil* distributed into the interior of a numeral from a position on the right of it, as shown below.

(64)   bedair mil a saithugeinmil (4 1,000 + 7 20 1,000) (= 144,000) (Revelations 14.1, 3)

saith mil a phedwar ugain mil (7 1,000 + 4 20 1,000) (= 87,000) (I Chronicles 7.5)

pedair mil a thri ugain mil a thri chant (4 1,000 + 3 20 1,000 + 3 100) (= 64,300) (Numbers 26.25)

gan mil ac wyth mil a chant (100 1,000 + 8 1,000 + 100) (= 108,100) (Numbers 2.24)

chwe chan mil a thair mil a phum cant a deg a deugain (6 100 1,000 + 3 1,000 + 5 100 + 10 + 2 20) (= 603,550) (Exodus 38.26, Numbers 1.46, 2.32)

tri chan mil a saith mil a phum cant (3 100 1,000 + 7 1,000 + 5 100) (= 307,500) (II Chronicles 26.13)

gan mil ac un ar ddeg a deugain o filoedd, a phedwar cant a deg a deugain (100 1,000 + 1 on 10 + 20 of 1,000s, + 4 100 + 10 + 2 20) (= 151,450) (Numbers 2.16)

onid un fil tri ugain mil a thri chant (minus 1 1,000 3 20 1,000 + 3 100) (= 59,300) (Numbers 1.23)

onid pedair mil pedwar ugain mil a phum cant (minus 4 1,000 4 20 1,000 + 5 100) (= 76,500) (Numbers 26.22)

(Recall that *o filoedd* is a variant of *mil*.) Distribution is the first of several processes that we shall discuss that treat *mil* and nouns exactly alike.

Distribution may copy a noun into the interior of a numeral more than once, as can be seen from the following examples.

(65)   gan mil ac onid tair mil tri ugain mil a chwe chant (100 1,000 + minus 3 1,000 3 20 1,000 + 6 100) (= 157,600) (Numbers 2.31)

gan mil a phedwar ugain mil a chwe mil a phedwar cant (100 1,000 + 4 20 1,000 + 6 1,000 + 4 100) (= 186,400) (Numbers 2.9)

naw can mlynedd a deng mlynedd a deugain mlynedd (9 100 years + 10 years + 2 20 years) (= 950 years) (Genesis 9.29)

bedwar can mil a deng mil a thri ugain [mil] (4 100 1,000 + 10 1,000 + 3 20 [1,000]) (= 470,000) (I Chronicles 21.5)

naw can mlynedd a deng mlynedd ar hugain [mlynedd] (9 100 years + 10 years on 20 [years]) (= 930 years) (Genesis 5.5)

can mlynedd a phymtheng mlynedd a thri ugain [mlynedd] (100
years + 15 years + 3 20 [years]) (= 175 years) (Genesis 25.7)
gan mlynedd a saith mlynedd ar hugain [mlynedd] (100 years +7
years on 20 [years]) (= 127 years) (Genesis 23.1)
dri chan mlynedd a deng mlynedd a deugain [mlynedd] (3 100
years + 10 years + 2 20 [years]) (= 350 years) (Genesis 9.28)

(In the last five of these examples a square-bracketed *mil* or *mlynedd*
is not actually present in the text of the Welsh Bible, but is assumed to
be present in the deep structure and to have been deleted by a transformation we shall discuss in the next section.)

Distribution of nouns into the interior of numerals is not obligatory,
as we see from the following examples.

(66)   onid tair deugain a chan mlynedd (minus 3 2 20 + 100 years)
(= 137 years) (Exodus 6.20)
tair ar ddeg a saith ugain o filoedd a chwe chant (3 on 10 + 7 20 of
1,000s + 6 100) (= 153,600) (II Chronicles 2.17)
cant a phedwar ugain mil (100 + 4 20 1,000) (= 180,000) (I Kings
12.21)
deucant a deg a deugain o filoedd (2 100 + 10 + 2 20 of 1,000s)
(= 250,000) (I Chronicles 5.21)
ddau cant a phedwar ugain mil (2 100 + 4 20 1,000) (= 280,000)
(II Chronicles 17.15)
deuddeg a thri ugain mil (12 + 3 20 1,000) (= 72,000) (Numbers
31.33)
cant ac ugain mil (100 + 20 1,000) (= 120,000) (Judges 8.10)
pump a thri ugain a thri chant a mil o siclau (5 + 3 20 + 3 100 +
1000 of shekels) (= 1,365 shekels) (Numbers 3.50)
chwe chant a thri ugain a chwech o dalentau (6 100 + 3 20 + 6 of
talents) (= 666 talents) (I Kings 10.14, II Chronicles 9.13)
pedair a phedwar ugain mlynedd (4 + 4 20 years) (= 84 years)
(Luke 2.37)

We have seen so far that a noun may optionally be distributed to one
or more places inside a numeral from a position on the right of it. There
are actually several qualifications that must be made to this statement
but I will first formulate the rule of Distribution and then describe the
necessary qualifications while illustrating the operation of the rule.

(67)   DISTRIBUTION

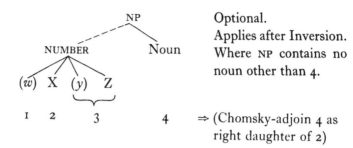

Optional.
Applies after Inversion.
Where NP contains no
noun other than 4.

$\Rightarrow$ (Chomsky-adjoin 4 as
right daughter of 2)

Constraint: if in a given structure there are two subtrees, A and B,
matching 2 in the structural index of this rule and A
dominates B, then the rule may not apply with respect
to A.

The broken line in this formulation indicates that NP must dominate
NUMBER, but need not necessarily immediately dominate it. That is,
other nodes may or may not intervene between NP and NUMBER; a
NUMBER indefinitely far down inside an NP may have a noun distributed
into it. In (67) X and Z are variables ranging over the categories PHRASE
and NUMBER. If Inversion has applied, X is NUMBER and Z is PHRASE;
otherwise X is PHRASE and Z is NUMBER. Distribution affects the leftmost
major category in a NUMBER, regardless of whether it is a PHRASE or a
NUMBER and this is why we have to use variables in our formulation of
the rule. *w* and *y* are also variables, ranging over the lexical items *onid*,
namyn, *ar*, and *ac*. The presence or absence of these elements in a
structure does not affect the applicability of Distribution and they are

(68)   (abbreviated)

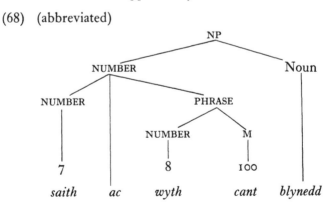

parenthesized for that reason. For the moment I will ignore the constraint on (67) and give some simple illustrations of the operation of the rule.

Consider the first example of (63), *saith mlynedd ac wyth gan mlynedd*. After lexicalization, Inversion, and insertion of *ac*, the structure of this expression is as in (68). Here *saith* matches 2 of the structural index of rule (67), *ac wyth cant* matches 3, and *blynedd* matches 4. The rule therefore tells us to Chomsky-adjoin *blynedd* as right daughter of *saith*. We do this, and derive (69). Phonological rules convert the

(69) (abbreviated)

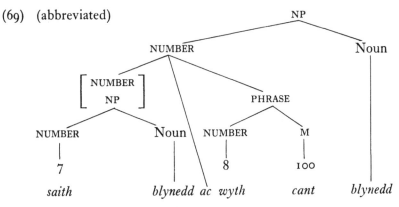

terminal string of this structure into *saith mlynedd ac wyth gan mlynedd*. Note that in structure (69) two things have happened. Firstly, the Chomsky-adjunction of rule (67) has made an extra copy of the node NUMBER dominating *saith*, while adjoining *blynedd* as right daughter of the original node. Secondly, convention (59) has assigned the categorial specification NP to the NUMBER node now dominating *saith* and *blynedd*. There is evidence that strings like *saith blynedd*, resulting from the operation of the Distribution rule, behave like noun phrases, in that they undergo the Pluralization transformation, which applies to plural NPs in general. We shall discuss the Pluralization transformation later.

Consider now a more complicated case, the first example in (65), *gan mil ac onid tair mil tri ugain mil a chwe chant*. (For convenience in discussing this example, assume that Agreement simply changes *tri* to *tair*, though in fact this is a later, phonological change, triggered by the marker [Fem] assigned by the Agreement rule.) After lexicalization, 1-Deletion, Agreement, Inversion, and insertion of *onid* and *ac*, the structure of this expression is as in (70). Here on one possible analysis the first *cant* matches 2 of the structural index of rule (67), *ac onid tair*

(70)   (abbreviated)

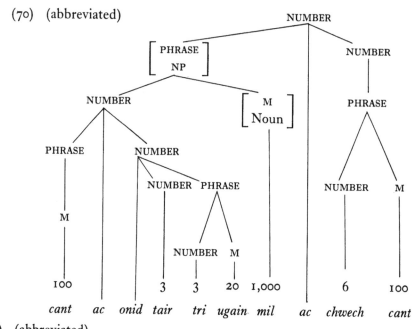

(71)   (abbreviated)

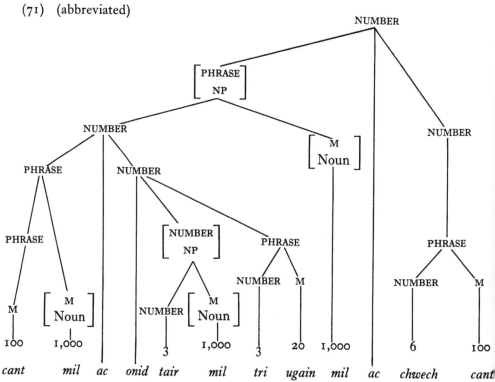

tri ugain matches 3, and *mil* matches 4. On another possible analysis *onid* matches 1, *tair* matches 2, *tri ugain* matches 3, and *mil* matches 4. Consequently *mil* can be Chomsky-adjoined as right daughter of either the first *cant*, or *tair*, or both. Chomsky-adjoining *mil* to both *cant* and *tair*, we derive (71). Phonological rules convert the terminal string of this structure to *gan mil ac onid tair mil tri ugain mil a chwe chant*. Note again that convention (59) has applied, assigning the categorial specification NP to *tair mil*.

The constraint mentioned in the formulation of rule (67) must now be explained. If there were no such constraint, rule (67) would state that a noun can be Chomsky-adjoined as right daughter of any node matching 2 in the structural index of the rule, but the possibilities are in fact somewhat more limited than this. It is not the case that there are as many opportunities for Distribution of nouns within NUMBERs as there are nodes matching 2 of the structural index of rule (67). Consider the following structure types, in which there are two levels of embedding of NUMBERs – numerals in the Welsh Bible are rarely more complex than this. In structure (72a) the nodes matching 2 of the structural

(72) (a)   (b)

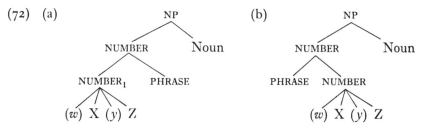

index of rule (67) are NUMBER₁ and X. In structure (72b) the nodes matching 2 of the structural index of rule (67) are PHRASE and X. Thus it might appear that we have in these two structure types six different possibilities for the application of the Distribution rule, namely those listed below.

(73) In structures like (72a), Chomsky-adjunction of a Noun at:
                              both NUMBER₁ and X
                              NUMBER₁ only
                              X only
      In structures like (72b), Chomsky-adjunction of a Noun at:
                              both PHRASE and X
                              PHRASE only
                              X only

Of these six possibilities, examples of the first two are not found in the Welsh Bible. We do not find examples such as:

(74)   *chwe mil a deugain mil a naw can mil (6 1,000 + 2 20 1,000 + 9 100 1,000) (= 946,000)

*pum mlynedd a thri ugain mlynedd a chan mlynedd (5 years + 3 20 years + 100 years) (= 165 years)

*chwech a deugain mil a naw can mil (6 + 2 20 1,000 + 9 100 1,000) (= 946,000)

*pump a thri ugain mlynedd a chan mlynedd (5 + 3 20 years + 100 years) (= 165 years)

In structures of type (72a), there are many examples of Chomsky-adjunction of a noun at just X.

(75)   dengwr a deugain a dau cant [wr] (10 man + 2 20 + 2 100 [man]) (= 250 men) (Numbers 26.10)

ddeng mlynedd ar hugain ac wyth cant [mlynedd] (10 years on 20 + 8 100 [years]) (= 830 years) (Genesis 5.16)

bymtheng mlynedd a phedwar ugain ac wyth gan mlynedd (15 years + 4 20 + 8 100 years) (= 895 years) (Genesis 5.17)

ddwy flynedd a thri ugain a chan mlynedd (2 years + 3 20 + 100 years) (= 162 years) (Genesis 5.18)

un fil ar bymtheg ar hugain [mil] (1 1,000 on 15 on 20 [1,000]) (= 36,000) (Numbers 31.38,44)

tair mil ar ddeg a deugain [mil] a phedwar cant (3 1,000 on 10 + 2 20 [1,000] + 4 100) (= 53,400) (Numbers 26.47)

bedair mil ar ddeg a thri ugain [mil] a chwe chant (4 1,000 on 10 + 3 20 [1,000] + 6 100) (= 74,600) (Numbers 1.27, 2.4)

ddwy flynedd a thri ugain a naw can mlynedd (2 years + 3 20 + 9 100 years) (= 962 years) (Genesis 5.20)

bum mlynedd a thri ugain a thri chant o flynyddoedd (5 years + 3 20 + 3 100 of years's) (= 365 years) (Genesis 5.23)

tair blwydd ar hugain a chant [blwydd] (3 years on 20 + 100 [years]) (= 123 years) (Numbers 33.39)

(As in previous examples, nouns in square brackets are not actually present in the text of the Welsh Bible, but are assumed to be present in deep structure and to have been deleted by a transformation to be discussed in the next section. *Blynyddoedd* and *blwydd* are eccentric variants of *blynedd* 'years', that will be explained later.)

Now consider constructions of type (72b). As examples of Chomsky-adjunction of a noun at both PHRASE and X, there are the examples of (65). As examples of structures of the (72b) type with Chomsky-adjunction of a noun at just PHRASE, there are:

(76)   gan mil ac un ar ddeg a deugain o filoedd, a phedwar cant a deg
       a deugain (100 1,000 + 1 on 10 + 2 20 of 1,000s, + 4 100 + 10 + 2
       20) (= 151,450) (Numbers 2.16)
       chwe chan mil a phymtheg a thri ugain o filoedd (6 100 1,000 + 15
       + 3 20 of 1,000s) (= 675,000) (Numbers 31.32)
       dri chan mil a dwy ar bymtheg ar hugain o filoedd, a phum cant
       (3 100 1,000 + 2 on 15 on 20 of 1,000s, + 5 100) (= 337,500)
       (Numbers 31.36,43)
       can mlwydd a deg ar hugain [mlwydd] (100 years + 10 on 20
       [years]) (= 130 years) (II Chronicles 24.15)
       saith gan sicl a deg ar hugain [sicl] (7 100 shekel + 10 on 20
       [shekel]) (= 730 shekels) (Exodus 38.24)
       tri chan niwrnod a deg a phedwar ugain [niwrnod] (3 100 day +
       10 + 4 20 [day]) (= 390 days) (Ezekiel 4.5,9)
       can mlynedd a dwy ar bymtheg ar hugain o flynyddoedd (100
       years + 2 on 15 on 20 of years's) (= 137 years) (Genesis 25.17)

Finally, as examples of structures of type (72b) with Chomsky-adjunction of a noun at just X, we have:

(77)   bedwar cant a dengwr a deugain [wr] (4 100 + 10 man + 2 20
       [man]) (= 450 men) (I Kings 18.22)
       gant a phedwar cufydd a deugain [cufydd] (100 + 4 cubit + 2 20
       [cubit]) (= 144 cubits) (Revelations 21.17)
       cant a'r saith dalaeth ar hugain [dalaeth] (100 + the 7 province
       on 20 [province]) (= 127 provinces) (Esther 9.30) (the article
       here may be disregarded for our present purposes)
       pedwar cant a deng mlynedd a deugain [mlynedd] (4 100 + 10
       years + 2 20 [years]) (= 450 years) (Acts 13.20)
       gant ac onid tair blynedd deugain [mlynedd] (100 + minus 3
       years 2 20 [years]) (= 137 years) (Exodus 6.16)

Rule (67) and its constraint have the effect shown diagrammatically in (78) below. In these structures a noun may be Chomsky-adjoined at any of the dark blobs and nowhere else. The nodes represented by blobs here and by the variable X in the structural description of (67) can be either NUMBERS or PHRASES.

(78)

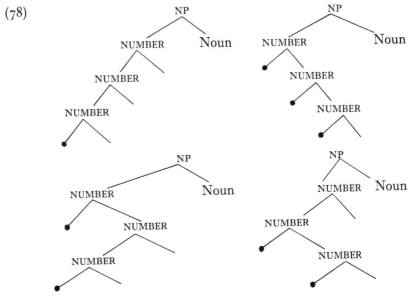

The condition 'Where NP contains no noun other than 4' in the formulation of rule (67) also prevents some unwanted applications of Distribution. Consider the following examples.

(79)   deuddeg a thri ugain mil o eidionau (12 + 3 20 1,000 of cattle)
(= 72,000 cattle) (Numbers 31.33)

bum mil ar hugain [mil] a channwr (5 1,000 on 20 [1,000] + 100 man) (= 25,100 men) (Judges 20.35)

chwe chan mil a phymtheg a thri ugain o filoedd o ddefaid (6 100 1,000 + 15 + 3 20 of 1,000s of sheep) (= 675,000 sheep) (Numbers 31.32)

ddeng mil a thri ugain [mil] o wŷr (10 1,000 + 3 20 [1,000] of men) (= 70,000 men) (II Samuel 24.15)

dwy fil ar hugain [mil] o wartheg (2 1,000 on 20 [1,000] of oxen) (= 22,000 oxen) (I Kings 8.63)

cant a phedwar ugain mil o wŷr (100 + 4 20 1,000 of men) (= 180,000 men) (I Kings 12.21)

In each of these examples, there is an occurrence of *mil* as well as of another noun. Note that the Welsh Bible contains no examples of such expressions where the outer noun is distributed, i.e. expressions such as:

(80)   *bum wr ar hugain [mil] a channwr
*chwe chan dafad a phymtheg a thri ugain o filoedd o ddefaid
*can wr a phedwar ugain mil o wŷr

The pre-Distribution structure of the last example in (79) is as in (81).

(81) (abbreviated)

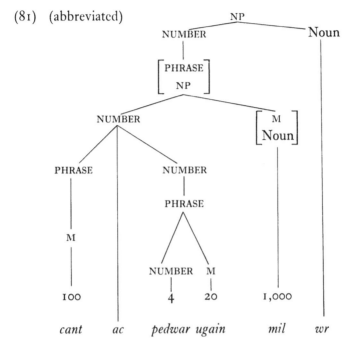

Given a structure such as this, the condition on rule (67) ensures that only the inner noun, here *mil*, may be distributed. There are, in other words, no instances in the Welsh Bible where a noun is distributed 'across' another noun.

Distribution must follow Inversion for reasons which I outline below. Inversion is, as we have seen, in many environments optional. Depending on whether or not Inversion applies, a node which begins a derivation as right-hand constituent of a NUMBER may or may not end up as its left-hand constituent; and similarly a node which starts as the left-hand constituent of a NUMBER may, through Inversion, become the right-hand constituent, or it may remain on the left. But regardless of whether Inversion applies or not, Distribution only Chomsky-adjoins nouns to the left-hand constituents of NUMBERs.

Consider the second example of (64), *saith mil a phedwar ugain mil* (= 87,000). The underlying structure of this expression corresponds to the string *pedwar ugain saith mil*. Inversion converts *pedwar ugain saith* to *saith pedwar ugain*. If *mil* is Chomsky-adjoined to *saith* before Inversion, we get the string *pedwar ugain saith mil mil*. If Inversion now applies, all is well, as we will have, ultimately, *saith mil a phedwar ugain mil*, as desired, but since Inversion is optional, we must also allow for the possibility that it may not apply, and in this case all is not well, as we get, ultimately, **pedwar ugain a saith mil mil*, which is not a wellformed expression for 87,000.

Conversely, consider the sixth example of (64), *tri chan mil a saith mil a phum cant* (= 307,500). The underlying string here is *tri cant saith mil pump cant*. Applying Distribution before Inversion, we Chomsky-adjoin *mil* to *tri cant*, deriving *tri cant mil saith mil pump cant*. If Inversion does not now apply, we derive, after application of other rules, *tri chan mil a saith mil a phum cant*, as desired, but if Inversion applies, as it may, then we derive ultimately **saith a tri chan mil mil a phum cant*, which is not a wellformed expression for 307,500.

We have shown how a wide range of numeral expressions from Biblical Welsh can be accounted for by a transformational rule, (67). Some space should be devoted to explaining why the same facts cannot be accounted for without the use of a transformation, i.e. by generating the structure of expressions like those of (63), (64), and (65) directly by the rules of the base component. There are a number of objections to such a treatment.

Consider, for example, the expression *tri chan mil a saith mil a phum cant* (3 100 1,000 + 7 1,000 + 5 100) (= 307,500) (II Chronicles 26.13). In the treatment I have proposed the first *mil* here is put in position by the Distribution rule. But consider a treatment in which the structure underlying *mil* is actually generated in this position by the phrase structure rules. The phrase structure rules we have proposed will generate a deep structure which can be lexicalized as *tri chan mil a saith mil a phum cant*, with no use made of the Distribution transfor-

(82) (abbreviated)

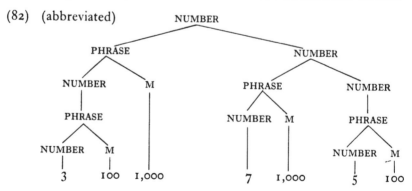

mation. This structure is as in (82). The phrase structure rules would indeed generate this structure, but note that the Packing Strategy, which we have reason to suspect is generally correct, would characterize this structure as illformed, because of the wellformedness of the PHRASE underlying *tri chant a saith mil* (3 100 + 7 1,000) (= 307,000). Consider, furthermore, what would be the effect of applying the Inversion rule to structure (82). If we apply Inversion on the first cycle only, we derive the ungrammatical **tri chan mil a phum cant a saith mil*, although the Inversion rule we have proposed appears to be otherwise well motivated.

The distribution in surface structure of *ar* and *ac* also justifies the existence of rule (67). In order to illustrate with examples the way in which the distribution of *ac* and *ar* justifies the transformational spreading of *mil*, I must unfortunately anticipate subsequent discussion by mentioning that there must also be a transformation in Biblical Welsh which deletes some occurrences of *mil* after the application of the transformation we are directly concerned with here. I can find no crucial example in which a nontransformational account of the distribution of *mil* conflicts with the regularities we have observed in the occurrence of *ar* and *ac* and in which an instance of *mil* has not been deleted. This appears to be a nonsignificant chance gap in the data. I ask the reader to accept on faith for the moment that there is a late transformation deleting some occurrences of *mil*. If this is accepted, there are quite a lot of crucial examples which show that the regular account I have given of the insertion of *ar* and *ac* is only possible if the spreading of *mil* is done by a transformation, rather than by the base component. In giving these examples, I will give a postulated deleted *mil* in square brackets, e.g. for the first example given below, what actually occurs in the Welsh Bible is *bum mil ar hugain*. Now consider:

(83) bum mil ar hugain [mil] (5 1,000 on 20 [1,000]) (= 25,000)
        (Judges 20.46)
      chwe mil ar hugain [mil] (6 1,000 on 20 [1,000]) (= 26,000)
        (Judges 20.15, I Chronicles 7.40)
      ddwy fil ar hugain [mil] (2 1,000 on 20 [1,000]) (= 22,000)
        (Judges 7.3, 20.21, Numbers 3.39, I Chronicles 18.5, II
        Samuel 8.5)
      ddeng mil ar hugain [mil] (10 1,000 on 20 [1,000]) (= 30,000)
        (Joshua 8.3, I Samuel 4.10, 11.8)

ddeuddeng mil ar hugain [mil] (12 1,000 on 20 [1,000]) (= 32,000)
(Numbers 31.35, I Chronicles 19.7)
dair mil ar hugain [mil] (3 1,000 on 20 [1,000]) (= 23,000)
(Numbers 26.62, I Corinthians 10.8)
bedair mil ar hugain [mil] (4 1,000 on 20 [1,000]) (= 24,000)
(Numbers 25.9)

Now if the distribution of *mil* is accounted for in the base component
rather than transformationally, the structure underlying *bum mil ar
hugain* [*mil*] (after Inversion) will be as in (84). The rules for inserting

(84) (abbreviated)

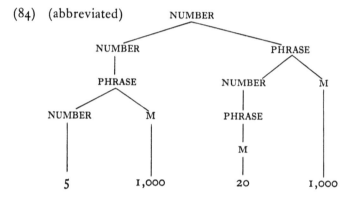

ar and *ac*, which otherwise account for all the relevant data, will in-
correctly insert *ac*, rather than *ar*, yielding the ungrammatical **bum
mil ac ugain* [*mil*].

Another argument for rule (67) is that the analysis given for *mil*
should be the same as for nouns generally and it is hard to see how the
base component could be arranged to generate nouns inside numeral
structures. The semantic component would also have to be complicated
to deal with such structures since the semantic relation between a number and a noun is not one of multiplication. I conclude on these grounds
that the distribution of nouns in examples such as those of (63), (64),
and (65) is properly handled by rule (67).

It is interesting to note that the Distribution rule (67) has an effect
which in a fairly clear sense parallels the mathematical Law of Distribution. A formulation of this Law is given below.

(85) $(a+b)c = (ac)+(bc)$

The bracketing produced by our rule (67) is more like $((ac)+b)c$, and so the parallel between it and the mathematical Law is not exact, but the ordering of elements, if not their bracketing, is shared by the mathematical Law of Distribution and the Biblical Welsh transformational rule of Distribution. In this respect Distribution resembles the rules of Inversion and 1-Deletion, which also parallel universally true statements of mathematics.

6.12 Deletion

Applicable after the operation of the Distribution rule there is an optional rule deleting the exterior, rightmost noun in a numeral expression provided that that noun has been copied into the interior of the numeral by Distribution. As examples of numerals whose derivations involve this deletion rule we have the last five examples of (65), the examples of (77), and those of (83). We formulate the Deletion rule as in (86). This rule applies to the output of the Distribution transfor-

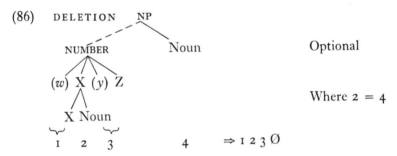

(86) DELETION

NUMBER   Noun   Optional

(w) X (y) Z

X Noun

1   2   3   4 $\Rightarrow$ 1 2 3 $\emptyset$

Where 2 = 4

mation. Here again the broken line in the formulation of the rule expresses the fact that the NUMBER involved may be embedded indefinitely far down inside the NP. Again X and Z are variables ranging over NUMBER and PHRASE and w and y are variables ranging over *onid*, *namyn*, *ar*, and *ac*. As an illustration of the operation of the rule, consider the derivation of the first example in (83), *bum mil ar hugain* (= 25,000). The structure, after Distribution, of this expression is as in (87). Rule (86) converts this to (88). Phonological rules convert the terminal string of this structure to *bum mil ar hugain*, as required.

There is a condition on rule (86) insisting that 2 and 4 be the same noun. As an illustration of the necessity of this condition, consider *ddeng mil a thri ugain o wŷr* (10 1,000 + 3 20 of men) (= 70,000 men) (II Samuel 24.15). The structure, after Distribution, of this expression

(87) (abbreviated)

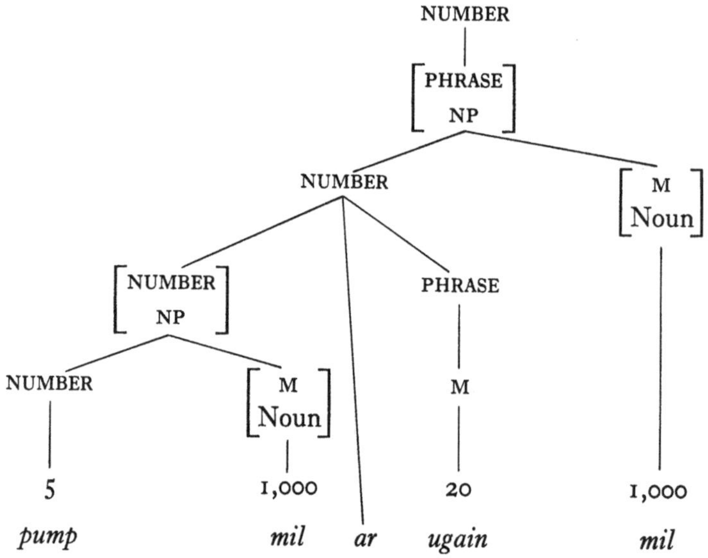

(88) (abbreviated)

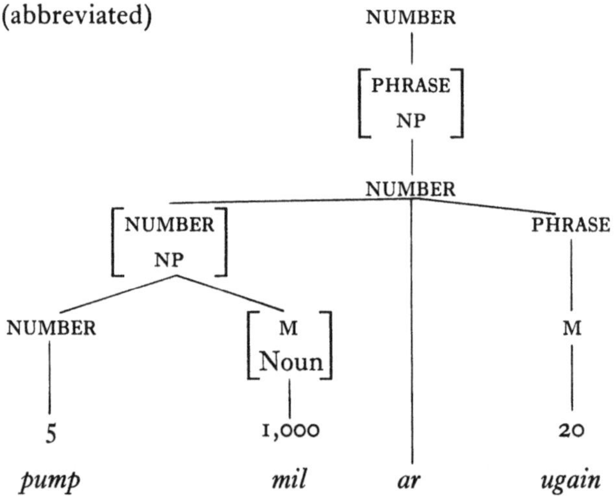

is as in (89). In this structure both the right-hand *mil* and *wr* match 4 in the structural index of rule (86), but only *mil* may be deleted. If we delete *wr* we lose all reference in the surface structure to the concept of 'men', although this concept is represented in the deep structure. This is, of course, undesirable. We prevent undesirable deletion of nouns in cases like this by insisting that the noun to be deleted be

(89) (abbreviated)

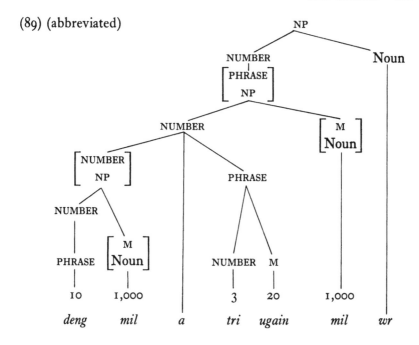

identical to some noun distributed into the interior of the numeral expression. This is the reason for the condition 'Where 2 = 4' in rule (86).

We can now mention an interesting and odd fact. It appears that numerals in Biblical Welsh may sometimes be ambiguous. The following expressions may, for example, have either of the meanings written in Arabic notation to the right of them.

(90) un fil a deugain   41,000   1,040
      naw mil a deugain   49,000   9,040
      dwy fil a thri ugain   62,000   2,060
      wyth mil a thri ugain   68,000   8,060
      tair mil a phedwar ugain   83,000   3,080
      saith mil a phedwar ugain 87,000   7,080

The fact that *ar* is used in some environments instead of *ac* protects some numerals from ambiguity. Thus *un fil ar hugain* can only mean 21,000, while *un fil ac ugain* can only mean 1,020. There are no examples in the Welsh Bible of exactly the same string of words used to refer to different numbers. To find such a string would be a great stroke of luck, but there can be no doubt that within the system we have described some numerals are ambiguous. There appears to be no sure way, for example, in which a reader, armed only with a copy of the Bible in Welsh, can tell whether *un fil a thri ugain o asynod* (Numbers 31.34) means '61,000 asses' or '1,060 asses'. In most cases he will be right if he guesses at the rounder figure, i.e. in this case 61,000, but there is nothing in the text to tell him whether his guess might be correct.

6.13 Pluralization

There are actually two ways of combining nouns with numeral expressions in Welsh. One way is to use the singular form immediately after and/or distributed within the numeral expression. Most of the examples we have so far discussed are of this type: *mil* is a singular form, the plural being *miloedd*. The noun *blwyddyn* 'year' behaves exceptionally when combined with a numeral in this way: its plural, *blynedd*, rather than its singular is used, as we have already seen in several examples. Regular examples of singular nouns used with numeral expressions are:

(91)   dwy wythnos a thri ugain (2 week + 3 20) (= 62 weeks) (Daniel 9.25,26)

chwe diwrnod a thri ugain (6 day + 3 20) (= 66 days) (Leviticus 12.5)

ddengwr a deugain a dau cant (10 man + 2 20 + 2 100) (= 250 men) (Numbers 26.10)

chwe enaid a thri ugain (6 person + 3 20) (= 66 people) (Genesis 46.26)

pedwar brenhin (4 king) (Genesis 14.9)

pum brenhin (5 king) (Joshua 10.5)

pedwar ugain sicl (4 20 shekel) (= 80 shekels) (II Kings 6.25)

The other way of combining numerals with nouns is to use the plural form after the numeral and separated from it by the preposition *o* 'of'. Examples are:

(92)   bump a phedwar ugain o wŷr (5 + 4 20 of men) (= 85 men) (I Samuel 22.18)

chwe chant a thri ugain a chwech o dalentau (6 100 + 3 20 + 6 of talents) (= 666 talents) (I Kings 10.14)

pump a thri ugain a thri chant a mil o siclau (5 + 3 20 + 3 100 + 1,000 of shekels) (= 1,365 shekels) (Numbers 3.50) chwech ugain mil o ddefaid (6 20 1,000 of sheep) (= 120,000 sheep) (I Kings 8.63)

wyth gan mil o wŷr (8 100 1,000 of men) (= 80,000 men) (II Samuel 24.9)

ddwy o wragedd (2 of wives) (Genesis 4.19)

saith o feibion a thair o ferched (7 of sons and 3 of daughters) (Job 1.2)

gant a phedair a deugain o filoedd (100 + 4 + 2 20 of 1,000s) (= 144,000) (Revelations 7.4)

bump a phedwar ugain a chant o filoedd (5 + 4 20 + 100 of 1,000s) (= 185,000) (II Kings 19.35)

gant a phedwar ugain a phump o filoedd (100 + 4 20 + 5 of 1,000s) (= 185,000) (Isaiah 37.36)

ddeucant a deg a deugain o filoedd (2 100 + 10 + 2 20 of 1,000s) (= 250,000) (I Chronicles 5.21)

I formulate a rule partially accounting for these facts below.

(93) PLURALIZATION

Optional.
Applies after Distribution.
Where the semantic representation of X is a number greater than 1.

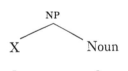

$$1 \quad 2 \Rightarrow 1\ 2 + \text{Plural}$$

This rule adjoins the marker Plural as right daughter of a noun node when the noun follows some semantically plural element. In (93) X is a variable ranging over categories, including NUMBER and PHRASE and a category such as Quantifier, to which items such as *faint*, *llawer*, and *ychydig*, the Welsh words for 'how many', 'many', and 'few', presumably belong. The condition 'Where the semantic representation of X is a number greater than 1' is necessary in order to prevent generation of expressions such as *un o wŷr, *un o dalentau, *un o siclau, *un o filoedd, which are not found in the Welsh Bible. Pluralization does not occur if the sole sister of the noun concerned is a NUMBER with the value 1. Rule (93) applies to derived structures, rather than to deep structures interpreted directly by the semantic component. The grammar expresses associations between arithmetic values and derived structures by means of the transformations which associate deep structures with derived structures.

As an example of the operation of rule (93), consider the first expression in (92), *bump a phedwar ugain o wŷr*. Before Pluralization, the structure of this expression is as in (94). NUMBER₁ in this structure is

(94) (abbreviated)

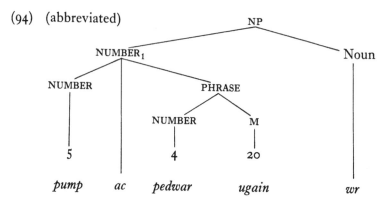

associated by the grammar with the value 85. Rule (93) converts (94) to (95). A later rule converts the string *wr* Plural into the irregular

(95) (abbreviated)

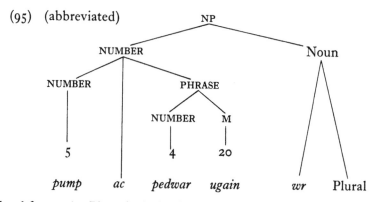

plural form *wŷr*. Phonological rules, and the rule inserting *o*, yet to be described, produce *bump a phedwar ugain o wŷr*.

Consider another example, *fil o filoedd a chan mil* (1,000 of 1,000s + 100 1,000) (= 1,100,000) (I Chronicles 21.5). Just before the operation of Distribution, the structure of this expression is as in (96). The grammar associates the PHRASE dominating the left-hand *mil* here with the value 1,000. Distribution converts this structure to (97). The PHRASE dominating just the left-hand *mil* here, being a downward copy of the left-hand PHRASE in (96) is associated by the grammar with the value 1,000. Rule (93) adjoins the marker Plural as right sister of the

(96) (abbreviated)

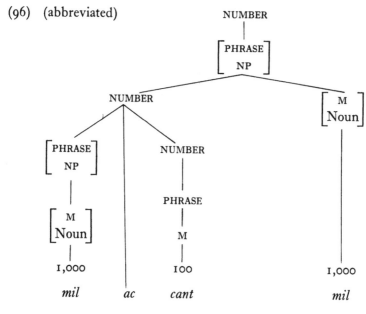

(97) (abbreviated)

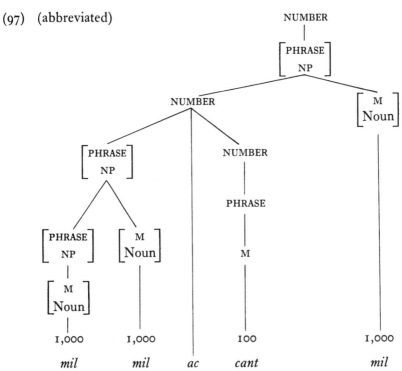

distributed *mil* (i.e. the second one) here. After *mil* the marker Plural is later lexicalized as the suffix *-oedd*: the plural of *mil* is *miloedd*. The rule inserting *o*, which we will discuss shortly, and phonological rules, yield *fil o filoedd a chan mil*.

Pluralization, which is optional, must apply after Distribution. The evidence for this is that, even when the 'original' noun is Pluralized, an internally distributed noun in the same expression need not be. Thus we have:

(98)   gan mil ac un ar ddeg a deugain o filoedd, a phedwar cant a deg
        a deugain (100 1,000 + 1 on 10 + 2 20 of 1,000s, + 4 100 + 10 + 2
        20) (= 151,450) (Numbers 2.16)
        chwe chan mil a phymtheg a thri ugain o filoedd (6 100 1,000 + 15
        + 3 20 of 1,000) (= 675,000) (Numbers 31.32)
        dri chan mil a dwy ar bymtheg ar hugain o filoedd (3 100 1,000
        + 2 on 15 on 20 of 1,000s) (= 337,000) (Numbers 31.36,43)
        can mlynedd a dwy ar bymtheg ar hugain o flynyddoedd (100
        years + 2 on 15 on 20 of years's) (= 137 years) (Genesis 25.17)

(The eccentric plural *blynyddoedd* will be explained directly.) Conversely, we have examples (99), in which a distributed noun has been Pluralized, while the original, external noun remains singular.

(99)   fil o filoedd a chan mil (1,000 of 1,000s + 100 1,000) (= 1,100,000)
        (I Chronicles 21.5)
        naw o flynyddoedd a dau can mlynedd (9 of years's + 2 100 years)
        (= 209 years) (Genesis 11.19)
        saith o flynyddoedd a dau can mlynedd (7 of years's + 2 100 years)
        (= 207 years) (Genesis 11.21)

If Pluralization preceded Distribution, then the Plural marker optionally attached to a noun would be carried along with it into the interior of a number expression by the Distribution transformation. Thus this ordering would predict that all instances of a noun in a number expression are Pluralized. The examples given above show this prediction to be incorrect. Therefore Distribution must precede Pluralization.

There are late lexicalization rules which associate phonological forms, such as the plural suffix *-oedd*, with markers such as Plural. These lexicalizations may take into account properties of the structures to which markers belong and are sequentially ordered so as to account for suppletive and irregular forms.

Let us deal now with the insertion of *o*. The rule for inserting *o* is shown in (100). Here again X is a variable ranging over categories such

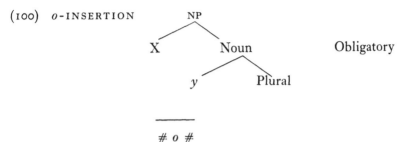

(100) *o*-INSERTION   NP

X   Noun   Obligatory

y   Plural

 # o #

as NUMBER, PHRASE, and Quantifier, and *y* is a variable ranging over lexical items (which are in this case, of course, nouns). Rule (100)

(101) (abbreviated)

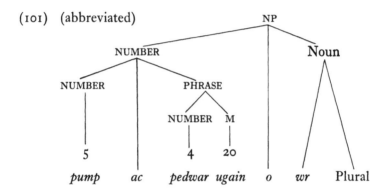

converts structure (95), for example, into structure (101). Conversion of the string *wr* Plural to *wŷr* and phonological rules yield *bump a phedwar ugain o wŷr*.

The foregoing is a tentative sketch of the rules that may be necessary to account for phrases indicating plurality such as *o wŷr, o siclau, o filoedd, o dalentau*. In the light of more general research into Welsh syntax, these rules might need revision. To end this description of the transformational processes affecting the Biblical Welsh numeral system I will describe briefly and without presenting any formal account the idiosyncrasies of the word for 'year'. The vagaries of this word are interesting, though not of importance as far as a theory of numeral systems is concerned.

The singular form for 'year' is *blwyddyn*. Grammars of Classical Welsh usually report that this word has two plurals, *blwydd*, used when referring to the age of a person or thing, and *blynedd*, used elsewhere.

In at least one respect, however *blwydd* and *blynedd* behave as singular nouns. They occur with numeral expressions without the preposition *o*. Thus parallel to expressions such as those in (91), we have expressions such as those in (63). *Blynedd* and *blwydd*, but never *blwyddyn*, occur after expressions with a value greater than 1. The matter is confused by the fact that we find examples in the Welsh Bible of both the singular *blwyddyn* and the 'plurals' *blwydd* and *blynedd* after *un*.

(102)   onid un flwyddyn chwech ugain mlynedd (minus 1 year 6 20 years) (= 119 years) (Genesis 11.25)

onid un mlwydd cant (minus 1 years 100) (= 99 years) (Genesis 17.1,24)

un mlynedd ar ddeg ar hugain (1 years on 10 on 20) (= 31 years) (II Kings 22.1, II Chronicles 34.1)

The form *blynyddoedd* is referred to as a 'double plural' by Morris-Jones (1931, p. 62). This characterization is apt; *-oedd* is a common Welsh plural ending and the formation of the plural frequently also involves a vowel change, as seen in the difference between *e* and *y* in the pair *blynedd–blynyddoedd*. In the Welsh Bible *blynyddoedd* is always the form which follows the preposition *o* after a numeral expression. Thus we have:

(103)   dri chant o flynyddoedd (3 100 of years's) (= 300 years) (Genesis 5.22)

bum mlynedd a thri ugain a thri chant o flynyddoedd (5 years + 3 20 + 3 100 of years's) (= 365 years) (Genesis 5.23)

pedwar ugain mlwydd a chwech o flynyddoedd (4 20 years + 6 of years's) (= 86 years) (Genesis 16.16)

As these examples show, *o flynyddoedd* is used both when expressing age, i.e. in the same expression as *blwydd*, and elsewhere, i.e. in the same expression as *blynedd*.

6.14 Summary of Biblical Welsh transformations

In summary, the numeral system of Biblical Welsh is remarkable for the richness of its transformational rule component. We have proposed the following rules, which apply in the order given. In this list rules connected by a broken line are intrinsically ordered and rules connected by a continuous line must be extrinsically ordered. A pair of rules is

(104)

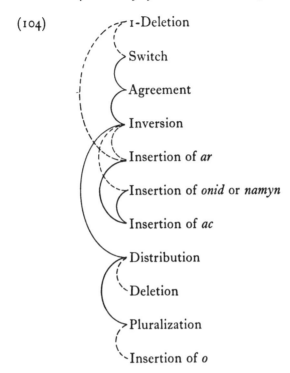

1-Deletion

Switch

Agreement

Inversion

Insertion of *ar*

Insertion of *onid* or *namyn*

Insertion of *ac*

Distribution

Deletion

Pluralization

Insertion of *o*

intrinsically ordered if the specific formulation given to one logically implies that it can only apply to a structure to which the other rule has already applied. Clear cases of pairs of intrinsically ordered rules, given the formulations proposed here, are the pair 1-Deletion, Switch and the pair Distribution, Deletion. For example, a structure matching the structural index of the Deletion rule (86) and meeting its condition 'Where 2 = 4' can only have come into existence through the application of the Distribution rule (67). It is therefore implicit in the formulation of the rules of the grammar that Distribution precedes Deletion and no special statement has to be made in the grammar stipulating the order of these rules.

In order to achieve proper results it is sometimes necessary to stipulate that pairs of rules which are not intrinsically ordered apply nevertheless in a particular order. Thus we have argued, on the basis of the illformedness of *dwyddeg, that Switch must precede Agreement, though these rules are not intrinsically ordered. Similarly, in order to account for the examples of (45), we have argued that Agreement must precede Inversion, though these rules are also not intrinsically ordered.

In cases such as these the grammar must include an explicit statement about the ordering of the rules concerned.

Some of the rules listed in (104) need not necessarily apply in the order in which they are listed. Thus Insertion of *ac*, for example, could just as well apply after Distribution as before it. I have formulated Distribution with parenthesized variables *w* and *y* so that it can (but not must) apply after the insertion of *onid*, *namyn*, *ar*, or *ac*.

In the event of further, more general research into Welsh syntax it may turn out that some of the rules we have postulated here should be formulated differently. It is quite possible, for example, that the rules inserting the prepositions *ar* and *o* should be formulated so that they in some way create prepositional phrase nodes dominating expressions such as *ar ddeg*, *ar bymtheg*, *ar hugain*, *o wyr*, *o dalentau*, *o siclau*, *o filoedd*. There is naturally no evidence within the numeral system that such expressions should be categorized as prepositional phrases and I have preferred not to complicate the rules I have given by supposing more than is indicated by a study of the numeral system.

Some of the rules we have postulated must apply cyclically (Inversion and Insertion of *ac*); some are optional; some obligatory; and some either optional or obligatory depending on the environment in which they apply; some rules involve conditions which may refer to semantic representations (Inversion, Insertion of *onid* or *namyn*, Pluralization); others involve conditions referring to the application of other transformations (Insertion of *ac*); the rules we have postulated make use of a wide variety of elementary transformational operations, including deletion, substitution, permutation, simple adjunction, and Chomsky-adjunction. Operating in tandem with the transformational rules I have proposed tentatively a convention (59) affecting categories in structures derived by transformations. The transformational rule component is, then, formally rather messy, permitting a great variety of different types of operations and conditions for their applicability. It appears that this messiness is necessary. I can find no more elegant way of capturing the generalizations that I have described.

Finally, there is one numeral, out of over four hundred in the Welsh Bible, which is not accounted for by the rules I have postulated. How to account for this example remains unexplained. The expression is:

(105)   chwe chan mil, a mil saith gant a deg ar hugain (6 100 1,000, + 1,000 7 100 + 10 on 20) (= 601,730) (Numbers 26.51)

I cannot explain why this expression is not *chwe chan mil ac un fil saith gant a deg ar hugain*. In the derivation of (105), a rule like the rule of 1-Deletion seems to have applied, but in an environment rather different from that in which *un* may normally be deleted. (105) is in any case quite unusual in that it contains a comma. There are less than five examples in the Welsh Bible of numerals containing an internal comma. I am, therefore, inclined to think that (105) is perhaps, for some reason, syntactically not a single numeral but a conjunction of two numerals. Assuming this, both numerals in the conjunction can be accounted for by the rules I have postulated.

7 Hawaiian numerals

The ancient Hawaiian numeral system is interesting and unusual in that it is a mixture of a decimal and a quaternary system. That is, the numbers 4 and 10 both play central roles in the formation of the expressions for the higher numbers. A reasonably complete picture of the ancient Hawaiian system can be pieced together from a small set of rather fragmentary accounts, many by nineteenth-century explorers and missionaries. It seems that no sooner was the ancient numeral system discovered and recorded than it began to be supplanted by a purely decimal system modelled largely on English, from which the loan words *haneri*, 100, *tausani*, 1,000, and *miliona*, 1,000,000, were taken. My data on the ancient system are from Humboldt (1832–9), Andrews (1854), Alexander (1864), an anonymous French Catholic missionary (1834), von Chamisso (1837), Beckwith (1918), Fornander (1878), Conant (1923), and Judd, Pukui, and Stokes (1945). I quote below the account of the anonymous French missionary.

Les insulaires, comptant sur leurs doigts, ont une espèce de calcul décimal. Ils comptent par unités jusqu'à 10, *umi*; par dizaines jusqu'à 40, *kanaha*; par quarantaines jusqu'à 400, *lau*; par quatre centaines jusqu'à 4000, *mano*; par quatre millaines jusqu'à 40,000, *kini*; par quarante millaines jusqu'à 400,000, *lehu*...Les unités une fois exprimées jusqu'à 10, ils recommencent, et s'arrêtent à quatre dizaines, puis ils recommencent de nouveau jusqu'au même nombre, et ainsi de suite, en disant: une quarantaine, deux quarantaines, jusqu'à dix quarantaines, après quoi viennent les quatre centaines, et ainsi de suite. Ils ont toutefois le nombre 20, *iwakalua*; mais ils ne comptent point par vingtaines. Les nombres 10, 40, 400, 4000, 40,000, 400,000 sont comme des touts, ou des nombres de repos ou ils reprennent haleine, et qui servent de point de départ...La quarantaine est exprimée par *kanaha*, *kokoha*, *kaau*, *iako*. Le premier mot est le seul usité dans les écrits...

Les unités simples sont *kahi*, *lua*, *kolu*, *ha*, *lima*, *ono*, *hiku*, *walu*, *iwa*, *umi*, auxquelles on ajoute toujours *a* ou *e*...*Kahi* ne prend jamais *e*, mais *a* ou *hoo*. *Umi* ne prend rien. (p. 10)

Les insulaires, n'ayant pas ordinairement de forts nombres à compter, s'accommodent aisément de la répétition des unités à chaque dizaine; cependant ils ont une manière d'exprimer les unités intermédiaires, c'est d'ajouter *kumama* entre la dizaine et l'unité excédante; exemple: Onze, *umikumamakahi*; douze, *umikumamalua*...Ceux qui tiennent à l'ancienne manière, et c'est le plus grand nombre, disent *umi keu* pour les dizaines intermédiaires des nombres indiqués plus haut, comme formant un tout: 30, *iwakalua a me na umi keu*; 50, *kanaha* ou *akahi kanaha a me na umi keu*; 70, *akahi kanaha a me iwakalua a me na umi keu*. 60 ne prendrait point *keu*, parce qu'il y a quarantaine et vingtaine sans dizaine excédante: ils l'y ajoutent quelquefois. Il en est de même de 40 et de 100. Le premier nombre ne renferme que deux quarantaines, et le second deux quarantaines et une vingtaine.

Les unités excédantes sont toujours précédées de *a me kumama: a me*, et avec, se met souvent entre chaque tout et devant l'excédant. Le dernier tout, fraction d'un plus grand nombre qui précède, prend toujours *keu*, qu'il y ait des unités excedántes ou non. *Keu* signifie *en sus*. On a vu par les exemples précédéns [sic], que *umi* excédant prend toujours *na*, quoiqu'il n'y ait qu'une dizaine en sus. On ajoute aussi *keu*...aux mots exprimant quarantaine, s'il y a des unités excédantes...Exemple d'un fort grand nombre rendu dans la langue: 609751, *ahahi leu, elima kini, elua mano, aha lau, ekolu kanaha, a me iwakalua, a me na umi keu a me kumama kahi*. Otez 10, et *keu* sera après *iwakalua*; ôtez 30, il sera après *kanaha*; ôtez 150, il sera après *lau*. (pp. 11–12)

From this account, supplemented by the other sources cited, we can establish a picture of the ancient Hawaiian numeral system as characterized in the table below.

(1)

11	10 + 1	19	10 + 9
21	20 + 1	29	20 + 9
30	20 + 10	36	20 + 10 + 6
40	40	47	40 + 7
50	40 + 10	59	40 + 10 + 9
60	40 + 20		
70	40 + 20 + 10	76	40 + 20 + 10 + 6
80	2 40	83	2 40 + 3
200	5 40		
320	8 40		
400	1 400		
4,000	1 4,000		
40,000	1 40,000		
400,000	1 400,000		

Beside the 'fort grand nombre' given by the French missionary in the quotation above, Conant gives 864,895 as $2 \times 400{,}000 + 40{,}000 + 6 \times 4000 + 2 \times 400 + 2 \times 40 + 10 + 5$ (p. 117). Judd, Pukui, and Stokes report that 'the ancient native system . . . rendered the number 968 as *elua lau me eha kanahakumamawalu*, lit. "two four-hundreds and four forties and eight"' (p. 22).

7.1 Phrase structure rules, semantic interpretation, and lexicon

Appropriate underlying structures for the ancient Hawaiian numerals can be generated by the following phrase structure rules.

(2)

$$\text{NUMBER} \rightarrow \left\{ \begin{array}{c} / \\ \text{PHRASE} \end{array} \right\} \quad (\text{NUMBER})$$

$$\text{PHRASE} \rightarrow \quad \text{NUMBER} \quad \text{M}$$

$$\text{M} \rightarrow \left\{ \begin{array}{c} 20 \\ 10 \; (\left\{ \begin{array}{c} 4 \\ \text{M} \end{array} \right\}) \end{array} \right\}$$

There is no evidence that the ancient Hawaiian system uses exponentiation in the interpretation of its Ms: multiplication is sufficient to account for their values. Thus *kanaha*, 40, is 10×4, *lau*, 400, is $10 \times 10 \times 4$, *mano*, 4,000, is $10 \times 10 \times 10 \times 4$, etc. In this system, then, the operation CALCULATE is never used at depth 3. The depth-assigning algorithm ((28) of ch. 2) postulated for the other languages we have discussed can actually be simplified to (3) below for the ancient Hawaiian system.

(3)   All NUMBERS are assigned depth 1.
      All other constituents are assigned depth 2.

Both PHRASEs and Ms are assigned depth 2 by (3). The same general projection rule can now apply to ancient Hawaiian as to the other languages we have discussed. It is repeated here as (4). The structure

(4) X_d

$$\overbrace{}$$
$$x \qquad y$$

$$= (\text{CALCULATE} + d \; x \; y)$$

of *lau*, 400, is as in (5). The lower M here is interpreted as (CALCULATE +

(5)

2 10 4), i.e. as 40, and the whole structure is therefore interpreted as (CALCULATE + 2 10 40), i.e. as 400, as required. The semantic interpretation of NUMBERs and PHRASEs is accounted for in exactly the same way as in most cases we have dealt with, i.e. by addition and multiplication.

The following lexical entries provide an illustrative sample of the lexicon of the ancient Hawaiian numeral system. (*Kahi* is the form for 1,

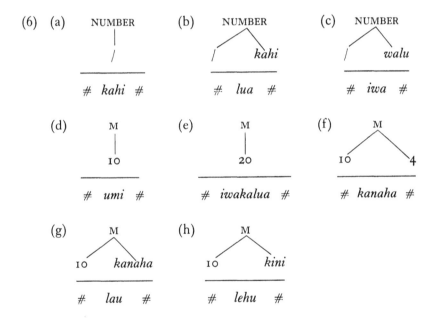

lua that for 2, *walu* for 8, *iwa* for 9, *umi* for 10, *iwakalua* for 20, *kanaha* for 40, *lau* for 400, *kini* for 40,000 and *lehu* for 400,000.) There is a problem with the form *iwakalua*, 20, which seems to contain the forms for 9 and 2. We shall leave *iwakalua* unanalysed in this chapter and return to this problem and other similar ones in chapter 9.

7.2 Wellformedness constraints

Just the same general constraints on the wellformedness of numeral deep structures (i.e. (77), (79), (82) of ch. 2) are valid for the ancient Hawaiian system as for the other systems that we have discussed. I illustrate below how these constraints interact to select just the correct underlying structures for the old Hawaiian numerals.

Constraint (79) of ch. 2 states that any MS generated by the phrase structure rules that are distinct from all MS specified in the lexicon are illformed. Thus structures as in (7) below, for example, are well-formed, being identical to MS specified in the lexicon. Structures as in

(7)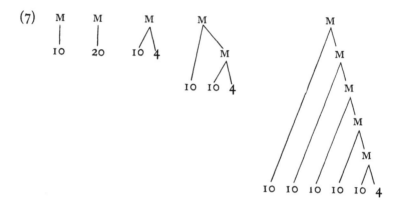

(8) below are, on the other hand, illformed, since they are distinct from all MS in the lexicon.

(8)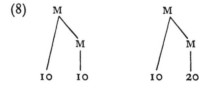

We now turn to the wellformedness of PHRASES in this system. The phrase structure rules (2) generate two PHRASES with the value 20. These are as in (9). The MS in both these structures are wellformed, since they

(9) (a)   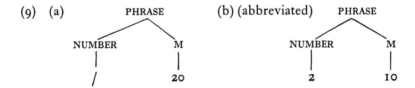   (b) (abbreviated)

are identical to MS appearing in the lexicon. The Packing Strategy ((82) of ch. 2) characterizes structure (b) as illformed in the following way. Let (9b) be the structure A of the Packing Strategy; then $x = 20$, $y = 10$, and Z is M; and the phrase structure rules do generate a wellformed M with value greater than 10 and equal to 20, i.e. the M found in structure (9a). Structure (9b) is therefore illformed.

Now consider PHRASES generated by the phrase structure rules with value 30. There is only one such PHRASE, that given as (10). Applying

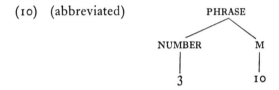

the Packing Strategy to this structure, X is PHRASE, $x = 30$, $y = 10$, Z is M. The phrase structure rules generate a wellformed M with a value greater than y, 10, and less than x, 30, namely that specified in the lexical entry for *iwakalua*, 20, (6e) above. Structure (10) is therefore illformed and this entails that there is no wellformed PHRASE with value 30 in the ancient Hawaiian system. This is true. The expression for 30 is not a PHRASE, but a NUMBER, *iwakalua a me na umi keu*, literally 'twenty and with ten more', which has the underlying structure given in (11).

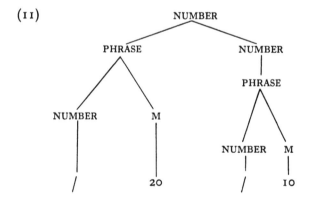

The phrase structure rules generate three PHRASES with the value 40. These are as in (12). All of the MS in these structures are wellformed. The Packing Strategy characterizes both (12b) and (12c) as illformed because of the wellformedness of the M in (12a), which has a higher value than either of the MS in (12b) and (12c). This is correct. The expression for 40 is *kanaha* or *akahi kanaha*, literally 'one forty'.

As a final example of the application of the Packing Strategy to PHRASES consider the expression for 400. Some PHRASES generated by the

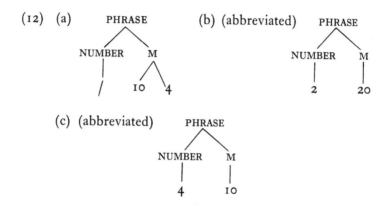

phrase structure rules with this value are given in (13). All of the MS in

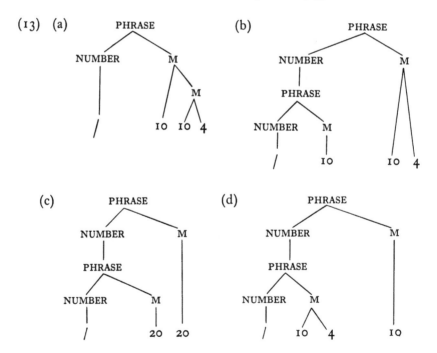

these structures are in themselves wellformed; and all of the PHRASES which are the left-hand constituents of structures (13b, c, d) are also wellformed in themselves. However, the Packing Strategy characterizes all of these structures except (13a) as illformed because of the wellformedness of the M which is its right-hand immediate constituent, which has a value higher than those of the MS which are the right-hand immediate constituents of the other structures. The structures given in (13) are by no means the only structures generated by the phrase structure rules with the value 400, but the reader may check for himself that any structure with this value other than (13a) is also characterized as illformed by the general constraints proposed in this study. This is appropriate, since the expression for 400 is *akahi lau* or *hookahi lau*, literally 'one four-hundred'.

The reader is by now familiar enough with the operation of the Packing Strategy to acertain without detailed illustrations that the constraints we have proposed will select just the wellformed NUMBER deep structures for the ancient Hawaiian numerals from among the structures generated by the phrase structure rules (2). I give below the structures underlying some of the longer numeral expressions we have mentioned.

(14) (abbreviated)

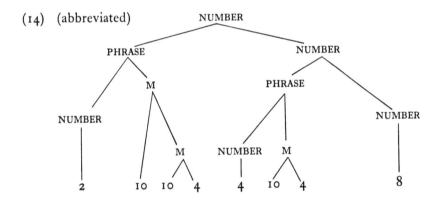

In (14) is the structure underlying *elua lau me eha kanahakumamawalu*, literally 'two four-hundreds and four forties and eight', 968.

A rule of 1-Deletion must be postulated for ancient Hawaiian. The required formulation turns out to be identical to that necessary for Welsh ((21) of ch. 6). The rule is given in (16). Thus we have *umi*, but not **akahi umi*; *iwakalua* but not **akahi iwakalua*; either *kanaha* or *akahi kanaha*; either *lau* or *akahi lau*, etc. I do not attempt here to give any account of the various connectives, such as *a me*, *a me na*, and

(15)   (abbreviated)

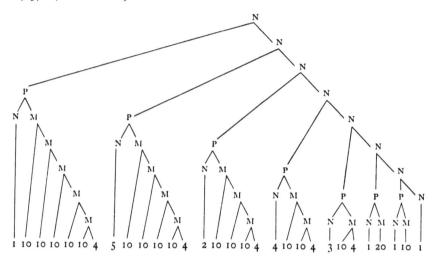

(Here N abbreviates NUMBER and P abbreviates PHRASE.) This is the deep structure of *ahahi leu, elima kini, elua mano, aha lau, ekolu kanaha, a me iwakalua, a me na umi keu a me kumama kahi* (1 × 400,000, 5 × 40,000, 2 × 4,000, 4 × 400, 3 × 40, +20, +10 + 1), (= 609,751).

(16)   I-DELETION

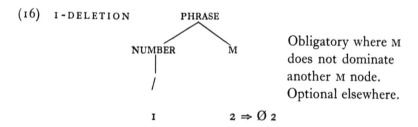

Obligatory where M does not dominate another M node. Optional elsewhere.

kumama which are used in Hawaiian numerals. Their use appears to be governed by somewhat complicated rules which are of little general theoretical interest. The theoretical interest of the ancient Hawaiian system lies in the fact that, though at first sight it seems to be highly unusual, it is in fact unusual only in one respect, namely the formation and interpretation of its MS. In all other respects, rules and constraints which are of near universal validity are applicable to this system.

8 Yoruba numerals

In Welsh and Danish we have seen examples of the use of subtraction. Subtraction is indeed used by a few scattered languages all over the world, but it is rarely used extensively through the whole numeral system. A spectacular exception to this general rule is Yoruba, whose very complicated numeral system uses subtraction to about the same extent as, and possibly even more than, addition. The most comprehensive description of the Yoruba numeral system is given by Abraham (1958). Less detailed descriptions occur in Rowlands (1969), Mann (1886), Bowen (1858), and Laṣebikan (1958).

Yoruba has what is probably the most unusual and complicated of any of the world's natural language numeral systems. This system presents a number of problems for the descriptive framework we have developed so far in this study and some of these problems are quite serious. Consequently, whereas in preceding chapters we have managed to give fairly complete and satisfactory accounts of the numeral systems of various languages, this chapter falls short of a comprehensive and satisfactorily explanatory account of Yoruba numerals. The problems are described in sections dealing with the three main phrase structure categories that have recurred throughout this work, namely NUMBER, PHRASE, and M. Problems with the semantic interpretation and well-formedness of these structures are discussed.

The numerals in Yoruba are often subject to fairly radical phonological modification. Abraham sketches the phonological processes leading to the modified forms and in each case the underlying morphemic structure can be discerned without too much difficulty. Examples of some typically elliptic Yoruba numerals (taken from Abraham) are as follows. The expression for 60 is ọgọ́ọ̀ta, derived by Abraham from ogún ọ̀ ẹ̀ta, literally '20 × 3'. The expression for 50 is àádọ́ọ̀ta, derived by Abraham from àádín ọgọ́ọ̀ta, literally '10 removed from 60'. It

211

seems clear from Abraham's description that *àádín* is itself derived from *èwàá dín*, '10 from'.

8.1 The structure of NUMBERS

Some examples of the use of subtraction in Yoruba are given below.

(1) 16   ẹ̀rìn dín lógún   4 from 20
     35   árùn dín lógójì   5 from (20 2)
     45   árùn dín láàádọ̀ọ̀ta
           (< árùn dín èwàá dín ogún ẹ̀ta)   5 from (10 from (20 3))
     190   igba ódín mẹ́wàá   200 minus 10
     215   okòó lẹ́ẹ̄ rúgba ódín márùn   (20 plus 200) minus 5
     350   òjì dín nírínwó ódín mẹ́wàá
           (< ogún èjì dín nírínwó ódín
           mẹ́wàá)   ((20 2) from 400)
                                                            minus 10

I assume that a depth-assigning algorithm assigns depth 1 to NUMBERS. A Yoruba-specific semantic rule, analogous to those postulated for Welsh ((8) of ch. 6) and Danish ((37) of ch. 5), but of greater generality, must stipulate which NUMBERS are to be interpreted by subtraction, that is by the inverse of operation CALCULATE at depth 1. This rule will have a form as in (2).

(2) If $d = 1$, and under certain other conditions, change $+$ to $-$.

The 'certain other conditions' referred to here cannot be specified with accuracy because of the limitedness of the Yoruba data available. It is clear that subtraction is used about as extensively as addition, and frequently the same number may be expressed either by addition or by subtraction. Abraham gives, for example, both *árùn dín láàádọ́fà* and *ogọ́ọ̀rùn ólé márùn*, respectively (5 from (10 from (20 6))) and ((20 5) plus 5), as forms for 105. A full description of the Yoruba numeral system must state the conditions determining whether numeral structures are interpreted by addition or subtraction. Abraham, who is by far the most comprehensive source for Yoruba numerals, only sporadically mentions alternative expressions and it is difficult to predict with confidence the wellformedness of numeral expressions not actually listed by him, so eccentric is the system. For example, just as there are two expressions for 105, given above, the mechanisms would appear to be available to form alternative expressions for 45, 65, 85, and 125, but Abraham only mentions one form for each of these numbers. It is not clear whether we should conclude that this is just a random omission, or whether the number 105 has some special status in the system which allows it to be expressed in two ways. Information on such matters is not likely to be easy to find, since the highly complicated Yoruba system seems to be falling out of use. Rowlands writes, 'The system is extremely cumbersome and is now for practical purposes obsolete' (p. 109). If completely comprehensive information on the Yoruba numeral system could be obtained, it would be highly interesting to ascertain the extent to which the Packing Strategy is responsible for selecting between expressions using addition and those using subtraction.

It is clear that some constraint quite similar in nature to the Packing Strategy accounts for the wellformedness of Yoruba NUMBERS interpreted by subtraction.

Consider, for example, the Yoruba expression for 199, *igba ódín kọn*, '200 minus 1'. Notice that, naturally enough, Yoruba does not express this number by any such expression as **igba ólé kọn dín nírínwó* '(200 plus 1) from 400'. Given that a language uses subtraction in its numeral system, the possibility exists in principle to express any number by first selecting some higher number, however great, and then specifying the difference. All the following formulas, for instance, have the value 199.

(3) 200 minus 1
     400 minus 201
     800 minus 601
     2,000 minus 1,801

Not surprisingly, Yoruba expresses 199 by an expression parallel to the first of these formulas and eschews the use of the others. The principle followed seems to be that the higher number in the subtraction sum be a 'round figure' as close as possible in value to that of the number ultimately being expressed. In the formulas of (3), for example, 200 is closer in value to 199 than either 400, 800, or 2,000, and therefore the preferred expression corresponds to the formula '200 minus 1'. This principle is exactly parallel to that embodied in the Packing Strategy, which guarantees that in numbers expressed by addition, the higher number in the addition sum be as close as possible in value to the value of the number ultimately being expressed. In French, for example, the Packing Strategy selects an expression corresponding to the formula '60 plus 10' to express the number 70: other expressions, corresponding to formulas such as '50 plus 20', '40 plus 30', etc., are characterized as illformed. The problem in a complete description of the Yoruba numeral system lies in specifying formally the content of such notions as 'round figure' and 'as close as possible in value to' used informally above. The latter notion can be characterized quite simply, as shown below, but the former, that is the notion of 'round figure', may be more difficult to capture in a natural way.

To capture the notion 'as close as possible in value to' the relevant constraints may in fact be imposed by stating a single quite natural extra condition in the formulation of the Packing Strategy. The general formulation of the Strategy ((82) of ch. 2) concludes with the condition '$y < z \leqslant x$'. This expresses the stipulation that the 'disqualifying' structure B has a value greater than that of the (non-NUMBER) immediate constituent of the structure A being considered and less than or equal to the value of A itself. Now we may make this a disjunctive condition:

(4) PACKING STRATEGY FOR YORUBA

A structure A generated by the phrase structure rules is illformed if

(a) it is of category X, has value x, and has as immediate constituents a NUMBER and some other structure with value y (not necessarily in that order), where

(b) the phrase structure rules generate a wellformed structure B of category Z with value z, where Z is on the right-hand side of a phrase structure rule expanding X and is not NUMBER, and EITHER $y < z \leqslant x$ OR $y > z \geqslant x$.

(A further revision of the Packing Strategy for Yoruba will be formulated in a later section.) The new condition above stipulates that the 'disqualifying' structure B may also have a value greater than or equal to that of A and less than that of A's (non-NUMBER) immediate constituent. We will now consider an application of this particular condition to some NUMBER structures interpreted by subtraction.

Phrase structure rules like those of previous chapters (e.g. (2) of ch. 2) generate the following NUMBERs, all of which, assuming that they are interpreted by subtraction, have the value 199. All of the PHRASES which are the left-hand immediate constituents of these NUMBERs are

(5) (abbreviated)   (a)

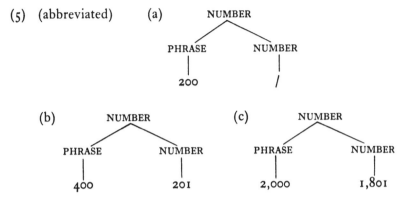

themselves wellformed. But we see that the Packing Strategy, as refor-
mulated in (4), will characterize (5b) and (5c), though not (5a), as illformed. In the case of (5b), for instance, *x* is taken as 199, *y* as 400,
and the phrase structure rules generate a wellformed PHRASE, namely
that found in (5a), which has a value less than 400 and greater than 199.
Structure (5b) is therefore illformed. Structure (5c) is similarly illformed.
Structure (5a) is not thus characterized as illformed by the (revised)
Packing Strategy. This is appropriate, since the Yoruba expression for
199 is *igba ódín kọn*, literally '200 minus 1'.

In both types of NUMBER structures, those interpreted by addition
and those interpreted by subtraction, the higher-valued constituent may
either follow or precede the lower-valued constituent. Examples are
given below.

(6) (a) 21 ⎰ ogún ólé ókọn   20 plus 1
          ⎱ ókọn lé lógún   1 plus 20

         43 ⎰ ogójì ólé ẹta   (20 2) plus 3
            ⎱ ẹta lé lógójì   3 plus (20 2)

        104 ẹrìn lé lógọ́ọ̀rùń   4 plus (20 5)
        105 ọgọ́ọ̀rùń ólé márùń   (20 5) plus 5
        201 igba ólé kọn   200 plus 1
        220 okòó léē rúgba   20 plus 200

     (b) 17 ẹtà diń lógún   3 from 20
          26 ẹrìn diń lógbọ̀n   4 from 30
         191 igba ódín mẹ́sọ̀ń   200 minus 9
         199 igba ódín kọn   200 minus 1
         320 òrìn diń nírínwó   (20 4) from 400
         360 òjì diń nírínwó   (20 2) from 400
         390 írínwó ódín mẹ́wàá   400 minus 10

These examples are typical of those given by Abraham. It is very hard to see any regularity in the use of *ólé*, *lé*, *dín*, and *ódín*. It does appear that *ódín* is never used to subtract a number greater than 10, but apart from this it is not possible on the basis of the data available to formulate systematic statements describing the variation of these forms. There may or may not be systematic variation: it is impossible to tell. Similarly it is not possible to decide which order of constituents in NUMBERS, higher-lower or lower-higher, is the unmarked order and we cannot decide which of the following two phrase structure rules should be postulated.

(7) (a)

$$\text{NUMBER} \rightarrow \left\{ \begin{array}{c} / \\ \text{PHRASE} \end{array} \right\} \; (\text{NUMBER})$$

   (b)

$$\text{NUMBER} \rightarrow (\text{NUMBER}) \left\{ \begin{array}{c} / \\ \text{PHRASE} \end{array} \right\}$$

The order of NUMBERS and PHRASES as constituents of NUMBERS in deep structure is not an issue of particular theoretical importance. It is clear that, whatever underlying order is chosen, transformational rules (e.g. Inversion) can be used to derive surface structures with the reverse order. What is lacking is evidence bearing on the correct choice of underlying structure and on the correct formulation of the appropriate transformational processes. In the rest of this chapter illustrations involving the structure of NUMBERS will arbitrarily assume whichever order of constituents simplifies the example under discussion.

We now come to a problem which does have some important bearing on the general theoretical framework we have developed in this study. The expression for 46 is *ẹ̀rìn dín láàádọ́ọ̀ta*, glossed by Abraham as '4 as-to-a-reduction off 60 − 10'. *Aádọ́ọ̀ta* is a contraction of *ẹ̀wàá dín ogún ẹ̀ta*, literally '10 from (20 3)'. Clearly the structure of this expression should reflect a bracketing as in (8).

(8)   [4[10[20 3]]]

In this structure 20 and 3 are to be combined by multiplication, yielding 60; after this 10 is subtracted from 60, giving 50; and finally 4 is subtracted from 50, giving 46. Note that the last two operations performed are both of subtraction. Within the framework developed in this study, we are led to postulate that both structure (8) and its right-hand immediate constituent are structures assigned depth 1 by the depth-assigning algorithm, since both structures are interpreted by operation CALCULATE (or rather its inverse) carried out at depth 1, i.e. by subtraction. We have not encountered in this study any cases where both constituents of a NUMBER are also NUMBERs themselves, of structures, that is, like (9). If we were to adopt such structures for

(9)   NUMBER

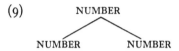

NUMBER   NUMBER

Yoruba, the general phrase structure rule expanding NUMBER (i.e. one of the rules of (7)), a rule whose constituent assignment we have found appropriate to a variety of other numeral systems, would need, in the Yoruba case, to be modified to (10).

$$(10) \qquad \text{NUMBER} \rightarrow \left\{ \begin{array}{c} / \\ \text{PHRASE} \\ \text{NUMBER} \end{array} \right\} \text{(NUMBER)}$$

While this possible analysis cannot be dismissed, it should be pointed out that it has some quite problematic consequences. If we allow such a rule in the grammar of a numeral system, then we shall have to devise some means of controlling its adverse consequences, that is, of filtering out illformed structures generated by it, and leaving behind as well-formed just the small set of structures which underlie the wellformed numerals of the language. This task has already been accomplished in previous chapters, working on the basis of a different set of phrase structure rules, specifically a set of rules which guaranteed that at least one constituent of every NUMBER was not itself a NUMBER. On the basis of those rules we developed a tight system of constraints which appears to be of very general validity. These constraints, and in particular the Packing Strategy, were justified by evidence from a variety of different numeral systems, for which they account. If we adopt phrase structure rule (10) for Yoruba, and with it structures such as (9), we shall have to develop a seriously different alternative constraint to the Packing Strategy specifically for Yoruba. This constraint will, for example, be responsible for selecting a wellformed structure from those below, all generated by rule (10), and all assigned the value 3 by the semantic interpretation component. There is, in fact, an infinite number of

(11)   (a)

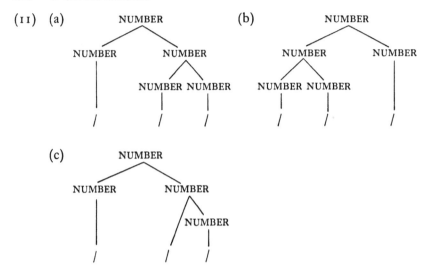

(c)

structures generated by rule (10) with the value 3. Those given in (11) are among the simpler ones. The Packing Strategy cannot be used to eliminate any of these structures since the Packing Strategy applies specifically to structures which have at least one non-NUMBER as an immediate constituent. Any decision to resolve the problem of structures like (8) by revising the structure of NUMBERs in the way proposed in (10) will necessitate the development of some alternative to the Packing Strategy.

Adopting rule (10) leads to the generation of structures such as (12).

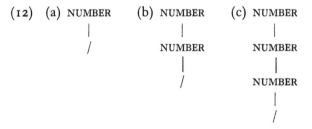

These structures, though distinct, are clearly equivalent. It is possibly not desirable to have infinite sets of distinct though equivalent structures corresponding to surface forms: this is no doubt an empirical matter which can be resolved by checking for possible adverse consequences of the existence of such sets, e.g. possible complications in the statement of lexical rules, or possible complications in the statements of trans- formational or phonological rules. I have not investigated these details in this study. It is clear, meanwhile, that should it be desired to eliminate such infinite sets of distinct though equivalent structures, a simple pruning rule, such as used elsewhere in syntactic studies (cf. Ross, 1969), will serve the turn. Such a rule may be graphically represented as in (13).

(13)   NUMBER

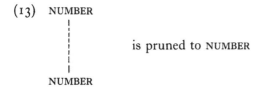

                    is pruned to NUMBER

        NUMBER

By this we state in effect that a NUMBER structure whose sole (not necessarily immediate) constituent is another NUMBER structure is to be reduced to a structure identical to the constituent NUMBER. By this process (12b) and (12c) may be reduced to (12a). The possible need to postulate such a pruning process is an inconvenience, but not a decisive factor in evaluating the proposal to solve the problem of structures such as (8) by revising the analysis of NUMBERS as in rule (10). The invalidation of the Packing Strategy by the postulation of rule (10) is, however, definitely a serious problem.

8.2 The structure of PHRASES

Can we suggest a way of solving the problem of structures such as (8) which does not lose the advantages of the general framework we have established, in particular of the Packing Strategy? It might seem possible that this could be done by modifying the rule expanding PHRASE (rule (2b) of ch. 2), but this proposal also has serious problems. The proposed modification would be peculiar to Yoruba and to perhaps just one other language, discussed in the next chapter. The revised rule is as in (14).

(14)   PHRASE → (M)   NUMBER

Under this possible analysis, then, the M constituent of a PHRASE in Yoruba is said to be optional. (Note too that the constituents of PHRASES in Yoruba are in the reverse of the usual order, i.e. M followed by NUMBER, rather than, as in the case of all other languages of which I am aware, NUMBER followed by M. This peculiarity of Yoruba has no significant consequences for the theoretical framework we are developing here.) With rule (14) in the grammar, a structure as in (15) could be generated as the more detailed structure of (8). This structure can

(15) (abbreviated)

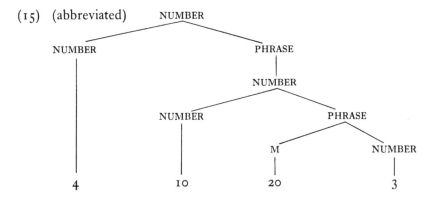

be interpreted in a straightforward manner by two processes of subtraction. In this way the right-hand immediate constituent of (15) is assigned the value 50, and the whole structure is assigned the value 46, as required.

Adopting rule (14) leads to the generation of structures as in (16).

(16)

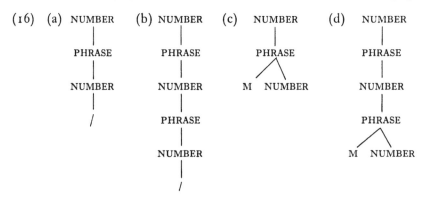

Clearly structures (16a) and (16b) are equivalent to structure (12a); and they may be reduced to (12a) by the pruning convention represented in (13). Similarly structure (16d), equivalent to (16c), may be reduced to (16c) by this convention. The existence of such sets of distinct though equivalent structures generated by rule (14) is thus not particularly problematic.

We now come to a more intractable problem resulting from the revision of the phrase structure rule expanding PHRASE. The revised rule for Yoruba (14) allows a PHRASE to be expanded to just NUMBER. This has the consequence that any NUMBER can also be a PHRASE. That is, PHRASES are no longer structures whose values are limited to multiples of the values of the wellformed MS. Informally speaking, the revised rule does not guarantee that PHRASES express 'round numbers', as they do in the other languages we have examined. An example will show how this is a serious problem for the Packing Strategy. The phrase structure rules generate the following structure which, assuming it is interpreted by addition, has the value 202. The NUMBER immediately dominated by

(17) (abbreviated)

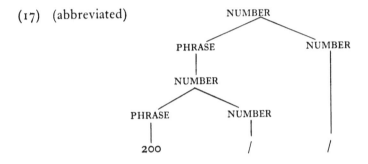

PHRASE in this structure is wellformed. It is in fact the underlying structure for the Yoruba expression for 201, *igba ólé kọn*, literally '200 plus 1'. Now if we apply the Packing Strategy to structure (17) we look for some wellformed PHRASE with a value greater than 201 and less than or equal to 202. This means, obviously, that we look for a wellformed PHRASE with the value 202. The revised phrase structure rules do generate a PHRASE with this value, a PHRASE whose sole constituent is structure (17). If we wish to take this PHRASE as the structure B of the Packing Strategy in trying to ascertain the wellformedness of structure (17), we cannot avoid entering into a viciously circular process, since the structure B of the Packing Strategy will actually contain structure A. The wellformedness of B depends on the wellformedness of A and vice versa. Let us say that this potential circularity can be overcome by an *ad hoc* stipulation in the formulation of the Packing Strategy that 'B does not contain A'. Even so we still face a problem with structure (17). This is because the phrase structure rules do not, of course, generate any wellformed PHRASE which does not contain (17) and which has a value greater than 201 and less than or equal to 202. The Packing

Strategy therefore does not characterize structure (17) as illformed. In fact, however, this structure is certainly illformed. The expression for 202 is formed by adding 200 to 2. Many similar examples of this problem could be constructed.

This misfunction of the Packing Strategy as a result of our tentative revision of the phrase structure rule expanding PHRASE is a strong argument against the revision. We are left with the problem of how to account for structures like (8) within the general framework we have developed. We have tried modifying the structure of NUMBERS; we have tried modifying the structure of PHRASES; and both attempts have resulted in undesirable consequences for the Packing Strategy. The question of the correct account of structures like (8) is left unresolved here. As far as I know, Yoruba is one of just two languages (the other is Ainu) in which this particularly difficult problem arises.

There is an unusual feature connected with the Yoruba forms for 2,000 and 20,000. Multiples of 2,000 and 20,000 are expressed by forms with *ẹgbàá* and *ẹgbàáwàá* respectively. (The detailed structure of these forms is discussed in the next section.) But, interestingly, these forms only occur in expressions for *exact* multiples of 2,000 and 20,000. We might expect, for example, the number 4,600 to be expressed as something like **ẹgbàájì ólé ẹgbẹ̀ta*, literally '(2,000 2) plus (200 3)', but such forms are not found. We only find *ẹgbẹ̀tà lé lógún*, literally '200 (3 plus 20)'. Similarly, in the expression for 70,000, where we might expect to find something like **ẹgbàáwàá ọ̀nọ̀n mẹ́ta ólé ẹgbàárùn*, literally '(20,000 times 3) plus (2,000 5)', we find only *ẹgbàa ọ̀nọ̀n márùn dín lógójì*, literally, '2,000 times (5 from (20 4))'. It seems that Yoruba has a definite preference for expressing the higher numbers as exact multiples of other numbers if possible. The situation is rather like what we would have in English if *one thousand, two thousand, three thousand*, etc., were wellformed, but expressions like *one thousand one hundred, two thousand eight hundred*, and *three thousand four hundred* were illformed, the only correct expressions for 1,100, 2,800, and 3,400, etc., being *eleven hundred, twenty eight hundred*, and *thirty four hundred*, etc.

This situation can be described by making a Yoruba-specific modification to the Packing Strategy. What is needed is a condition that ensures the wellformedness of PHRASES expressing exact multiples of 200, 2,000, and 20,000. The wellformedness of these structures will in turn predict the illformedness of semantically equivalent NUMBERS. The revised Packing Strategy for Yoruba is given below.

(18) PACKING STRATEGY FOR YORUBA (second version)

A structure A generated by the phrase structure rules is illformed if

(a) it is of category X, has value x, and has as immediate constituents a NUMBER and some other structure with value y (not necessarily in that order), where

(b) EITHER A is a PHRASE containing an M with a value greater than 20 and the phrase structure rules generate a wellformed M with value z, where $z > y$ and (CALCULATE -2 x z) is a natural number.

OR the phrase structure rules generate a wellformed structure B of category Z with value z, where Z is on the right-hand side of a phrase structure rule expanding X and is not NUMBER, and EITHER $y < z \leqslant x$ OR $y > z \geqslant x$.

The difference between this formulation and (4), presented earlier, is that the Yoruba-specific formulation now contains the extra condition following the first 'EITHER' in (b). This condition is explicitly restricted to PHRASES with values of 200 or greater. The stipulation that (CALCULATE -2 x z) be a natural number ensures that any 'disqualifying' structure, i.e. B in the formulation, will contain an M with a value which divides exactly into the value of the structure being considered, i.e. A in our formulation. The application of this condition to several PHRASES is illustrated below.

The phrase structure rules generate the following PHRASES, among others, with the value 4,000. Neither of the MS in these structures are

(19) (abbreviated)

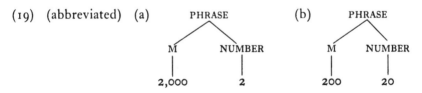

illformed themselves, since there are structures identical to them specified in the lexicon. The Yoruba-specific condition to the Packing Strategy applies to both these structures since they are both PHRASES containing MS with values greater than 20. Consider first PHRASE (19b). x is then 4,000 and y is 200. The phrase structure rules do indeed generate a wellformed M, namely that in structure (19a), with a value greater than 200 and which divides exactly into 4,000. Structure (19b) is therefore characterized as illformed. The Packing Strategy (18) does not similarly characterize structure (19a) as illformed, since there is no wellformed M with a value greater than 2,000 which divides exactly into 4,000. This is as required, since the Yoruba expression for 4,000 is *ẹgbàājì*, contracted from *ẹgbàā èjì*, literally '2,000 2'.

Consider now structure (20), a PHRASE generated by the phrase structure rules with the value 4,600. The Yoruba-specific condition is

(20) (abbreviated)

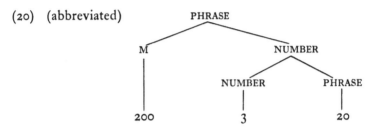

applicable to this structure, since it is a PHRASE containing an M with a value greater than 20. Applying the Packing Strategy, x, is 4,600, y is 200. Now although the phrase structure rules generate a wellformed M, namely that underlying the form for 2,000, which has a value greater than 200, 2,000 does not divide exactly into 4,600. In fact the phrase structure rules do not generate a wellformed M which meets the condition and structure (20) is therefore wellformed. This is appropriate, as the Yoruba expression for 4,600 is *ẹgbẹ̀tà lé lógún*, literally '200 (3 plus 20)'.

Now the phrase structure rules also generate NUMBERS with the value 4,600. One of these, in a sense the most plausible one, is given in (21).

(21) (abbreviated)

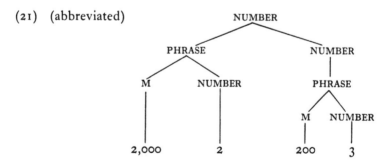

Applying the general version of the Packing Strategy to this structure, i.e. considering the condition following the word 'OR' in (18), X is

NUMBER, x is 4,600, y is 4,000. Now the phrase structure rules do generate a wellformed PHRASE, namely (20), with a value greater than 4,000 and equal to 4,600. Structure (21) is therefore illformed. This appears to be appropriate, since forms like **egbàāji ólé egbèta*, literally '(2,000 2) plus (200 3)' are not found in any of the accounts of Yoruba numerals.

The proposed modification to the Packing Strategy may have some relevance outside Yoruba, since we may suspect that the notion 'z exactly divides into x' is also pertinent to the problematic case, discussed in ch. 2, of English forms like *eleven hundred, twenty two hundred*, etc. We found that the Packing Strategy undesirably characterized such expressions as illformed, while permitting semantically equivalent forms such as *one thousand one hundred* and *two thousand two hundred*. So far, this is the most serious clear exception to the Packing Strategy we have discovered and it is noteworthy that here too, as in the Yoruba case just discussed, the class of expressions involved is a class of PHRASES containing MS whose values exactly divide the values of their PHRASES. Unfortunately there are not enough cases of exceptions of this sort to provide clear indications of a correct solution to the problem.

8.3 The structure of MS

A further odd aspect of the Yoruba numeral system is the range of values for which it has special lexical items. In most languages there is a regular series, with each member of the series being in some fairly obviously systematic relationship with the preceding members. In American English, for example, we have words for the values, 10, 100, 1,000, 1,000,000, 1,000,000,000, and 1,000,000,000,000, and structures with just these values can be generated by a simple rule. The values for which Yoruba has special lexical items are as follows.

(22)   10   èwàá
       20   ogún
       30   ogbòn
       200   igba
       300   òódún (or òódúnrún)
       400   irinwó

The apparent lack of regularity here is not a serious problem, however, for a closer inspection of the numeral system reveals that only the expressions for 10, 20, and 200 are used as MS. *Ogún* and *igba*, for example, systematically occur in multiplicational relationships with NUMBERS. Examples are given below.

(23) 40   ogóji   (<ogún èjì)   20 × 2
      60   ọgọ́ọta   (<ogún ẹta)   20 × 3
      80   ọgọ́ọrin   (<ogún ẹrin)   20 × 4
      600   ẹgbèta   (<igba ẹta)   200 × 3
      800   ẹgbẹ̀rin   (<igba ẹrin)   200 × 4
      1000 ẹgbẹ̀rùń   (<igba àrùń)   200 × 5

Ogbọ̀n, *ọọ́dún*, and *irinwó*, on the other hand, are never found in a multiplicational relationship with NUMBERS. This leads to the conclusion that these words are not MS. They must be analysed as suppletive forms for quite complex structures. *Ogbọ́n*, for example, must be analysed as a suppletive variant of what would otherwise be expressed as something like *àádogóji*, a contraction of *ẹwàá diń ogún èjì*, literally '10 from (20 2)'. This latter hypothetical form is constructed on the basis of an expression like that for 50, *àádọ́ọ̀ta*, a contraction, ultimately, of *ẹwàá diń ogún ẹta*, literally '10 from (20 3)'. Under this view the lexical entry for *ọgbọ̀n* would look something like (24). The words for

(24)   NUMBER

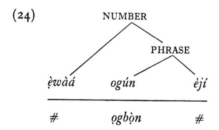

300 and 400, *ọọ́dún* and *irinwó* are presumably to be treated in a similar way.

It is not uncommon for languages to use suppletive variants in this way for quite high numeral expressions. In Russian, for example, all the multiples of 10 (but one) up to 80 are expressed bimorphemically as obvious compounds of the form for 10. Thus we have *dvadzatj*, 20; *tridzatj*, 30; *pjatjdesjatj*, 50; *sestjdesatj*, 60; *semdesatj*, 70; and *vosemjdesatj*, 80. But the word for 40 is a suppletive form *sorok*, a single morpheme phonologically unrelated to anything else in the numeral system. Similarly in Turkish the forms for 60, 70, 80, and 90 are clearly bimorphemic, containing the forms for 6, 7, 8, and 9 respectively, but the forms for 30, 40, and 50 'have no connection whatever with the names of the units' (Menninger, 1969, p. 82). Examples like thus turn up in a variety of languages and lend credence to the analysis of Yoruba *ọgbọ̀n, ọ̀ọ́dún,* and *irinwó* as suppletive forms for quite complex underlying structures.

Although *igba* is the highest-valued monomorphemic M in Yoruba, it is quite likely that certain other morphologically complex expressions are actually MS in the language. The expression for 2,000 is *ẹgbàā*, a contraction of *ẹgbẹ̀wàá*, literally '200 times 10'. Multiples of 2,000 are expressed by combining *ẹgbàā* with a NUMBER, as for example in the expression for 4,000, *ẹgbàājì*, a contraction of *ẹgbàā èjì*, '(200 times 10) 2'. Similarly the expression for 20,000 is *ẹgbàāwàá*, a contraction of *ẹgbàā ẹ̀wàá*, '(200 times 10) 10'. *Egbàāwàá* is itself used in the expressions for multiples of 20,000, as for example in the expression for 40,000, *ẹgbàāwàá ọ̀nọ̀n méjì*, literally '((20 times 10) 10) 2'. Similarly the expression for 60,000 is *ẹgbàāwàá ọ̀nọ̀n mẹ́ta*, literally '((200 times 10) 10) times 3'.

An analysis of these facts within the framework presented in this work is as follows. We may regard the expressions for 2,000 and 20,000 as MS, despite the fact that they are morphologically complex, since these expressions do clearly enter into multiplicational relationships with NUMBERS. (We will describe directly the way in which the morphological complexity of these forms is to be accounted for.) If we postulate that *ẹgbàā* and *ẹgbàāwàá* are MS, then we have in Yoruba a series of MS with the values 10, 20, 200, 2,000, and 20,000. A single simple rule generating structures with these values can be postulated as in (25).

$$(25) \qquad \text{M} \rightarrow \text{10} \left(\left\{ \begin{matrix} 2 \\ \text{M} \end{matrix} \right\} \right)$$

(Here and below, 2 is used as abbreviation for the semantic representation $//$.) This rule will generate a set of structures such as in (26).

These structures are to be interpreted by multiplication. Clearly Yoruba, which uses the series of values 10, 20, 200, 2,000, and 20,000 as 'stages' in its numeral system, makes no use of the operation of exponentiation. None of these numbers is a higher power of any natural number. Yoruba is, then, like Hawaiian in this respect, and as in the Hawaiian case, the depth-assigning algorithm ((28) of ch. 2) can be simplified. In these and some other languages operation CALCULATE

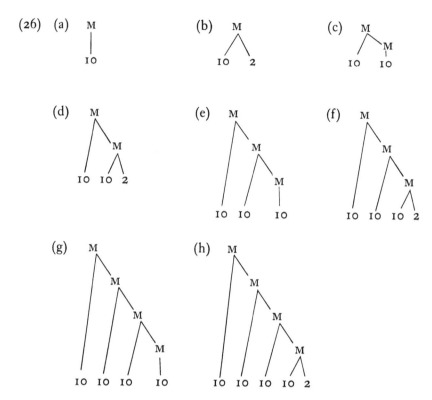

never functions at a depth greater than 2. The simplified depth-assigning algorithm ((3) of ch. 7) is repeated here as (27).

(27)   All NUMBERS are assigned depth 1.
         All other constituents are assigned depth 2.

Structure (26a) is the structure underlying *èwàá*, 10, and this structure is in the lexical entry for this form. Structure (26b), which is interpreted as 20, is the underlying structure for *ogún*, 20, and this structure appears in the lexical entry for this form. These two lexical entries are presented in (28). Now by our general constraint on the

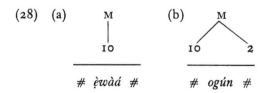

wellformedness of MS ((79) of ch. 2) structures (26a) and (26b) must
be wellformed since they occur in lexical entries. Structure (26c) does
not occur in any lexical entry, since there is no single lexical item for
100 in Yoruba. Furthermore the Packing Strategy characterizes the
structure as illformed because the phrase structure rules generate a
wellformed M, namely (26b), with a value greater than the value of its
right-hand immediate constituent and less than the value of the whole
structure.

(26d) is the structure underlying *igba*, 200, and is characterized in the
lexical entry for this form, given in (29). There are two further entries

(29)

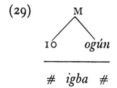

for MS in the Yoruba numeral lexicon, both of them 'incomplete'. They
are given in (30) and (31). The existence of these two entries in the

(30)

(31)

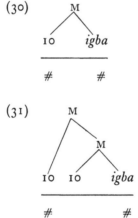

lexicon ensures that structures (26f, h) are wellformed. By our general
constraints all further structures generated by rule (25), and in particular
structures (26e, g), are characterized as illformed. We have, then, a
series of M structures with the required values 10, 20, 200, 2,000, and
20,000. We describe below the way in which the last two of these M
structures are associated with the appropriate phonetic forms by means
of the lexical extension component.

The phrase structure rules generate the following structure, which is interpreted as 2,000. I assume that a rule of 1-Deletion is applicable

(32)

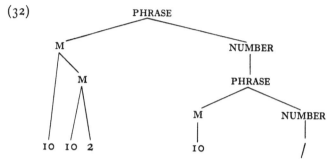

in Yoruba. This will delete the lower right-hand NUMBER from the above structure. The M dominating just 10 is lexicalized as ẹ̀wàá (by rule (28a)), and the M which is the left-hand immediate constituent of the whole structure is lexicalized as igba by rule (29). The resulting phonological string is igba ẹ̀wàá. A lexical rule, not explicitly formulated here, inserts the morpheme ẹ̀ẹ̀ 'times', yielding igba ẹ̀ẹ̀ ẹ̀wàá. According to Abraham, regular vowel harmony and tone-modifying rules will convert this string to ẹgbẹ̀wàá, and, again according to Abraham, this form is contracted to ẹgbàà. The grammar thus generates a derivation expressing the following relationship.

(33)   The value 2,000 is related to the phonetic form ẹgbàà.

This information allows the lexical extension component, in accordance with principle (76) of ch. 2, repeated below as (34), to fill out the incomplete lexical entry (30) with the phonetic representation ẹgbàà.

(34)   Given an incomplete lexical entry associating a structure G with morphological information M, where the semantic interpretation of G is S; and given also a derivation which associates S with a phonetic representation P; the incomplete lexical entry is filled out with the phonetic representation P.

Accordingly the incomplete lexical entry (30) is converted to the complete lexical entry (35). Given this lexical entry, it is clear that expressions like ẹgbàájì, contracted from ẹgbàà èjì, literally '2,000 2', can be accounted for. Ẹgbàájì, for example, is a PHRASE with the underlying structure shown in (36). By the process we have just described, the left-hand immediate constituent of this structure is lexicalized as ẹgbàà, and

(35)

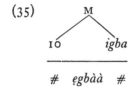

ẹgbàà

(36) (abbreviated)

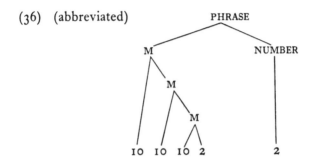

the right-hand NUMBER is lexicalized as *ẹ̀jì*. The resulting string *ẹgbàā ẹ̀jì*, is contracted by rules, which, according to Abraham, are regular, to *ẹgbàājì*.

In a similar way expressions containing *ẹgbàāwàá*, the expression for 20,000, can, by means of the lexical extension component, be accounted for. I will not go over the details of the workings of the lexical extension component in this case, as they are exactly parallel to the particulars of the illustration just given. In the case of *ẹgbàāwàá*, of course, the lexical entry filled out by the lexical extension component is (31).

It does not matter for the purposes of the operation of the lexical extension component in the cases just discussed that the structures such as (32) which give rise to the phonetic forms which ultimately fill out the incomplete lexical entries are themselves characterized as illformed (by the Packing Strategy). We have already encountered a situation such as this in the case of Welsh *pymtheg* (see section 4 of ch. 6). Our grammar generates derivations of both wellformed and illformed expressions: it is the function of a particular component of the grammar, namely the 'general constraints', to characterize certain structures, and by implication the derivations in which they figure, as illformed or wellformed. The principle upon which the lexical extension component works ((76 of ch. 2, repreated as (34) above) utilizes *any* derivation generated by the grammar and not, less simply and less generally, just the derivations involving wellformed structures.

Despite the difficulty in finding crucial information in the sources, it is conceivable that some complete account of Yoruba numerals can be given that is fairly soundly motivated. This language certainly presents the weightiest challenge for a general theory of numerals that we have encountered.

9　Some further problems

In this chapter I discuss briefly several languages which have not received detailed treatment in this study, but which appear to have interesting characteristics and may well reward further study.

9.1 'Correct misinterpretations'

In ch. 2, when discussing the words *billion*, *trillion*, etc. in American English, we saw that in the semantic interpretation of these words by exponentiation a special rule is needed adjusting the values of the prefixes *bi-*, *tri-*, etc., to 3, 4, etc., since the words *billion* and *trillion*, for example, mean $1,000^3$ and $1,000^4$ respectively. The user of these words in American English is in general not aware of this anomaly, which appears only when a detailed linguistic description of the numeral system is formulated. The user of American English apparently understands these words without performing any actual calculation involving exponentiation. The skewed relationship between the prefixes *bi-*, *tri-*, etc., and the natural number sequence is evidently not an obstacle to the correct use of words. We might be tempted to attribute this to the impossibility of conceiving realistically such large numbers as are expressed by *billion*, *trillion*, etc. But there are languages where a similar skewing apparently takes place in the expressions for quite small numbers. I give examples of these below.

The first example is from Hawaiian. As seen in ch. 7, the Hawaiian word for 20 is *iwakalua*. *Iwa* is Hawaiian for 9, and *lua* is the word for 2. Humboldt noticed this discrepancy: 'Man kann das Zahlwort 9 (*iwa*) und 2 (*lua*) nicht verkennen, und müsste also annehmen, dass hier eine Verwirrung der Begriffe stattgefunden und man 9 × 2 gesagt hätte; *ka* könnte der numerische Vorsatz sein' (pp. 776–7). In assigning an interpretation to *iwakalua*, ancient Hawaiian speakers presumably ignored the fact that it was made up of *iwa* and *lua*.

233

A number of further examples of this phenomenon are given by Seidenberg. I cite below the relevant passages.

We now come to the etymology of -*mtandatu*, or *tandatu*, a form which is frequently found. The almost universal word for 5 in Bantu is *tano*, or *tanu*, sometimes abbreviated to *tan*...The almost universal word for 3 in Bantu is -*tatu*, also frequently found in the form -*datu*. Then *tandatu* clearly derives from $5+3 = tan+datu$. This etymology is quite clear and would no doubt readily be accepted but for the fact that *tandatu* means 'six'...The real problem, however, is not the etymology of this word, but the question of how a word meaning 'eight' was displaced and came to mean 'six'.

I shall not try to explain this shift, but will give a few examples in which it is quite clear that such a shift has taken place; in other words, place beyond doubt the fact that such shifts do take place.

H. H. Johnston supplies the first example. He says: ' "Six" is represented in Ba-kusu and Kele by Li-*ambi* and in Ba-mbole [who are near the Bakusu] by Li-*ame*, a root which seems to be related to the -*ambi* so often used in Congoland and the Cameroons languages for "eight".' (That is, the -*ame* seems related to the -*ambi*.) The word 'eight' is usually found in the form *Mo-ambi*; here one should keep in mind that the *Li* and *Mo* are merely prefixes.

For Ma-sango, he gives:

1 = moshi   7 = kambo-moshi [Johnston adds a question mark]
2 = bei   8 = kambo-bei
3 = i-rero   9 = kambo-irero (also kambo-moshi in some dialects)

Here, then, *kambo moshi* in some dialects stands for 9 and in others 7. (Johnston does not explain his question mark.) There is something else quite strange about these number words. The *kambo* is the same root as *hambo*, encountered with the Herero; and the words for 7, 8, 9 are quite what one might expect for 6, 7, 8. Of course, looking at Ma-sango in isolation, we might suppose that it was a 6-system. However, there can be little doubt that the words for 6, 7, 8 were shifted into positions 7, 8, 9 respectively (pp. 255–6).

Seidenberg notes the North Wintuns'

...remarkable word for 11. They have:

1. ketet
2. palel
9. cemaketet
10. cema
11. cema-palel

$12 = 3$, $13 = 4$, $14 = 5$, $15 = 3 \times 5$, $16 = 15 + 1$, $17 = 2$, $18 = 3$, $19 = 4$ [Seidenberg clearly means here that 12 is expressed as $10 + 3$, 13 as $10 + 4$, and 14 as $10 + 5$.] Had we confined our study to the first ten number words only, we might conclude that the word for 9 exhibits the quite familiar equation $9 = 10 - 1$. On the other hand, 11 shows that an additive principle is involved, but we get $11 = 10 + 2$. What happened was that the word for 11 got displaced to position 9, perhaps under the influence of a familiar subtractive principle, and then the words after fell back one step.

Incidentally, it is quite conceivable that the investigator got his notes mixed up – there exist vocabularies (reported by other persons) in which, it seems quite certain, this happened – but in the present case it would appear that it was the Indians who got mixed up (p. 256).

I have not investigated the question of how shifts such as these described by Humboldt and Seidenberg are to be accommodated within a formal grammar. The problem that must be faced is that, in the Hawaiian case for example, it is surely more than a coincidence that the word for 20 is built up out of two other numeral morphemes of the language; however no non-*ad hoc* interpretation rules will yield the value 20 from a combination of the values of these two morphemes. It does not seem to me satisfactory to rule that the composition of the word for 20 out of the morphemes for 9 and 2 is 'not significant' or 'a coincidence'. Somehow the odd fact that *iwa* 9 and *lua* 2 make *iwakalua* 20 must be stated in the grammar.

9.2 Overcounting

In previous chapters we have seen the use of what might be called the 'standard' arithmetic operations, addition, subtraction, multiplication, division, and exponentiation. A further arithmetic operation, referred to here as 'overcounting' (after Menninger, 1969), is used extensively in certain Maya languages. I quote below from Gallatin (as quoted in Pott, 1847, pp. 94–5).

The word for 20 [in Maya] is *kal* or *hunkal* (one 20); and the words for 40, 60, 80, 100, etc., are *cakal*, *oxcal*, *cankal*, *hocal*, etc.; meaning respectively twice 20, three times 20, four times 20, and five times 20, etc. The numerals from 21 to 39 are compounds of *kal*, or *hunkal*, 20, and of the numerals 1 to 19. But after 40, each subsequent series of twenty numbers is considered as belonging to what may be called the third, fourth, fifth score, etc. Thus the numeral 41, instead of being expressed by a word meaning 'twice twenty

plus one', is *huntuyoxkal*, viz. the first (*huntu*) of the third score; *oxkal* being
three times twenty, or sixty. In the same manner the numeral 42 is *catuyoxkal*,
or the second (*catu*) of the third score. *Can* is 4 and the numeral 61 is *hun-
tucankal*, or the first of the fourth score; and so on, till you come to the last
or twentieth score, where, as *bak* or *hunbak* means 'four hundred', the word
for 381 is *huntuhunbak*, or the first of the twentieth score.

The existence of this form of counting in Maya is corroborated by Aulie
(1957), Menninger (1969), and Merrifield (1968). An example given by
Merrifield for Ch'ol (a Mayan language) is an expression for 45,
hóˀp'ehl iyuš k'àl, literally '5 towards (3 20)'. (*p'ehl* is one of several
numeral classifiers in this language.) Such an expression would presumably have a structure like (1). A bracketing as in (1) is clearly

(1)   (abbreviated)

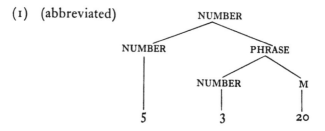

appropriate and it is also clear, since *ˀús k'àl* in isolation means 60, that
the operation needed to interpret the PHRASE is multiplication, as in the
other systems we have discussed. But what of the interpretation of the
whole structure, that is, of the topmost NUMBER? We must in some
way combine the numbers 5 and 60 and come out with 45.

An example of the same phenomenon, given by Aulie, is an expression
for 500, *hoˀk'al i čaˀbahk'*, literally '(5 20) towards (2 400)'. This expression presumably has a structure as in (2). Again, interpretation of the
right-hand PHRASE is unproblematic. It is interpreted by multiplication,

(2)   (abbreviated)

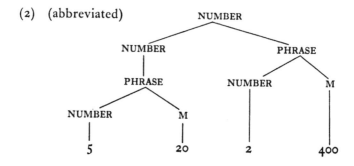

as is usual for PHRASES, and assigned the value 800. This is appropriate, as the expression *čaʔbahk'* in isolation means 800. Similarly, the left-hand PHRASE, interpreted by multiplication in a regular way, is assigned the value 100, again appropriately, since the expression *hoʔk'al* in isolation means 100. But now we have to combine the values 100 and 800 and somehow arrive at 500.

A further example comes from Gallatin. It is an expression for 385, given as *hotuhunbak*, literally '5th (1 400)'. This presumably has a structure as in (3). Having interpreted the right-hand PHRASE here as

(3) (abbreviated)

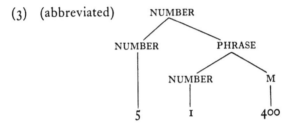

400, which is desirable, since *hun bak* in isolation means 400, we face the problem of combining 5 with 400 and arriving at 385.

Within the framework proposed in this book, a way to handle these examples seems to be as outlined below. The values of the right-hand PHRASES in each of the examples presented must be adjusted in some way. 60 in (1) must be treated as 40 for the purposes of interpreting the higher NUMBER; 800 in (2) must be treated as 400; and 400 in (3) must be treated as 380. These adjustments can be stated in approximately the same way as the adjustment used earlier to account for the interpretation of the American English *-illions* ((31) of ch. 2), but they cannot be formulated so simply and their effects on the numeral system are more far-reaching. I assume that the depth-assigning algorithm (28) of ch. 2, the general projection rule (29) of ch. 2, and the definition of the operation CALCULATE as in (26) of ch. 2, supplemented by (32) of ch. 5 are all applicable to the Maya numeral systems in question, as they are to the great majority of the world's numeral systems. The necessary adjustment rules, then, may be stated as in (4).

(4) If $d = 1$ and $y > 20$, then if $x < 20$, set y to (CALCULATE $- 1$ y 20)
       otherwise, set y to (CALCULATE $- 1$ y 400)

This rule is obviously language-specific and applies after the application of the general projection rule (29) of ch. 2 and before the operation

CALCULATE computes the values of the topmost NUMBERs in structures
(1), (2), and (3). In the case of structure (3), for example, the left-hand
NUMBER is assigned the value 5 and the right-hand PHRASE is assigned the
value 400, as desired. The general projection rule ((29) of ch. 2) now
states that the value of the whole NUMBER structure in (3) is (CALCULATE
+ 1 5 400), i.e. 5 + 400. Our Maya-specific adjustment rule (4) modifies
this to (CALCULATE + 1 5 380), i.e. to 5 + 380. When this is computed by
operation CALCULATE, the value assigned to the whole NUMBER structure
is 385, as desired. In a similar way the values 45 and 500 are assigned to
structures (1) and (2) respectively.

The adjustment rule (4) just proposed is certainly cumbersome, not
least in so far as it makes reference to the quite high number 400. There
is not enough data available on the Mayan numeral systems or on other
numeral systems which make use of overcounting to make it fruitful
to pursue the question of whether adjustment rule (4) is optimal. It
accounts for the examples just mentioned and all the other similar
examples found in the sources.

The use of overcounting in Maya is not comprehensive and perhaps
not consistent. Both Merrifield and Aulie mention alternative expressions
for the same number, one using overcounting and the other making
use of normal addition. Thus besides *ho²k'ali ča²bahk'*, '(5 20) towards
(2 400)', for 500, Aulie also gives *humbahk' yik'ot ho²k'al*, '(1 400) plus
(5 20)'. Notice also from these examples that when overcounting is used
the lower-valued constituent precedes the higher-valued one, whereas
in the case of simple addition, the lower-valued constituent follows
the higher-valued one. It is quite conceivable that these numerals
should be handled rather like the Welsh expressions discussed in ch. 6.
All NUMBERs may be generated in deep structure with the constituents
in the same order; and then the application of the adjustment rule (4)
accounting for overcounting may be made optional, just as in the case
of the rule accounting for subtraction in Biblical Welsh ((8) of ch. 6);
and finally an Inversion transformation could be made sensitive to
the semantic values assigned to the structures meeting its structural
description, as in the case of the Welsh Inversion rule ((33) of ch. 6).

It is a pity that more comprehensive information is not available on
the extent of overcounting in Mayan. It seems unlikely that more
information will be forthcoming, since, according to Merrifield, 'the
native system is being modified or replaced in many towns by the use
of Spanish number-names, with the result that few people really

control the native system' (p. 98). It would be of great interest to have a comprehensive and reliable account of the interaction between overcounting and normal addition. Just which numbers, for example, may be expressed in either form? And which numbers, if any, may only be expressed in the overcounting form? And which numbers may only be expressed by means of normal addition? If the answers to these questions were provided for the complete range of values, they would constitute an interesting test for the system of general constraints on numeral structures (e.g. the Packing Strategy) that has been developed in this book.

Traces of overcounting systems occur in several languages, among them Russian, where the expression for 90 mentions the word for 100, in this case quite redundantly. The expression for 90 is *devjanosto* glossed by Menninger as '9 before 100' (p. 75); *sto* means 100 in Russian and *devjatj* 9. A description of the Russian numeral system must mention in some way that the expression for 90 contains the word for 100.

9.3 Ainu numerals

The Ainu numeral system makes use of subtraction. There are single words for the numbers 1–5, and the expressions for 6 to 9 are said by most sources to make use of subtraction. The system I discuss here is a vigesimal one as described in Pott (1847). The account given there is confirmed by Menninger (1969), Pfizmaier (1851), Batchelor (1887), Hattori (1964), and Peng and Brainerd (1970). In the latter two works there are references to elements of a decimal system in some dialects: here I discuss only the vigesimal system. I use the spellings of Pott. Pott, citing Krusenstern, gives the following:

(5)   1. schnepf   9. schnebischambi (1 von 10)
      2. tup   8. tubischambi (2 von 10)
      3. repf   7. aruwambi (3 von 10? oder 3 + (4)?)
      4. inipf   6. juwambi (4 von 10? oder 2 + (4)?)
      5. aschiki 10. wambi   (p. 86)

The numbers expressed here by subtraction present no particular problem from the point of view of the framework developed in this study. They could be described in a way quite analogous to the description of the Biblical Welsh expressions which make use of subtraction.

But there is one other type of expression in Ainu which uses subtraction and these expressions are indeed problematic in the same way as the Yoruba numerals discussed in the previous chapter. In Ainu, the odd decades, i.e. 30, 50, 70, 90, 110, 130, etc., are expressed by subtracting 10 from the next higher decade. Examples are as follows:

(6)   30. wambi i-dochoz   (10 from (2 20))
       50. wambi i-richoz   (10 from (3 20))
      130. wambi aruwanochoz   (10 (7 20))

Now the expression for 31, for example, is *schnepu igaschima wambi idochoz*, literally '1 plus 10 from 2 20'. This expression must clearly have a bracketed structure as in (7) below.

(7)   [1[10[2 20]]]

In interpreting this structure, 2 is first multiplied by 20, giving 40; 10 is then subtracted from 40 to give 30; and finally 1 is added to 30 to give 31. Note that the last two operations are respectively subtraction and addition, both versions of operation CALCULATE carried out at depth 1. Here again, as in Yoruba, we meet the situation of a complex NUMBER which apparently has no PHRASE as an immediate constituent, but rather further structures interpreted by addition (or its inverse). Several potential solutions to this problem were discussed in connection with Yoruba, in sections 1 and 2 of ch. 8. The discussion there is equally applicable to the Ainu case. As in the Yoruba case, no solution to the problem of structures such as (7) is proposed here.

There is a further anomaly in the Ainu numeral system. The highest valued single word is the word for 20, *choz* in Pott's spelling, and yet the system can be used to count at least as high as 2,000, the expression for 200 being used for this purpose in a way typical of an M, although it appears to have the structure of a PHRASE. The expression for 200 is *schnewanochoz*, '1 10 20'. Given the general framework developed in this study, one would postulate that this has a structure as in (8). This structure would be lexicalized as *schnewanochoz*. It is clear that Ainu uses both 10 and 20 as MS. In a vigesimal system with no higher valued lexical item than that for 20, one would expect the expressions for 220, 240, 260, 280, 300, 320, 340, 360, and 380 to be expressed as multiples of 20 (as they are, for example, in Mixtec). Only if there existed a higher-valued word, such as, for example, *cant*, 100, in Welsh, or *igba*, 200, in Yoruba, would one expect a new 'tier' in the numeral system to be

(8)

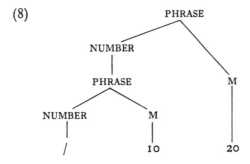

begun, using this new word. Thus Welsh, for example, counts in multiples of 20 as far as 100, for which it has a word, and then it counts by multiples of 100 as much as possible thereafter. Similarly Yoruba counts in multiples of 20 as far as 200, for which it has a word, and then by multiples of 200 as much as possible thereafter. But the Ainu expression for 300, for example, is *aschikinichoz igaschima schnewano choz*, literally '(5 20) plus (1 (10 20))'. One could very well postulate a structure as in (9) for this expression. This structure, however, is problematic

(9) (abbreviated)

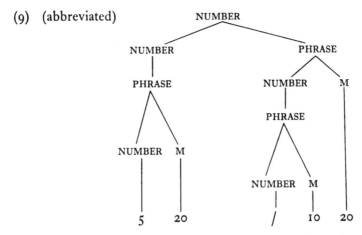

from the point of view of the general framework developed here. It would be characterized as illformed by the Packing Strategy, since there appears to be no reason not to prefer a structure corresponding to the formula (15×20).

Note that if we could postulate an M with the value 200 for Ainu and somehow associate this with the expression *schnewanochoz*, then a quite unproblematic structure for the expression for 300 could be adopted, as shown below. Given a wellformed M with the value 200 the

(10) (abbreviated)

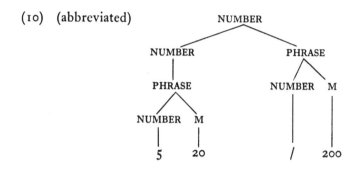

general constraints proposed in this study would not reject structure (10) as illformed; and they would, as required, reject a structure corresponding to the formula (15 × 20) as illformed. Thus we see that there is some attraction to the idea of postulating an M with the value 200 in Ainu even though there exists no single lexical item with this value.

Further support for this proposal emerges when we consider expressions for numbers like 400, 600, 800, and 1,000. 600, for example, is expressed as *re schiniwanochoz*, literally '3 (1 (10 20))'. Clearly this expression is to be interpreted by several operations of multiplication, the last being the operation of multiplying 3 by 200. Within the general framework we have developed, structures interpreted by multiplication are PHRASES, whose constituents are generally a NUMBER followed by an M. Here again we see the attraction of postulating an M in Ainu with the value 200. Postulating such a structure, we can generate a structure as in (11) as the structure underlying the expression for 600. Given the

(11) (abbreviated)

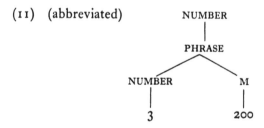

existence of a wellformed M with the value 200, the general constraints on the wellformedness of numeral deep structures would characterize this structure as wellformed.

The major task remaining is that of associating an M with the value 200 with the string *schnewanochoz*. It is clear that this can be done in a straightforward way by the use of the lexical extension component discussed in earlier chapters. I assume that the Ainu rule expanding M will be as follows.

(12)   M → (10) (20)

This rule states that M may be expanded to 10, or to 20, or to the sequence 10 20. That is, I assume that the structure of the M with value 200 in Ainu is as in (13). (Rule (12) assumes a convention stating that

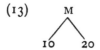

(13)

when all the elements on the right-hand side of a phrase structure rule are parenthesized, at least one of them must be chosen.) There will be an incomplete lexical entry for the M with value 200 as in (14). This

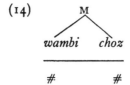

(14)

will be filled out by the lexical extension component with the phonetic representation of *schnewanochoz*. I will not repeat the details of this mechanism here. Finally, it remains to be stated that the depth-assigning algorithm ((28) of ch. 2) can be simplified in Ainu just as in the cases of Yoruba and Hawaiian. In these and some other languages, operation CALCULATE never functions at a depth greater than 2, i.e. no use is made of exponentiation. The simplified depth-assigning algorithm ((3) of ch. 7, (27) of ch. 8) is repeated here as (15).

(15)   All NUMBERs are assigned depth 1.
       All other constituents are assigned depth 2.

9.4 Indian MS

In most Indian languages, both Indo-European and Dravidian, there is a series of MS with the values 10, 100, 1,000, 100,000, and 10,000,000. Siromoney (p. 83), for example, mentions the following for Tamil.

(16)   10   paththu

100   nūru

1,000   ayiram

100,000   laksham

10,000,000 kōdi

In languages where MS are interpreted by exponentiation, e.g. English, Chinese, Mixtec, it is regularly the case that the values of the MS may be arranged into a series $m_1, m_2, \ldots, m_n$ such that for all adjacent pairs of values m_i, m_j, either $m_j = m_i^2$ or there exists some m_x and some whole number y such that $m_i = m_x^y$ and $m_j = m_x^{y+1}$. This is true of British English, for example, where we have the series of values 10, 10^2, 10^3, $(10^3)^2$, $((10^3)^2)^2$, $((10^3)^2)^3$. It is true in Chinese also where we have a series of MS with the values 10, 10^2, 10^3, 10^4, $(10^4)^2$, and $(10^4)^3$. Clearly the Indian MS, if they are interpreted by exponentiation, are an exception to this general pattern.

In languages whose MS are interpreted by multiplication, e.g. Hawaiian, Yoruba, and Ainu, it is usually the case that the values of the higher-valued MS can be arranged into a series $m_1, m_2, \ldots, m_n$ such that for all adjacent triples of values m_i, m_j, m_k there exists some whole number y such that $m_k = m_j \times y$ and $m_j = m_i \times y$. Thus in Hawaiian we have the series 40, 40×10, $40 \times 10 \times 10$, $40 \times 10 \times 10 \times 10$, etc. In Yoruba we have 20, 20×10, $20 \times 10 \times 10$, and $20 \times 10 \times 10 \times 10$. The Indian MS, if they are interpreted by multiplication, are an exception to this pattern.

Within the framework developed in this book there are several possible analyses of the Indian MS, all of them involving some Indian-specific statement. The analysis which is perhaps preferable, in so far as it makes the least implausible Indian-specific statement, is suggested below. The phrase structure rule expanding M for the Indian languages is as in (17).

(17)   M → (M) 10.

This rule generates structures as in (18). M structures in the Indian languages are interpreted by multiplication, so the depth-assigning algorithm for these languages is the simplified version as in (3) of ch. 7, (27) of ch. 8, and (15) of this chapter. There is an Indian-specific semantic rule, which applies after the operation of the general projection

(18) (a) M   (b)   M   (c)   M

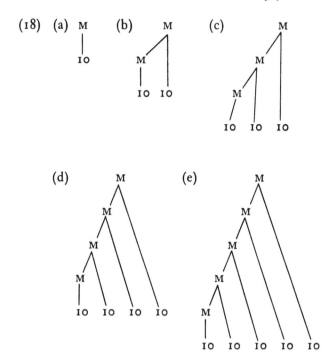

rule ((29) of ch. 2) and before the functioning of operation CALCULATE. This semantic rule is as in (19).

(19) If $d = 2$, $x > 100$, and $y = 10$, set y to (CALCULATE $+ 2$ y 10).

This rule applies just once in the interpretation of a given M. To illustrate its application, consider structures (18c) and (18d). The former is interpreted straightforwardly by multiplication as 1,000: the semantic rule (19) does not apply in its interpretation, because no numbers greater than 100 are involved in the calculation which arrives at the figure 1,000. Structure (18d), however, contains structure (18c) as an immediate constituent. According to the general projection rule, this structure is to be interpreted as (CALCULATE $+ 2$ 1,000 10), i.e. as 1,000 × 10. The semantic rule (19) adjusts this formula to (CALCULATE $+ 2$ 1,000 100), i.e. to 1,000 × 100. This formula is computed to the value 100,000 and this is the value assigned to structure (28d). We postulate that this is the structure underlying Tamil *laksham*. Structure (18e), which we postulate to be the structure underlying Tamil *kōdi*, is interpreted by a similar process as 10,000,000.

9.5 Chinese *ling*

A peculiarity unique, as far as I know, to the Chinese numeral system, is its use of the word for 'zero' as a kind of placeholder in certain numerals, although the presence of this word contributes nothing to the meaning of the whole numeral expression. The Chinese word for 'zero' is *ling*. Examples are:

(20) (a) ichian ling ell.shyrsyh   (= 1,024)
           1 1000 0   2 10   4
      (b) erh pai ling erh   (= 202)
           2   100 0   2

These examples are from Chao (1968), p. 575, and Brainerd and Peng (1968), p. 78, respectively. In both cases I have used the romanization of the source.

I do not offer any analysis of the Chinese numeral system here and leave open the matter of the proper treatment of the morpheme *ling*.

10 *Summary: a basis for typology*

In this chapter we give a brief summary of the principal conclusions that can be drawn concerning the formal organization of the numeral systems of natural languages. We concentrate here on the more plausibly universal properties of numeral systems and ignore idiosyncratic, language-specific features. Furthermore we will not repeat here the detailed arguments for our conclusions. These may be traced by referring to the index. The salient features of numeral systems in general, isolated here, may obviously be used to provide a general typology of numeral systems.

10.1 Phrase structure rules

For most languages three syntactic categories, NUMBER, PHRASE, and M are relevant and the phrase structure rules expanding the first two of these are essentially the same for most languages. These rules generally take the form below.

(1) (a)
$$\text{NUMBER} \rightarrow \left\{ \begin{array}{c} / \\ \text{PHRASE} \end{array} \right\} \text{(NUMBER)}$$

(b) PHRASE → NUMBER M

In some languages the constituents defined by these rules may be in the reverse order, but no issue of any theoretical significance arises from this difference.

The phrase structure rules expanding M are less uniform across languages and fall into two general types, depending on whether Ms are interpreted by multiplication or exponentiation. The rules expanding M also differ in the particular values which they mention explicitly, e.g. 5, 10, 15, 20. These differences account for the most obvious differences between counting systems, i.e. whether they are decimal, quinary, vigesimal, etc. In the schemata given below these various possible bases will be represented as m_1, m_2, m_3, etc. In languages whose MS are interpreted by multiplication, another value is sometimes mentioned explicitly in the phrase structure rule expanding M, e.g. the value 4 in Hawaiian, and the value 2 in Yoruba. Such values will be represented as x in the schemata below. Schemata representing the general types of rules expanding M are given in (2).

(2)   (a) Multiplication type

$$ M \rightarrow \left\{ \begin{array}{c} [m_1] \\ m_2(\left\{ \begin{array}{c} [x] \\ M \end{array} \right\}) \end{array} \right\} $$

   (b) Exponentiation type

$$ M \rightarrow \left\{ \begin{array}{c} m_1 \\ [m_2] \\ [m_3] \\ \text{NUMBER} \quad M \end{array} \right\} $$

In these schemata square brackets enclose elements which may or may not be found in the phrase structure rule expanding M in any given language. Thus in Mixtec, for example (see (1) of ch. 3), three separate values for MS, 10, 15, and 20, are listed in the rule expanding M, corresponding to m_1, m_2, and m_3, but in English (see (2c) of ch. 2) only one value, 10, is mentioned explicitly in the rule expanding M.

The terminal symbols of these phrase structure rules, i.e. those symbols that do not occur on the left-hand side of any rule, are semantic representations of the numbers that have particular significance for the language in question, e.g. 1 and 10 for English, 1, 4, 10, and 20 for Hawaiian.

The phrase structure rule components of numeral systems are highly recursive, as can be seen from (1) and (2).

10.2 Semantic interpretation

Structures generated by phrase structure rules ('deep structures') are assigned semantic representations by the following general rules and conventions. A depth-assigning algorithm first associates each node in a deep structure with an integer denoting its 'depth'. There are two versions of this algorithm, depending on whether exponentiation is used in a language or not. These two versions are given below.

(3) Depth-assigning algorithms
  (a) (simpler version – no exponentiation)
    All NUMBERS are assigned depth 1. All other constituents are assigned depth 2.
  (b) (version for languages using exponentiation)
    Where there exists a phrase structure rule X → Y Z, and X is a constituent at depth n, all Ys and Zs in the phrase structure rules are marked as constituents at depth $n+1$ unless they have already been assigned a depth by a previous application of this convention. All NUMBERS in phrase structure rules are assigned depth 1.

There is a general projection rule which appears to be valid for all languages. This is expressed as (4). This rule states that the value of any

$$(4) \qquad X_d \qquad = (\text{CALCULATE} + d \, x \, y)$$

constituent with depth d and immediate constituents with values x and y is to be computed by the formula $(\text{CALCULATE} + d \, x \, y)$. There is a further rule that the value assigned to any structure which has but a single immediate constituent is the value of the constituent.

$(\text{CALCULATE} + d \, x \, y)$ is a general arithmetical operation defined procedurally as follows.

(5) $(\text{CALCULATE} + d \, x \, y)$
    declare z as a variable to be used in the procedure
    set z to the value of y
  A if $d = 1$ and $x = \emptyset$, or if $d \neq 1$ and $x = 1$, return z as the value of the procedure
    otherwise,
    set z to $(\text{CALCULATE} + (\text{CALCULATE} - \emptyset \, d) \, z \, y)$
    set x to $(\text{CALCULATE} - \emptyset \, x)$
    go back to the instruction labelled A and continue

This operation is a conflation of the operations of addition, multiplication, and exponentiation. If d is 1, operation CALCULATE does addition, if d is 2, CALCULATE does multiplication, and if d is 3, the operation is exponentiation. The above definition relies crucially on an undefined operation, represented as (CALCULATE + ø x), which is the basic counting operation, or the operation of 'adding one'. Semantic representations for numbers expressed in any language are assumed to be sets of marks. (Arabic notation is used simply as a convenient shorthand for these representations. Thus '3' is an abbreviation for the semantic representation ///.) The basic operation of counting, i.e. (CALCULATE + ø x) can be defined pragmatically as 'making another mark'. Also assumed in the above definition (5) of CALCULATE is the notion of its inverse, expressed by a 'minus' sign rather than a 'plus' sign as the first argument of the operation. The inverse of operation CALCULATE is defined generally as follows:

(6)   If and only if (CALCULATE + d x y) = z, then (CALCULATE − d z y) = x.

This definition subsumes definitions of 'counting backwards', subtraction, division, and logarithm, which are, respectively, the inverses of counting, addition, multiplication, and exponentiation. Since the input to operation CALCULATE or its inverse is always (disregarding for the moment the initial plus or minus sign) a trio (or a pair) of semantic representations in the form of sets of marks, and since the operation is defined in terms of the basic operations of 'making another mark' and 'taking away a mark', the output of the operation is then always itself in the form of a set of marks, i.e. the semantic representation of some number.

The definitions given here of operation CALCULATE and its inverse are valid in general for all natural languages, since all languages make use of the same familiar arithmetic operations, which do not differ from language to language. For several languages it is, however, necessary to postulate certain idiosyncratic extensions to the general arithmetic framework set up in definitions (5) and (6). That is, in certain languages it is necessary to postulate semantic adjustment rules operating after the application of the general projection rule (4) and before the actual functioning of operation CALCULATE. Such adjustment rules are usually quite restricted contextually and play a fairly peripheral role in the interpretation of numeral structures, although there are some exceptions, e.g. languages which make extensive use of 'overcounting' or subtraction.

Operation CALCULATE and its inverse, as defined in (5) and (6), actually subsume an infinite number of different, successively more complex, arithmetic operations, since it is possible in principle for the argument represented by the variable d in (5) to be any natural number. In fact, however, the universal phrase structure rule types (1) and (2) and the two depth-assigning algorithms (3) together ensure that operation CALCULATE never functions at a depth greater than 3 in interpreting the numeral structures of natural languages. Furthermore, since numeral structures are only interpreted by the inverse of operation CALCULATE in the relatively infrequent instances where a semantic adjustment rule must be stated, the inverse of CALCULATE is used less frequently than CALCULATE itself. The order of frequency of use of the basic arithmetic operations is addition, multiplication, exponentiation, subtraction, and division.

The semantic representations used here can only represent natural numbers: fractions and negative numbers cannot be represented. This has the consequence that certain numeral structures containing substructures interpreted by division are assigned their appropriate semantic representations by means of a process of deduction involving various arithmetical universals in addition to operation CALCULATE and its inverse. Some examples of such arithmetical universals are given below.

(7) (a) (Law of Commutativity of Multiplication)
         (CALCULATE + 2 x y) = (CALCULATE + 2 y x)
     (b) (Law of Distribution)
         (CALCULATE + 2 (CALCULATE + 1 x y) z) = (CALCULATE + 1
         (CALCULATE + 2 x z) (CALCULATE + 2 y z))

An example of the use of such a deduction process was given in section 5.4, on Danish.

10.3 Wellformedness constraints

Three general constraints on the wellformedness of numeral deep structures appear to be of universal or near-universal validity. These are given below.

(8) Any structure containing an illformed structure is itself illformed.

(9) Any M generated by the phrase structure rules but distinct from all M types characterized in the lexicon is illformed.

(10) PACKING STRATEGY

A structure A generated by the phrase structure rules is illformed if

(a) it is of category X, has value x, and has as immediate constituents a NUMBER and some other structure with value y (not necessarily in that order), where

(b) the phrase structure rules generate a wellformed structure B of category Z with value z, where Z is on the right-hand side of a phrase structure rule expanding X and is not NUMBER, and $y < z \leqslant x$.

The notion of 'M type' used in (9) is understood in the following sense. Sets of structure specifications in lexical entries which are not distinct from each other because they include variables together characterize structure types. Various problems with and possible alternative formulations of (10), the Packing Strategy, have been discussed. Constraints (8), (9), and (10) characterize numeral deep structures as illformed, but do not cause structures to disappear in any way. Thus it is useful for other statements in the grammars of numeral systems (in particular the central principle of the lexical extension component – see below) to refer to derivations involving structures characterized as illformed by these constraints.

The wellformedness constraints (8), (9), and (10) apply in an intrinsically determined order. Thus constraint (10), for example, the Packing Strategy, depends on certain constituents of the structure to which it applies having been previously characterized as wellformed (more accurately, not characterized as illformed) by one of the other constraints, either (8) or (9). Constraint (8) similarly depends crucially on the previous operation of one of the other two constraints. Constraint (9) does not depend on the prior application of either of the other two constraints and may thus be said intrinsically to precede them in order of application.

Two of these constraints are 'global' in that they refer to information not explicitly represented in the structures to which they apply, but associated with them by other components of the grammar. Thus constraint (9), for example, refers to information which is contained in the lexicon and can only be retrieved through access to the lexicon. Similarly the Packing Strategy, in applying to a structure A, refers to the semantic representations associated with A and one of its immediate constituents by the semantic component of the grammar. The Packing

Strategy is, furthermore, not merely a global constraint, but also a 'transderivational' constraint, since it refers to information which cannot be retrieved from the derivation of the structure to which it applies, but only from the derivations of other structures generated by the phrase structure rules. That is, in applying the Packing Strategy to a structure A, it is necessary to refer to the semantic representation and wellformedness of some other structure B.

In some languages there may be a need to postulate idiosyncratic language-specific wellformedness constraints on numeral deep structures. We have seen examples in French (see (3) of ch. 4) and in Danish (see (4) of ch. 5).

10.4 Lexicon

For all natural language numeral systems it appears to be valid to postulate a lexicon in the form of a set of 'lexical entries' or 'lexicalization rules'. Each such entry associates a particular syntactic structure with a specific phonological representation and specific morphological information. Each lexical entry takes the form of a characterization of some syntactic structure, in the form of a tree diagram, below all or a proper substructure of which is drawn a line; below the line is a phonological representation of the form associated with the structure above the line. The phonological representation may have a # symbol at one or both ends; if it has a # symbol at both ends, it is a word in the language, if it has a # just at the beginning, it is a prefix, and if it has a # at the end, it is a suffix. Some of these boundaries may be deleted during the course of a derivation of a numeral expression by language-specific, or sometimes possibly universal, conventions. In this study we have used conventional orthography as a convenient expository shorthand for phonological representations, which we assume to take the form generally proposed in generative grammars, namely that of a matrix of distinctive phonological features.

The structure represented above the line in a lexical entry may be characterized in syntactic and semantic terms, as, for example, in the entry for English *one*, given in (11). Here NUMBER and / are categories mentioned by the phrase structure rules and / is also a terminal symbol, i.e. a symbol found only on the right-hand side of a phrase structure rule and having intrinsic semantic content. The structure above the line in a lexical entry may be characterized, at least in part, by reference to

(11) NUMBER

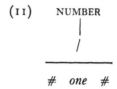

\# *one* \#

phonological information, as in, for instance, the entry for English *two*, given in (12). Here the phonological form *one* is used as a systematic

(12) NUMBER

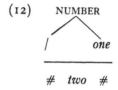

\# *two* \#

shorthand (i.e. an abbreviation which has significance within the theory) for the syntactic structure represented above the line in (11). By means of this abbreviatory convention, lexical entries are simplified. Variables ranging over syntactic categories may also sometimes figure in lexical entries.

The phonological form mentioned in a lexicalization rule is associated just with the underlined part of the given syntactic structure. In cases where only a proper substructure of the given structure appears directly above the line, the lexical entry is context-sensitive, associating the phonological form in question with the underlined structure just in the environment specified by the non-underlined part of the structure. A convention associated with the application of lexicalization rules that appears to be valid for some languages and may well be universally valid is that context-sensitive rules apply before context-free ones.

There are cases where a lexicalization rule may be collapsed with a non-lexical transformational rule (see next section). This implies that the insertion of lexical items does not necessarily precede the application of all transformational rules.

Some lexical entries are 'incomplete' in the sense that they contain no phonological information below the line. In cases such as this the entry is filled out by the lexical extension component, operating in accordance with the principle set out below.

(13) Given an incomplete lexical entry associating a structure G with morphological information M, where the semantic interpretation of G is S; and given also a derivation which associates S with a

phonetic representation P; the incomplete lexical entry is filled
out with the phonetic representation P.

The lexical extension component is thus responsible for synthesizing
new lexical entries on the basis of information contained in derivations
generated by the grammar. We have seen a variety of evidence from
different languages for the existence of some such component.

10.5 Transformations

A number of transformational rules turn up in substantially the same
form in many different numeral systems. These are the rules that we
have called 1-Deletion, Switch, Inversion, and Conjunction Insertion.
In particular languages there may be idiosyncratic conditions on the
applicability of these rules, which are given in their most general form
in (14), (15), (16), and (17).

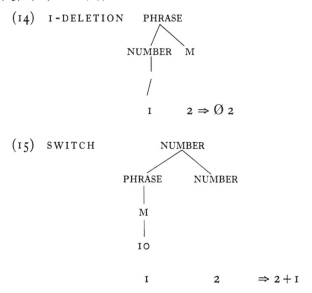

There are numeral systems (e.g. that of Welsh) in which some quite
considerable transformational apparatus must be set up in order to
account for the surface forms of numeral expressions, but these are not
common. In the case of Welsh, we have seen that it is necessary to
postulate a transformational component that is formally quite uncon-
strained in the sense that a variety of transformation types must be

(16) INVERSION

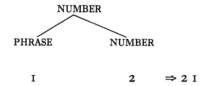

$$I \qquad\qquad 2 \quad \Rightarrow 2 \ I$$

(17) CONJUNCTION INSERTION

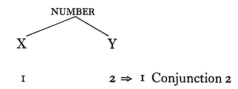

$$I \qquad\qquad 2 \Rightarrow I \text{ Conjunction } 2$$

formulated and these rules are, furthermore, subject to a wide variety of conditions on their applicability, conditions which are often 'global'.

II   *Some other numeral grammars*

We have given in the preceding chapters a fairly copious illustration of what the linguistic theory of numerals is; we have described the form of the theory that is necessary to express the significant generalizations that can be made about numeral systems. In this chapter we will give some examples of what the linguistic theory of numerals is not. Over the past few years a number of authors have tried their hand at writing formal descriptive grammars of numeral systems. The results have been, in general, very inadequate. None of the grammars concerned seems to account in a satisfactory way for the major characteristic properties of numeral systems. We have selected several grammars for examination here, not because any one of them can be said to have made any particular contribution to our understanding of numeral systems, but rather as representatives of five rather widely differing 'schools' of linguistic theory. These 'schools' are: 'functional grammar', tagmemics, early transformational grammar, stratificational grammar, and generative semantics. These are by no means unified bodies of thought and it is possible that other proponents of these schools will disown the grammars of numerals reviewed here. But the rubrics we have given them are all those chosen by the authors themselves, with the exception of Sanders' grammar. He does not actually use the term 'generative semantic' of his work, but his ideas have most in common with workers in that school of thought. In discussing each grammar, we will not make a comprehensive survey of all its failings, but will concentrate on the major inadequacies and on those which appear to result from characteristic properties of its approach to the subject. It must be also emphasized that the writers mentioned here do not necessarily still adhere to the views discussed.

11.1 Van Katwijk's functional grammar

Van Katwijk's 1968 grammar is in fact, though he does not say so, attacking the problem of set-systems versus concatenation-systems outlined by Chomsky (1965, pp. 123–7). Briefly a set-system is a system for stating grammatical relationships without at the same time imposing an order on grammatical elements. Phrase structure rules do both. For example, the first of the phrase structure rules proposed for most of the numeral systems dealt with in previous chapters states a grammatical relationship between a NUMBER, a PHRASE, and another NUMBER. Speaking figuratively, we can say that the rule defines a NUMBER and a PHRASE as 'sister' constituents, whose 'mother' constituent is another NUMBER. The semantic component interprets the grammatical relationship 'is the sister of' as 'is added to' and the grammatical relationship 'is the mother of' as 'is the sum of'. Besides defining these grammatical relationships, the rule states a sequential ordering between the two 'sisters', i.e. it states that the PHRASE precedes the NUMBER and, except where transformational processes affect it, this is the ordering of the constituents in the surface structure of actual numeral expressions. The rule 'concatenates' the constituents between which it defines a grammatical relationship. Phrase structure rules belong, then, to 'concatenation-systems'. With a 'set-system' the two functions of phrase structure rules are fulfilled by two different types of rules, one stating grammatical relationships between unordered elements, and the other type imposing a sequential order on these elements. Chomsky writes,

A priori, there is no way of determining which theory is correct; it is an entirely empirical question, and the evidence presently available is overwhelmingly in favor of concatenation-systems over set-systems, for the theory of the categorial component. In fact, no proponent of a set-system has given any indication of how the abstract underlying unordered structures are converted into actual strings with surface structures. (p. 125)

Van Katwijk faces this challenge. He proposes, in constructing his grammar of Dutch numerals,

The *positions* of terminal elements within numerical expressions are determined by *functional* rules; and the terminal symbols themselves are generated by *category* rules. In the derivations of numerical expressions both types of rules are interdependent with respect to their applicability. I.e. the inputs of most of the functional rules are introduced by the outputs of category rules and vice versa...To give an example, *vijfhonderd* (five hundred) is derived from, π which produces the multiplicative relation $\beta.C$. The relation $\beta.C$ is a single symbol. It may also be represented by $C.\beta$, for order of constituents has no meaning in functional relations. The relation is then to be replaced by a positional relation $\beta\frown C$, which is a complex symbol. This complex symbol then turns out to be a sequence of symbols with positional indices with respect to category rules, replacing β by *vijf* and C by *honderd*. (pp. 1–2)

Van Katwijk describes this type of grammar as 'double-decked'. It separates the definition of grammatical relations from the concatenation of constituents by using different types of rules for these purposes. Empirical justification for this separation is most appropriately sought by studying Van Katwijk's grammar and seeing whether it permits expression of significant linguistic generalizations which could otherwise not be expressed.

The grammar is for the most part conveniently laid out in pairs of rules, one of each type to a pair. For each functional (position determining) rule, there is just one corresponding category rule. Some category rules have no corresponding functional rule, and these are just those category rules which rewrite a single category symbol as a one-member set (as we shall have to say since Van Katwijk insists that β.C, for example, is a 'single symbol'). Naturally no ordering can be imposed on a set with only one element and so no functional rule is necessary in these cases. Thus Van Katwijk's category rules are of two types, those which generate one-member sets, upon which no ordering can logically be imposed, and those to each of which corresponds *a single* functional rule imposing a certain order on the constituents which it generates. Note that there is never, in Van Katwijk's grammar, more than one possible ordering of constituents generated by his category rules. This surely demonstrates, at least as far as the Dutch numerals are concerned, that there is a definitely preferred order of elements in grammatical categories, and separation of their enumeration from their ordering is both artificial and unnecessary. The usual phrase structure rules of generative grammars would account for the syntactic structure of Dutch numerals more efficiently than the rules proposed by Van Katwijk.

Van Katwijk's justification of his treatment is in fact rather lame. The nearest thing to a piece of evidence is in a note, 'That order of elements is unimportant in relations, is in agreement with language intuition. Incidentally, 25 is expressed in Dutch as *vijfentwintig* (five and twenty), whereas in English, e.g. it is "twenty-five"' (p. 8*n*). Van Katwijk neglects the ease, illustrated by his article, with which one can generate Dutch numerals without having to resort to functional relations.

The double-deck grammar is actually generative in two senses. It generates a syntactic analysis of a string and a functional representation of it at the same time. As an example, the string *tweeduizendvijfhonderd* (two thousand, five hundred) is associated with the structure diagram (1). (In this diagram horizontal arrows represent application of functional

(1)

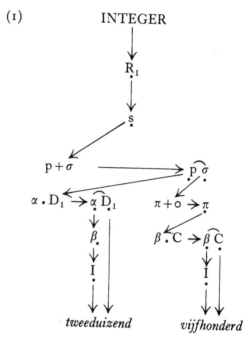

rules, vertical arrows represent application of category rules that generate one-member sets, and slanting arrows represent application of other category rules. A dot between letters indicates a multiplicational relationship; a + sign indicates a relation of addition; a dot under a symbol indicates that it has been assigned an order and may be operated on by a category rule; ⌢ is a concatenation sign.) The nodes at the bottom end of the slanting arrows in this diagram express semantic relations of multiplication and addition between the various constituents of *tweeduizendvijfhonderd*. The node $\pi + o$ serves no useful purpose and it is unclear why Van Katwijk did not write his rules so that π could be derived directly from σ. As it is, the symbol o is generated only to be deleted immediately by a functional rule and therefore has no syntactic significance. Adding zero to a number does not affect its value and so the treatment is not motivated semantically either. There are similar examples in the grammar, where a letter is said to be in a multiplicational relationship with 1, which is immediately deleted. But these are minor irritants and do not detract from the interest of generating functional representation and syntactic analysis in one grammar.

The most common semantic relations with which one has to deal when considering most numeral systems are those of addition and multiplication, which are both symmetric relations. Thus there is no objection in this particular case to the non-ordering of constituents in 'functional' relations. It is indeed true that, according to the general conventions for interpreting plus-signs and 'Polish dots', $p + \sigma$ is indistinguishable from $\sigma + p$ and $\beta.C$ is indistinguishable from $C.\beta$. But natural languages assuredly have semantic relations which are asymmetric. Some numeral systems, for example, use subtraction. Since the semantic relations which may exist between constituents of deep structures are not always symmetric, some method for representing relations without the property of symmetry is needed. For example, we will wish to convey, in numeral systems that use subtraction, which number is to be subtracted from which. Ordering of constituents in deep structures provides a useful convention for representing certain properties of relations existing between constituents. We have shown that from the point of view of generating syntactic structures for the Dutch numerals the choice of a particular ordering for constituents of deep structures is not an arbitrary matter, but is dictated by the facts of the Dutch numeral system itself. This system associates certain 'functional' or 'semantic' relations existing between elements of deep structure with certain sequential orderings of those elements. And, as we have seen, Van Katwijk's mapping of functional relations onto ordered sequences of symbols is essentially a one-to-one mapping. The Dutch numeral system is, then, an example of the non-ambiguity, from a functional or semantic point of view, of underlying syntactic phrase markers. The nodes at the bottom ends of the slanting arrows in diagram (1) are, therefore, entirely superfluous, as is Van Katwijk's dichotomy between functional and category rules.

The assumption underlying Van Katwijk's grammar seems to be that representations such as $p + \sigma$ and $\beta.C$ are in some sense more real or true semantically or arithmetically than representations such as $p \frown \sigma$ and $\beta \frown \underset{.}{C}$. No such claim can be made. In either case a set of interpretive conventions is needed. One set of conventions would interpret the plus sign and the dot as relations of addition and multiplication respectively; the alternative set of conventions would interpret the elements of any ordered pair in which the second element is Ç (or any other member of the same well-defined syntactic class as Ç) as being in a multiplicational relationship, and the elements of any ordered pair in which the second element is σ (or any other member of the same well-defined syntactic class as σ) as being in a relationship of addition. Since the task of linguistics is not only to represent abstract semantic relations, but also to map these relations on to temporally or spatially ordered strings of elements (i.e. of 'words' or 'sounds'), the concatenating or ordering type of representation is obviously more appropriate than the other. Phrase structure rules, which express an abstract relation between elements and at the same time impose an ordering on them, embody symbolically the basic function of language which is to relate non-linear reality with linear strings of symbols.

11.2 Merrifield's tagmemic grammars

The issue of expressing functional relations in a grammar is also relevant to Merrifield's (1968) article. Merrifield's analysis of numerals in Otomi, Mixtec, Tarahumara, and Ch'ol is tagmemic. (For an introduction to tagmemics, see Cook, 1969.) Merrifield's syntagmemes can be interpreted in the manner suggested by Bach (1964, pp. 41–4). I would differ from Bach in the following respect, though. It seems to me that there are no equivalents in the notation of phrase structure rules for tagmemic 'slots'. I take 'fillers' to correspond to the categories of phrase structure rules and slots to correspond to functional, essentially relational terms such as 'subject' and 'object' which are not mentioned explicitly in phrase structure rules. When Bach writes, 'it is sometimes advantageous to build in an intermediate node (for purposes of transformational manipulations)' (p. 42), he does not have in mind a concept of the same significance as that of the tagmemic slot, as Pike 1967, p. 496) points out. I would therefore interpret Merrifield's syntagmemes for Mixtec (2) as the phrase structure rules (3).

(2) (a) NML(1) = +H:CLS(1) ±M:DGT(1)
    (b) NML(2) = +Q:DGT(1,2), NML(1) +H:CLS(2)
                  ±M:DGT(1,2), NML(1)
    (c) NML(3) = +Q:DGT(1,2), NML(1) +H:CLS(3)
                  ±M:DGT(1,2), NML(1,2)

(Merrifield's syntagmeme for NML(3) has CLS(2) in the Head slot. This is surely a misprint for CLS(3). We assume this here.)

(3) (a) NML1 → CLS1 (DGT1)

(b) NML2 → $\left\{ \begin{array}{c} \text{DGT1} \\ \text{ĐGT2} \\ \text{NML1} \end{array} \right\}$ CLS2 $\left(\left\{ \begin{array}{c} \text{DGT1} \\ \text{DGT2} \\ \text{NML1} \end{array} \right\} \right)$

(c) NML3 → $\left\{ \begin{array}{c} \text{DGT1} \\ \text{DGT2} \\ \text{NML1} \end{array} \right\}$ CLS3 $\left(\left\{ \begin{array}{c} \text{DGT1} \\ \text{DGT2} \\ \text{NML1} \\ \text{NML2} \end{array} \right\} \right)$

Grammatical relations which the tagmemic rules label explicitly as M(odifier) and H(ead) are not represented in the structures generated by the rules (3). It should be apparent from a comparison of (2) and (3) that nothing of syntactically explanatory significance is lost by omitting such terms as Head and Modifier from phrase structure rules. Indeed, seen from the point of view of accounting purely for the forms of linguistic structures, these terms are *merely* labels. 'Head' is the name which the analysis gives, for example, to a Classifier of type 1 when it occurs as an element in a Numeral construction of type 1. What is important, from the point of view of describing the forms of the language in the most natural manner, is that a Classifier of type 1 is in fact used in this way: attaching another label to it is superfluous.

The explicit mentioning of 'functions' in syntax is characteristic of tagmemic theory, as may be seen from the following two quotations from Pike (1967):

The semantic nature of the labels is a mnemonic device, not essential in any respect to the presentation of the system as a formal structure.

The semantic labels are, however, of high value when one is presenting the system as part of a pedagogical device to teach people to speak the language. Just as a lexicon must be provided the learner in order that he may have the meanings of the words which he wishes to use, if he is to use them at all, so the meanings of the tagmemes must be presented to the learner if he wishes to use them for communication. (p. 491)

Tagmemes do not have to be represented by semantic symbols... It is then clear that in the presentation of the system as a whole no semantic component need obtrude itself. The tagmemic grammar would then be available for evaluation in terms of its formal characteristics, alongside of any other type of grammar description available...

This is not to say, however, that we ourselves prefer a tagmemic symbolism which is devoid of all reference to structural meaning and the like. The burden on the memory imposed by a symbolism which has no great reference to tagmemic function such as subject, object, head of a construction, modifier, or time relation, etc., etc., is exceedingly great. (p. 493)

Subject, object, head, modifier, etc., are, then, seen by tagmemics as elements in some kind of fixed universal semantic vocabulary. To say that a constituent acts as subject of a sentence is more than just to label it; it is, tagmemics would claim, to say something about its meaning, about the response it evokes when used in this way. A tagmemic grammar is, very much like Van Katwijk's grammar, generative in two senses. It generates both form and meaning alongside each other. These quotations from Pike (1967) confirm this:

In our view, however, we reject both the start from meaning *and* the start from pure form, by insisting on treating language as a form-meaning composite, and by insisting on the necessity of working with both of them from the beginning, and of keeping both of them in our definitions. (p. 149)

Note that my emphasis does not at all set up semantics independently of the grammar, but emphasizes a form-meaning composite, to avoid a trap of totally independent meaning, or a trap of a totally independent form. (p. 279)

Tagmemics is, then, likely to be vulnerable to the same kind of criticism as I have made of Van Katwijk's grammar. There a node such as β.C turned out to have no more information content for the reader of a grammar than a node such as $\beta \frown$ C. We will examine the use of the functional terms H(ead), M(odifier), and Q(uantifier) in Merrifield's Mixtec grammar to see whether they really tell us anything about the meaning of the constituents of Mixtec numerals.

In syntagmeme (2a) a member of the class of Classifiers of type 1 is said to be the H(ead) of a Numeral construction of type 1, and a member of the class of Digits of type 1, if one occurs, is said to be the M(odifier) in such a construction. The class of Classifiers of type 1 consists of two words, whose meanings, symbolized in Arabic numerals, are 10, and 15. The class of Digits of type 1 consists of four words, whose meanings are 1, 2, 3, and 4. The meanings which may be expressed by Mixtec Numeral constructions of type 1 are, symbolized in Arabic numerals, 10, 11, 12, 13, 14, 15, 16, 17, 18, and 19. It is clear that the semantic relation which exists between a Classifier and a Digit in these constructions is one of addition. One might conclude from this that the term

Modifier, supposedly, as we have seen, an element in a universal semantic vocabulary, indicates a relationship of addition.

But 'Modifier', as is well known, is the function which is attributed by many grammarians, including tagmemicists, to an adjective in relation to a noun. Does this mean, to transfer to an English example without losing the point of the argument, that in the two expressions 'brown cow' and 'twenty six', the word 'brown' bears the same semantic relation to 'cow' as 'six' does to 'twenty'? Obviously the relations are logically quite different. Pike himself expresses uncertainties about the applicability to various structures of the terms 'modifier, modifies, modification', and discusses the issue at some length (Pike, 1967, pp. 247–50). Whereas Merrifield, in the grammars discussed here, treats 'Modifier' as (the slot half of) a single tagmeme, Pike states that 'two or more separate tagmemes can be identified within a single distribution class of "modification" tagmemes' (p. 247). Merrifield does not appear to be as aware as Pike of the difficulties involved with terms such as 'M(odifier)'.

Similar difficulties exist with the other functional slots which Merrifield posits, such as Q(uantifier), and H(ead). One could, for the sake of argument, give tagmemics the benefit of the doubt and say that Merrifield has used these terms carelessly and ask whether, had he used others, such as Additive for M(odifier) and Multiplicand for Q(uantifier), our objections would then be met. Would the grammars then specify the relational meanings of the tagmemes? In some of the grammars, the way Merrifield has written them, such would not be the case. In the grammar for Otomi, for example, 'Multiple' constructions consist of a Quantifier followed by a Head. The semantic relation between these tagmemes is one of multiplication. 'Numeral' constructions consist of a Head, followed by a Conjunctive, followed by another Head. The semantic relation between the two Head tagmemes is one of addition. Clearly no single term used as a substitute for Head can specify the relational meaning of this posited tagmeme. Actually, as a comparison of ch. 3 of this book and Merrifield's syntagmemes (2) will illustrate, Merrifield's data can be accounted for in terms of phrase structure rules which express much more neatly the patterns inherent in his material and in these rules one can insert, if one wishes, names for functional slots specifying correctly the semantic relations which exist between constituents. But insertion of these names would be entirely superfluous, since the semantic relations are in any case unambiguously derivable from the syntactic structures themselves. The arguments which applied to Van Katwijk's grammar apply here.

The example of Otomi 'Numeral' constructions, referred to above, illustrates a further inadequacy of the theory which insists on giving a functional label to every element in an observed linguistic expression. Otomi 'Numeral' constructions consist of a Head, followed by a 'Conjunctive', followed by another Head. The class of forms which can be 'fillers' for the 'Conjunctive' slot are called by Merrifield 'Conjunctions'. One immediately suspects that the analyst has been embarrassed by the theoretic necessity to postulate two entities, a slot and a filler, and to give them different names. If slot-names carry semantic information, then it seems clear that the name 'Conjunctive' is intended to denote a relation of addition between the two Heads in the construction, and if this is the case, the two 'Head' labels are themselves superfluous. There is only *one* semantic relation obtaining between the constituents of this construction, and it is, of course, inappropriate to express this relation by postulating *three* theoretical entities. Tagmemics, in attaching a functional label to every constituent in a construction, fails to capture the basic dichotomy in language between 'lexical meaning' and 'structural meaning'. 'Structural meaning' is not a property of individual constituents, but of relations between constituents.

Consideration of conjunctions leads one to another objection to tagmemic theory. It will be convenient here to consider an example from English. The expressions *two hundred and four* and *two hundred four* are for many Americans equivalent. Presumably constructions of this sort would be characterized by tagmemics as follows:

(4)   DGT = *two, four*
      CLS = *hundred*
      MLT = +Q:DGT +H:CLS
      NML = +H:MLT ±C:CNJ +H:DGT

Thus in 'Numeral' constructions the 'Conjunctive' slot, filled by a Conjunction, is optional. As we have seen its inclusion or omission makes no difference to the semantic interpretation of the construction. The 'Conjunctive' slot, therefore, *has no meaning*. The inclusion of a Conjunction in these expressions merely makes explicit a relational meaning between other constituents of the same construction, a meaning which is in any case implicit in the structure of the phrase. Tagmemics of the vintage of Merrifield's grammars makes no allowance for the difference in semantic status between various elements in the surface structure of expressions and in fact fails to capture at all the important distinction between deep and surface structure.

Pike writes that if the 'semantic component' of a tagmemic grammar is excluded (i.e. if functional terms such as 'Head', 'Modifier' are not labelled explicitly) 'the Tagmemic grammar would then be available for evaluation in terms of its formal characteristics, alongside of any other type of grammar description available' (ibid., p. 493). We may, then, compare the phrase structure rules (3), which are symbol-for-symbol translations of Merrifield's syntagmemes (2) stripped of their semantic labels, with the grammar for Mixtec numerals proposed in ch. 3 of this book. It is obvious that a number of significant generalizations are missed in Merrifield's rules, i.e. not stated explicitly as generalizations but left for the user of the grammar to detect for himself. The clear similarity between the constructions Merrifield calls NML, for example, only emerges when one looks at three separate statements and compares them. Implicit in Merrifield's choice of category labels lie several generalizations which are not made explicit, but only hinted at. Obviously, for example, the notion represented by the term NML has some central significance in the Mixtec numeral system, but this notion is not characterized explicitly in a single clear statement. Merrifield's grammar only does half of the job of stating the patterning inherent in the data of Mixtec numerals, since one can discover in Merrifield's own statements further patternings which are not noted or remarked on.

Merrifield's grammars for Otomi and Tarahumara may similarly be improved upon, although in the case of Ch'ol he has used a recursively defined syntagmeme and a system of variables to present concisely the facts of a complicated system. Presentation of the Ch'ol data in any other way would have been very cumbersome, and in using this abbreviatory notation, Merrifield clearly captures certain significant linguistic generalizations, in particular the recursive nature of the system, which would not otherwise be made clear. In the case of the systems of Mixtec and Otomi, however, Merrifield is curiously reticent about the use of abbreviatory notations. After his grammar for Otomi he writes:

The reader will have noticed that the syntactic rules (or syntagmemes) above are susceptible of abbreviation. I use the word abbreviation advisedly, since I do not believe the revision presented below (or any other of the same general nature) *changes* the grammar in any important sense.

This is not to say that abbreviation is unimportant. The fact that rules may be abbreviated indicated the iterative nature of these particular rules. (pp. 94–5)

We naturally concur with the last sentence above, but find the earlier statements perplexing, because they give the impression of taking issue with other opinions. But, to my knowledge, no linguist would disagree with Merrifield on this matter. If by 'the grammar' Merrifield means the abstract system which the linguist is describing, then clearly nothing we do on paper can affect that in any way. If, on the other hand, Merrifield has in mind the linguist's representation (on paper) of the abstract system, then he is just as clearly wrong.

11.3 Some transformational grammars

F. C. C. Peng and B. Brainerd have also written generative grammars for numerals and give the impression that they regard their efforts as contributory to the Chomskyan enterprise, in that they give brief sketches of transformational grammar in the preambles to their papers. These papers have many inadequacies, which are in general of a superficial nature, not involving the deeper theoretical issues which were raised by Van Katwijk's and Merrifield's papers. In particular, Brainerd and Peng show about as little, or less, regard for economy in their descriptions as Merrifield, and consequently fail to express many significant generalizations about their data.

Peng's (1965) description of the standard Chinese numeral system is especially redundant. Although he summarizes such technical matters as the difference between context-free and context-sensitive phrase structure rules, he appears not to have come across the use of parentheses to express optional elements in rules. His grammar of phrase structure rules and transformations makes use of the brace notation but not parentheses. This causes Peng to resort to an extremely clumsy, and unnatural, method of expressing optionality. All possible elements are introduced mandatorily by phrase structure rules and are later optionally deleted by transformations. As an example of the redundancy which is involved, consider the following from a grammar of Chinese numerals.

(5) Initial string # I #

$I \rightarrow E_4 + E_3 + E_2 + E_1$

$$E_4 + E_3 + E_2 + E_1 \Rightarrow \left\{ \begin{array}{l} E_4 + E_3 + L + E_1 \\ E_4 + L + E_2 + E_1 \\ E_4 + L + E_1 \\ \left. \begin{array}{l} E_n + E_{n-1} + E_{n-2} \\ E_n + L + E_{n-2} \end{array} \right\} \ (n = 3, 4) \\ E_n \ (n = 1, 2, 3, 4) \\ E_n + E_{n-1} \ (n = 2, 3, 4) \end{array} \right\}$$

The generalizations missed in (5) jump to the eye; much of the rest of Peng's grammar is similarly redundant.

As an exercise in linguistic analysis, Peng's grammar would not normally deserve the attention it has been given here. One is dismayed to find, however, that the most prolific producer of number-name grammars, B. Brainerd, has not only taken Peng's grammar seriously, but even experimented with making a principle out of Peng's most notable shortcoming. His intentions, as he states them, sound laudable enough. He writes:

By now a vast literature on transformations has grown up. However, many of the transformational grammars appearing in this literature lack precision and rigor...

These shortcomings can be remedied, provided the class of transformations considered is somewhat restricted. For example, if the class of transformations under consideration is restricted to those which delete symbols, then a rigorous definition is possible. (Brainerd, 1966, p. 33)

Accordingly, Brainerd defines a class of 'deletion grammars' in which all transformations are deleting transformations. Exploration of the consequences of formal restrictions on grammars is certainly worthwhile, but only if one knows how to tell the difference between a good and a bad result. Brainerd does not. He writes a 'deletion grammar' for Chinese numerals and within the first half-page it becomes clear that this is a singularly inappropriate way of accounting for linguistic data. A set of simple phrases structure rules generates expressions for all sixteen-digit numbers and sixteen-digit 'non-numbers', such as 0,000,000,000,000,000. The task of the transformations is now to get rid of the *lings* (zeros) and accompanying superfluous elements in the non-numbers to whittle them down to acceptable Chinese numerals.

While a 'deletion grammar' is inappropriate for accounting for numerals, it is unworkable for natural language data as a whole. Brainerd defines such a grammar as a set of context-free phrase structure rules followed by a series of obligatory deletion transformations. In terms of strong generative capacity, Brainerd's 'deletion grammars' are quite hopelessly inadequate. One has only to contemplate attempting to account for simple English declarative sentences and their corresponding interrogatives and passives without being allowed to resort to permutations and adjunctions to become convinced that this is the case. The structures of these types of sentences appear quite unrelated, which is of course unsatisfactory. The fault common to almost all numeral grammars mentioned here is that they appear to have been motivated not by a desire to learn about linguistic structure from a particular body of data, but rather by an urge to tame, to subjugate the data and to force them into some or other predetermined descriptive framework.

Failure to modify notational conventions (and thus the theory) in ways obviously demanded by the nature of the data is found in other articles by Brainerd and one that he published with Peng. In Brainerd and Peng (1968) the following rule for Chinese appears:

$$(6) \quad \# \, I \, \# \; \rightarrow \quad \# \left\{ \begin{array}{c} E_4 \, (E_3 \, (E_2 \, (E_1))) \\ E_3 \, (E_2 \, (E_1)) \\ E_2 \, (E_1) \\ E_1 \\ o \end{array} \right\} \; \#$$

While this is a definite improvement on Peng's 1965 rules (5), it is still extremely cumbersome and fails to capture an obvious generalization. In Brainerd's various grammars, covering a relatively limited range of data, there are at least half a dozen examples of rules which could be sharply simplified in the same way as (6). One example is (7), from a grammar for English numerals (Brainerd, 1968, p. 15).

$$(7) \quad R_0 \; \rightarrow \; \left\{ \begin{array}{c} (U \quad 100 \quad +) \left\{ \begin{array}{c} U \quad 10 \quad (U) \\ U \end{array} \right\} \\ U \quad 100 \end{array} \right\}$$

One wonders why the obvious inadequacies of rules such as this do not trouble Brainerd. Perhaps the answer lies in his persuasion that 'there can be a number of different grammars for a given corpus, and in general there will be no "best" grammar for the corpus' (1966, pp. 34–5). This belief is perhaps reassuring if one's interests lie in toying with any of the infinite number of observationally adequate grammars for a given body of data. After 'deletion grammars', why not 'substitution grammars', or 'permutation grammars', in which only transformations of substitution or permutation respectively are permitted? The possibilities are endless but in general promise to be unilluminating. If one's purpose is to describe as closely as possible the formal properties of the organization of linguistic data, then clearly there will generally be a 'best' grammar. Finding the general properties of the best grammars for all natural languages is the task of much meaningful linguistic research.

11.4 Sampson's stratificational grammar

Sampson's work 'offers an analysis of the English numeral system as a brief example of a stratificational grammar' (p. 7). One of the goals of stratificational theory is said to be that of embodying 'linguistically significant generalizations' (p. 16) and we are interested in seeing whether Sampson's grammar of English numerals achieves that goal. We shall not examine Sampson's grammar in all its details, since that would involve a detailed review of stratificational theory, but we will proceed far enough to see that it fails to capture some of the generalizations which are most central to the English numeral system.

We begin by quoting some of Sampson's introductory statements concerning stratificational grammars.

The stratificational theory of language includes a small set of types of relation...A stratificational grammar of a particular language consists of a set of semantic units, a set of phonetic units, and a large unordered set of relations, of the type specified in the theory, whose terminals are either semantic or phonetic units or terminals of others of the relations. The grammar must of course be faithful to the facts, in the sense that given semantic inputs should produce only appropriate phonetic outputs, and vice versa. (pp. 13–14)

It is a claim of stratificational grammarians that, for any given language, a grammar...including on the one hand a 'realisation portion', showing the various possibilities of diversification, neutralisation, portmanteau and composite realisation for different units, and on the other a certain number of 'tactic patterns', giving the set of permissible sequences of units at various levels, and thus determining the choices in case of diversifications and neutralisations, will be both the simplest...and, in its internal form, will correspond well with our intuitions about language. (pp. 14–15)

A stratificational grammar is a graphic representation of a network of relationships bridging the gap between sequences of semantic units ('meanings') and sequences of phonetic units ('sounds'). The relationships are stated with reference to sequences of units of intermediate kinds, e.g. morphemic units, lexemic units. There are thus several 'strata' of representation in a stratificational grammar. The level of representation which will concern us most here is the 'top' level, that of the sequences of semantic units. The portion of the grammar which defines the permissible sequences of semantic units is the 'semotactics'. Sampson presents the semotactics of English numerals in a complicated diagram. We will give a few simplified examples extracted from this diagram to illustrate the diagramming conventions.

The pattern 'Digit teen' as in *thirteen, fourteen, ..., nineteen* is represented as in (8). The triangle at the top of this diagram is known as

(8)

a 'downward ordered and'. The two lines descending from it represent the two constituents, in their correct sequential order, of this pattern. The right-hand line connects with the node *teen*, which other statements in the grammar relate to the semantic unit 10. The left-hand line leads to a device known as a 'downward unordered or', represented as a bar with downward curving ends. The lines descending from this bar represent the alternative choices which may be made to obtain the left-hand constituent of the pattern, i.e. either 1, or 2, or 3, or 4, ..., or 9. Other statements in the grammar relate these to the forms *one, two, three,* etc., and account for the realization of *one-teen* and *two-teen* as *eleven* and *twelve* respectively. Diagram (8) thus corresponds to the configuration (9) in the more familiar notation of phrase structure grammar.

(9)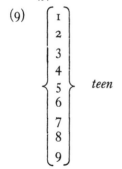

As a somewhat more complicated example of this notation, take Sampson's description of the pattern that would be described in familiar phrase structure notation as in (10), where Digit is one of the symbols 1, 2, 3, ..., 9. Sampson's graph is as in (11). This is the pattern of

(10) $\left\{ \begin{array}{l} \text{Digit} \quad \text{teen} \\ \text{(Digit times ten) (Digit)} \end{array} \right\}$

(11)

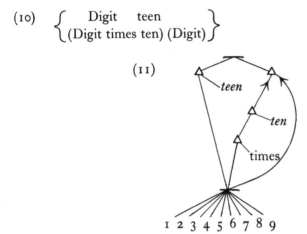

semantic units corresponding to any English numeral with a value up to 99. It will be seen that diagram (8) is a subpart of diagram (11). The two nodes *teen* and *ten* are related by other statements in the grammar to the semantic unit 10. This treatment misses the generalization that *teen* and *ten* are obviously similar phonetically; the two forms are introduced independently, as if they bore no resemblance to each other at all. The device at the top of diagram (11) is a 'downward ordered or'. According to Lamb (1966, p. 10), in an 'ordered or', the line 'which comes first takes priority over the second if both are possible'. Sampson seems to be claiming, then, that the choice of Digit *teen* is in some sense 'preferred' to that of (Digit times *ten*) (Digit). I can see no reason to make this claim. The device at the top of diagram (11) could just as well be an 'unordered or'. These are minor objections to Sampson's grammar and can easily be rectified within the stratificational framework.

The lines descending from the top right 'and' in (11) have arrowheads on them. This is Sampson's notation to indicate optionality. Where both of two lines descending from an 'and' have an arrowhead on them, either constituent may occur by itself, or both may occur together in the sequential order indicated; but at least one of the options represented must be chosen. This is equivalent to a convention in phrase structure rule notation to the effect that where all elements on the right-hand side of a rule are parenthesized, then at least one of them must be chosen as the expansion of the element on the left-hand side of the rule. Confusingly, Sampson's convention holds that where just one of two lines descending from an 'and' carries an arrowhead, then the constituent represented by the other line is optional.

By starting at the top of diagram (11) and descending to the bottom by any of the 'pathways' available, i.e. by taking just one line at an 'or' and both lines in succession at an 'and' (except, optionally, where there are arrowheads), always exploring lower pathways fully before returning to travel higher unexplored ones, we can arrive at strings of units such as those in the left-hand column below.

(12) | | |
|---|---|
| 4 *teen* | fourteen |
| 9 *teen* | nineteen |
| 5 times *ten* | fifty |
| 8 times *ten* | eighty |
| 3 times *ten* 3 | thirty three |
| 9 times *ten* 9 | ninety nine |
| 2 | two |
| 6 | six |

Other statements in the grammar relate the strings in the left-hand column here to the corresponding English numerals on the right. Since *teen* and *ten* are related to the semantic unit 10, the grammar successfully states in these cases a relationship between strings of semantic units (e.g. 4 10, 5 times 10) and the appropriate English numerals.

At this point we can give some consideration to the 'semantic representations' Sampson employs. The representation of *eighty* at the level of content is for Sampson '8 times 10'. This is clearly not a universally valid representation; the representation of the French translation of *eighty*, *quatre-vingts*, would be '4 times 20'. Sampson's grammar stops short of providing universal semantic representations. Sampson claims that this is a matter of principle:

Except insofar as empirical research (for instance, acoustic phonetics) shows that universals exist, the semantic and phonetic units, and the structures of sets of respective units, are to be discovered independently for each individual language. (p.14)

It is, of course, impossible that acoustic phoneticians working independently should 'show that universals exist'. It is the phonologist who initially hypothesizes about phonetic/phonological universals, and the acoustic phonetician may then formulate appropriate physical definitions for some of them. And for semantic universals there is no science that seems likely to be able to provide extralinguistic definitions, and here too the 'empirical researcher' could do nothing unless he were first provided by the linguist with a set of hypothetical universals. It is, then, the responsibility of the linguist to formulate theories of universals, and in so far as they claim that a stratificational grammar is the most appropriate for any natural language, stratificationalists also are in pursuit of a theory of universals. But in the case of universal semantic representations for numerals, stratificationalists meet an insoluble problem caused by the very form of their theory. It is simply impossible to relate formulas like '8 times 10' and '4 times 20' to any plausible form of universal semantic representation, such as we have used in this book, with any generality by means of the kinds of statements that are available within the stratificational framework. A grammar such as Sampson's cannot explain the synonymy of equivalent formulas such as '(1 times 1,000) plus (1 times 100)' and '(1 plus 10) times 100', which are realized in English as *one thousand one hundred* and *eleven hundred* respectively, because there is no way of relating these formulas to a common, more basic representation. This is a serious inadequacy of stratificational theory, which Sampson's grammar exemplifies. (Actually Sampson's semotactics fails to generate any strings of semantic units corresponding to expressions of the class *eleven hundred, twelve hundred, ..., ninety nine hundred,* but this failure could be rectified within a stratificational grammar.)

The sequences of semantic units defined by Sampson's semotactics are, then, more like the deep structures we have proposed in earlier chapters than universal semantic representations. We can evaluate the generality with which the semotactics performs the task of defining a set of underlying formulas like those given in (12).

Relations of addition and multiplication are of course of central importance in the formulas defined by Sampson's semotactics, as they are in the underlying structures of any but the most primitive numeral system. Ignoring for the moment the matter of exponentiation, one can say that numerals in almost any language are built of combinations of two kinds of formulas, 'addition formulas' and 'multiplication formulas'. In previous chapters we have expressed this concisely in two phrase structure rules. Each of these rules states the existence of a particular type of formula. The rule expanding NUMBER generates *all* 'addition formulas' and the rule expanding PHRASE generates *all* 'multiplication formulas'. And formulas of these two kinds are always in the same relationship to one another, which fact is expressed by the particular deployment of the terms NUMBER and PHRASE in the rules.

These generalizations are not made in Sampson's grammar. In his semotactic graph an addition formula is specified by a configuration of 'downward ordered ands' as in (13). Such a pattern defines sequences of

(13)

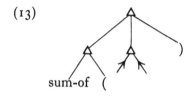

sum-of (

units like 'sum-of (X Y)' and 'sum-of (X)', where X and Y stand for the constituents of the pattern defined by the lower right 'and' in (13). (The left and right parentheses are treated by Sampson as 'semantic units' of similar status to units such as 1, 2, 3, etc.) In Sampson's graph of the semotactics of English numerals, the configuration (13) occurs in three separate places. Clearly a generalization, namely that there is a single *type* of formula, characterized in (13), is missed in presenting this configuration three times. Thus one of the major generalizations about English numerals is not captured. (In connection with Sampson's treatment of addition we may note that his semotactics defines the sequence of semantic units corresponding to English *one* as 'sum-of (sum-of (sum-of (1)))'. All three occurrences of 'sum-of' and the left and right parentheses are entirely superfluous here, of course.)

Sampson's treatment of multiplication similarly misses the obvious generalization. In his semotactic graph, multiplication formulas are defined by two separate kinds of configuration of nodes, which are given in (14). These patterns define sequences of the form 'X times Y',

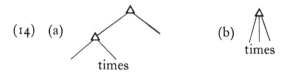

where in the case of (14a) X stands for the left-hand constituent of the pattern characterized by the lower 'and' and Y stands for the right-hand constituent of the pattern represented by the upper 'and', and in the case of (14b) X and Y are the left- and right-hand constituents respectively of the pattern defined by the 'and'. In Sampson's graph of the semotactics of English numerals there are four distinct occurrences of the configuration (14a) and three separate occurrences of the configuration (14b). Here again, an obvious generalization is missed, a generalization which is only discovered in Sampson's grammar by searching carefully through his complicated graph for repetitions of a specific type of pattern. The single general statement that 'there exist "multiplication formulas" of just such and such a form' is not to be found in the grammar.

The constant relationship between addition formulas and multiplication formulas is also not made explicit as a single generalization in Sampson's grammar. In his semotactic diagram, for each of the three occurrences of a configuration as in (13), which defines addition formulas, the left-hand arrowheaded line connects with the topmost 'and' of a configuration as in (14). But again one has to search carefully through the graph to discover this generalization. It is not made explicit in the grammar. Sampson's grammar, then, does not attain the ideals of linguistic analysis, as they are expressed by Lamb (1966), the originator of stratificational theory.

Linguistic analysis...is a process in which the analyst finds recurrences of similar entities having such relationships among themselves and with other entities that they can be regarded, at some level, as repetitions of one another. Once found, such recurrent entities may be extracted and described only once instead of repeatedly. This process amounts to a simplification, and it also involves generalization. The phenomena dealt with are then better understood and are better treated in whatever applications may be desired. (p. 3)

It remains to be shown that the major generalizations about numeral systems can be expressed within a stratificational framework.

An obvious formal device for capturing the missed generalization in (3), (5), (6), (7), and in Sampson's grammar, namely the recurrence of a particular type of element, is recursion. We have seen in preceding chapters the vital role played by recursion in numeral systems. Almost all of the numeral grammars reviewed here fail to express even this fundamental fact. This failure may be attributed to a general lack of awareness of the notion 'significant linguistic generalization'.

11.5 Sanders' generative semantic grammar

Sanders (1968) has sketched an account of the English numeral system and all others within a transformational framework. His account explicitly and emphatically makes several theoretical claims that are quite at odds with our account and these will be discussed in this section.

It is convenient to begin by pointing to a similarity between our account of numerals and Sanders'. Our semantic representations for numbers may be regarded as conjunctions of 'marks'. Sanders argues that 'all numerals must be derived by lexicalization of numerational bases of the form ((K, ONE), (K, ONE, OTHER), (K, ONE, OTHER, OTHER), ...)' (p. 128). K is Sanders' non-phonological representation for *and*; Sanders uses capitals for all non-phonological symbols, so ONE and OTHER are also non-phonological representations; the difference between ONE and OTHER and between one OTHER and all other OTHERS is a difference of reference. This difference need not concern us here, so Sanders' 'numerational bases' can be regarded as conjunctions of 'marks', or OTHERS. Sanders' 'numerational bases' do not have the status, in his account, of semantic representations; they are, rather, produced transformationally from underlying simple non-numerated sentential coordinations. Thus, for Sanders there are derivations which we may characterize informally as in (15) and (16).

(15)   I saw one sparrow and I saw another sparrow and I saw another sparrow
    ⇒ I saw one and another and another sparrow
    ⇒ I saw three sparrows

(16)   One boy ran, and another boy ran
    ⇒ One and another boy ran
    ⇒ Two boys ran

The difference between our account and Sanders' with which we are centrally concerned is one of the type of rule which is needed to relate surface structure numerals to conjunctions of marks or OTHERS. We shall not investigate here the relation between phrasal and sentential conjunction. Sanders' treats the relation between surface structure numerals and conjunctions of marks or OTHERS solely by processes of lexicalization; we treat the relation by an interpretive semantic component, as described in section 2 of ch. 2, as well as by a small number of lexicalization rules (and, trivially here, sometimes a few transformations). Sanders has a lexicalization rule (ONE) = (*one*) and 'an infinite number of multi-unit rules such as

(xxi) (a) (K, ONE, OTHER) = (*two*)
  (b) (K, ONE, OTHER, OTHER) = (*three*)
  (c) (K, ONE, OTHER, OTHER, OTHER) = (*four*), etc. . . .' (p. 130)

The significant difference between our proposals and Sanders' is that he postulates an infinite number of lexicalization rules, whereas we postulate a finite number. Sanders is not unaware that postulating an infinite number of rules for a language is problematic. He writes,

Since no scientific theory can contain an infinite number of rules, however, and since a language requiring an infinite number of rules for the proof of its theorems could obviously never be learned, some finitizing abbreviation of (xxi) would appear to be necessary. But, although various types of abbreviation are, of course, possible here, there appears to be *no* way of reducing numeral lexicalization to a *finite* process except by means of rule conventions which are required only for numerals and, even then, only if we accept some arbitrary numerational base as the base for a *highest numeral name*, with all strings longer than this specifiable only by conjunctions of lower numeral names. (pp. 130–1)

Sanders conquers these adversities in the following way:

This obviously does not indicate any inadequacies in *grammars* or *linguistic metatheories*. In fact, if our grammars did *not* characterize numeral lexicalization as distinct from all other lexicalization processes, *that* would indicate inadequacy, since we know that there are obvious differences between the ways in which numbers are learned and used, and thus we *require* that adequate grammars characterize this distinction in some way. (p. 131)

There are three flaws in this argument: firstly it is not obviously true that numeral lexicalization differs from all other lexicalization. Although Sanders deems the differences too obvious to mention, one may surmise that the unique characteristic of numeral lexicalization, as he sees it, is that it associates an infinite set of names with an infinite set of formally higher similar structures which are differentiated from each other in a very simple and systematic way, namely by the number of elements they contain. But this characteristic is not unique to numerals. The infinite set of terms *father, grandfather, great grandfather, great great grandfather*, etc. must be associated by a grammar with the infinite set of structures whose members are something like FATHER, FATHER'S

FATHER, FATHER'S FATHER'S FATHER, FATHER'S FATHER'S FATHER'S FATHER, etc. Several other similar examples can be found in kinship terminology. Another possible example of this sort of thing is the system of expressions which used to be used in maritime navigation for expressing directions. The four cardinal points of the compass are called North, East, South and West. A point between North and East is called North-East; a point between North and North-East is called North-North-East. There is, of course, an infinite number of points which can be named, if this is found useful, just as there is an infinite set of numbers and certainly a very large number of ancestors in the series referred to by *father, grandfather, great grandfather*, etc. The system for naming compass-points could be described by a small recursive grammar, augmented by some device for eliminating undesirable expressions such as **East-North*. Three other sets of expressions which seem to be potentially infinite in the same way as numerals are *post-script, post-post-script*, etc., *ultimate, penultimate, antepenultimate*, etc., and *quaver, semiquaver, demisemiquaver, hemidemisemiquaver*, etc. It can be argued that the non-occurrence of forms such as *?post-post-post-script, ?pre-antepenultimate*, and **halfhemidemisemiquaver* has the same theoretical status as the non-occurrence as forms such as *quadrillion, quintillion*, etc., in everyday speech. These forms are simply not useful enough to have found an established place in English. Admittedly the phenomena mentioned in this paragraph are somewhat peripheral, but they do show that numerals are certainly not unique, though they are definitely the most interesting expressions of this general type.

Secondly, Sanders' argument contains contradictory assertions. On the one hand he claims, as we have seen, that numerals are in a sense different from the rest of language and that therefore it is required that an account of numerals violate certain assumptions of his metatheory; on the other hand he writes,

it should be obvious that we have chosen to discuss at length the inadequacy of the 'morphemic view' in respect to numerals *not* because numerals are assumed to be abnormal in respect to other words. On the contrary, it is clear that, in respect to the general theory assumed here, numerals are essentially derived in *exactly the same way* as all other words and that they differ from other words only in respect to minor properties of their respective lexicalization rules. (p. 106)

The properties which differentiate Sanders' numeral lexicalization rules from other lexicalization rules do not seem to be 'minor'. The question of whether, for example, phonological rules make reference to syntactic information has always been considered an important issue in linguistic theory; the question of whether lexicalization rules make reference to phonological information is surely of about equal importance to our view of what language is like. It is in referring to phonological information that Sanders' numeral lexicalization rules differ from his other lexicalization rules.

Thirdly, Sanders argues only that numeral systems are different in some way from most of the rest of language. He presents no arguments at all to show why they should be characterized as different in the particular way he does it. Sanders' grammar characterizes numerals as different in two respects: (a) as necessitating the postulation of an *ad hoc* finitizing convention for infinite sets of rules as stated in a quotation above, and (b) as necessitating a further violation of his metatheory, described in the quotation below:

Now we would soon find that our efforts to achieve maximal numerational abbreviation are greatly facilitated if we introduce a convention allowing phonologically specified contexts for numeral lexicalizations, with perhaps even greater facilitation if we also allow for substitution of one phonological string for another in respect to such rules. Both of these powers are, of course, metatheoretically excluded by the general theory that is assumed here, which requires that all simple equivalence, or substitutability, relations hold *only* between a non-phonological string and a non-semantic string, and, if context-sensitive, *only* in respect to non-phonological contexts. Thus the toleration of these powers in respect to numeral lexicalization would again explicitly differentiate this process from all other types of lexicalization. (p. 132)

Thus Sanders finds that the facts of numeral systems require him to renounce several of the specific assumptions about the general nature of language with which he begins his study. Another specific assumption with which Sanders begins is,

that it is presently neither empirically necessary nor intuitively reasonable to maintain that there is any discrete or fundamental distinction between what has conventionally been called 'semantics' and what has conventionally been called 'syntax 'or 'grammar'. Thus all linguistic metatheories which, like that of Katz and Fodor (1963), allow for metatheoretically-distinctive semantic and syntactic theories or 'components' are here assumed to be excessively powerful and thus empirically unmotivated and scientifically inadequate. (p. 15)

This quotation is from a section entitled 'Basic Assumptions' in Sanders' first chapter. We are not told why Sanders did not choose to renounce this specific assumption rather than the others he mentions, and, as far as we can see, there is no good reason. We believe that we have in previous chapters made a good case that interpretation of quite complex structures by an interpretive semantic component permits one to state the major significant generalizations that apply to a numeral system and we shall briefly show later that Sanders' alternative of treating the relation between numerals and conjunctions of marks or OTHERS as 'lexicalization' necessarily involves missing significant generalizations.

Because of the assurance with which Sanders states his case and the sweeping conclusions for which it forms a basis, it is worth taking more space to show that this case is misconceived. Sanders' calls the semantic representations of values such as 3, 36, 507, 1,000 'numerational elements'. He writes,

if numerational elements were accepted as possible constituents of underlying structures, then one or the other of the following clearly unacceptable consequences would follow: (p. 103)

The first of three 'unacceptable consequences' which Sanders lists is not a consequence at all of the acceptance of some numerational elements as possible constituents of underlying structures, but rather the consequence of a different 'if':

(1) If each numeral were assumed to be a distinct unanalysable element, then, since the number of numerals is infinite, the number of distinct elements of the general theory would be infinite. (p. 103)

The 'if' statement in this quotation is, of course, correct, but has no relevance to what Sanders undertook to show in the quotation before, because the 'if's are different. Sanders' second 'unacceptable consequence' is relevant to the issue at hand.

(2) If each non-unitary numeral were assumed to be inherently complex with all underlying numerational constituents being drawn from a finite set of semantic elements (i.e. if, for example, the underlying structure of *eighteen* is (K, (EIGHT, TEN)) and that of *eighty* is (TIMES, (EIGHT, TEN)), then there would obviously be no non-arbitrary way of determining what the correct underlying representation of any numeral is. For, although it could be shown that the derivation of English *eighty* is facilitated by the assumption of a base (TIMES, (EIGHT, TEN)), rather than (TIMES, (FOUR, TWENTY)), precisely the opposite argument would hold for the derivation of the French *quatre-vingt*.

If one sought to avoid this problem, on the other hand, by postulating different underlying structures for *eighty* and *quatre-vingt*, this would obviously contradict the unquestionable fact that *eighty* and *quatre-vingt* are synonymous. (p. 103)

If we take 'underlying representation' and 'underlying structure' here to mean what we have called 'deep structure', then the first part of this quotation fairly accurately describes the analysis we propose of numerals, and we do in fact postulate different deep structures for *eighty* and *quatre-vingt* (see ch. 4 for our discussion of French numerals). But our analysis does not 'contradict the unquestionable fact that *eighty* and *quatre-vingt* are synonymous', because these different deep structures are assigned identical semantic representations by an interpretive semantic component. Sanders, as we have seen, simply assumes *a priori* that there is no difference between deep structure and semantic representation.

Sanders' third 'unacceptable consequence' is this:

(3) If it were assumed that there are underlying numerals such that each distinct numeral is a conjunction of a distinct number of instances of a single semantic numerational element, i.e. if the underlying representations of *one, two, three*, etc., are respectively (ONE), (ONE & ONE), (ONE & ONE & ONE), etc., then the unacceptable consequences of alternatives (1) and (2) would be avoided. However, this alternative, like the others, would not only make it impossible to explain any synonymity relations involving numerational alternants, such as

(pp) (1) I saw thirteen blackbirds
    (2) I saw seven and six blackbirds
    (3) I saw three and ten blackbirds, etc. (p. 103)

Let us pause there. These three sentences are not synonymous. One would say (pp) (2) only if one had seen seven blackbirds on one occasion and six blackbirds on a separate occasion. A person who had seen thirteen blackbirds all at once would not say Sanders' (pp) (2). The third sentence similarly refers to two separate events. It is true that the second and third sentences entail the first, but that is a different matter. A theory of entailment within generative grammar has yet to be developed. When one is developed, it will probably be significantly similar to a theory of synonymy, and the proof that, for example, (pp) (2) entails (pp) (1), will almost certainly involve some kind of 'calculation' of the equivalence of $(7+6)$ and 13. Sanders assumes *a priori* that the statements in a grammar which comprise such calculations can only be statements of coordinative reduction. He gives no empirical grounds for rejecting other types of statement, such as the interpretation procedures we have proposed. In view of our present lack of a theory of entailment, it would be clairvoyant to claim that with any given general theory containing a method for making these arithmetical calculations the proof of true entailment theorems is impossible.

Sanders continues that the assumption referred to in the last quotation 'would also imply that there are an infinite number of distinct numeral "morphemes"' (p. 104). This is true, but again not relevant to the issue here, since our proposals make use of a finite number of numeral morphemes.

Thus we see that the 'unacceptable consequences' of assumptions other than Sanders' are either consequences of assumptions which we both reject and which are therefore not relevant to the issue here, or else 'unacceptable' because Sanders has assumed them *a priori* to be so. His assumption that a distinction between semantics and syntax is unacceptable is based on an *a priori* notion of metatheoretical simplicity and not on any indication that the drawing of a distinction between semantics and syntax necessarily involves contradictions or loss of generalizations. It can easily be shown, on the other hand, that Sanders' proposals do involve a serious contradiction. Sentences (pp) (1–3) are not synonymous; Sanders' proposals allow a proof that they are synonymous. We will later show briefly that Sanders' proposals also involve loss of generalizations. Sanders' rejection of the distinction between semantics and syntax is, furthermore, arbitrary, since he is quite prepared to permit his account of numerals to violate certain other of his fundamental metatheoretical assumptions.

Finally, we propose to show that Sanders himself implies in several passages that a treatment such as ours would succeed in capturing generalizations which are missed by his treatment. Sanders gives the following as 'an illustration of the general lines which numeral lexicalization abbreviations will follow' (p. 133).

(K, ONE, OTHER) = (*two/three/four/five/six/seven/eight/nine/ten/eleven/twelve/*
thirteen/fourteen/fifteen/sixteen/seventeen/
eighteen/nineteen/twenty/thirty/forty/fifty/sixty/
seventy/eighty/ninety/one & (hundred/(thousand/(million/
billion)))...)

IN THE CONTEXT   *(one/two/three/four/five/six/seven/eight/nine/ten/eleven/*
twelve/thirteen/fourteen/fifteen/sixteen/seventeen/
eighteen/nineteen/twenty & nine/thirty & nine/forty & nine/
fifty & nine/sixty & nine/seventy & nine/eighty & nine (/ø(ø/(ø/
nine & hundred & million) nine & hundred & thousand)
nine & hundred & ninety & nine) (ø/hundred/thousand/
million/billion) ———.

As Sanders rightly says, this rule 'is, of course, subject to much further abbreviation', but note that to get this far, he has already had to violate several of his initial assumptions, as we have seen. There are obviously a number of generalizations missed by Sanders' rule and the reader is invited to try to abbreviate it further so as to capture these generalizations without further violating Sanders' assumptions that the number of rules in a grammar must be finite (here, of course, he is correct) and that only one type of statement may be used to relate conjunctions of marks or OTHERS to surface numerals. The enterprise seems fruitless and we will show how some of Sanders' own remarks tend to indicate a more satisfactory alternative, which is like the grammar we have proposed.

Sanders admits, as we have seen, that

it could be shown that the derivation of English *eighty* is facilitated by the assumption of a base (TIMES, (EIGHT, TEN)), rather than (TIMES, (FOUR, TWENTY))...(p. 103)

This is tantamount to saying that the assumption of a base (TIMES, (EIGHT, TEN)) for *eighty* leads to the capture of a significant generalization about *eighty*. If a derivation is 'facilitated', then surely it is simplified and we agree with Sanders that 'simplicity and generality are essentially alternative names for the same metric property' (p. 45). Sanders implies, then, that his treatment misses a generalization. Sanders also states that his treatment is possible 'only if we accept some *arbitrary* numerational base as the base for the *highest numeral name*, with all strings longer than this being specifiable only by conjunctions of lower numeral names' (p. 131). Thus his treatment misses the obvious generalization that there is *one* system, rather than two, for naming very high numbers. It is, however, a common characteristic of our analysis and Sanders' that we postulate a dichotomy between types of numerals. Sanders' dividing line comes at a relatively high numerical value, which he admits is arbitrary. Our dividing line comes, for English, at the value 10; names for values up to 10 are simple, whereas names for values beyond that are syntactically complex. It is an obvious fact about the English numeral system that the value 10 has a special significance, and Sanders' analysis fails to express this fact.

In summary, Sanders' account suffers from the fault of the other numeral grammars discussed in this chapter, that it is more concerned with squeezing data into some predetermined framework than with discovering the essential properties of numeral systems.

Bibliography

Abraham, R. C. (1958) *Dictionary of Modern Yoruba*, University of London Press Ltd, London.

Alexander, W. D. (1864) *A Short Synopsis of the Most Essential Points in Hawaiian Grammar*, H. M. Whitney, Honolulu.

Andrews, L. (1854) *Grammar of the Hawaiian Language*, Mission Press, Honolulu.

anonymous French Catholic missionary (1834) *Notes grammaticales sur la langue sandwichoise*, Paris. (British Museum catalogue no. 12901.bb.47.)

Aulie, W. (1957) 'Higher Layered Numerals in Chol (Mayan)', *International Journal of American Linguistics*, Vol. XXIII, No. 4, pp. 281–3.

Bach, E. (1964) *An Introduction to Transformational Grammars*, Holt, Rinehart, and Winston, New York.

Batchelor, J. (1887) *A Grammar of the Ainu Language*, in Chamberlain (ed.).

Beckwith, M. W. (1918) *The Hawaiian Romance of Laieikawai*, Bureau of American Ethnology, Washington, D.C.

Bierwisch, M. and K. E. Heidolph (eds. 1970) *Progress in Linguistics*, Mouton, The Hague.

Bowen, J. T. and T. J. Rhys Jones (1960) *Teach Yourself Welsh*, English Universities Press, London.

Bowen, T. J. (1858) *Grammar and Dictionary of the Yoruba Language*, Smithsonian Institute, Washington, D.C.

Brainerd, B. (1966) 'Two Grammars for Chinese Number Names', *Canadian Journal of Linguistics*, Vol. 12, pp. 33–51.

(1968) 'On the Syntax of Certain Classes of Numerical Expressions' in Corstius (ed.), pp. 9–40.

Brainerd, B. and F. C. C. Peng (1968) 'A Syntactic Comparison of Chinese and Japanese Numerical Expressions', in Corstius (ed.), pp. 53–81.

Bredsdorff, E. (1956) *Danish: An Elementary Grammar and Reader*, Cambridge University Press, Cambridge.

Brunot, F. (1906) *Histoire de la Langue Française des Origines à 1900*, Tome II: *Le Seizième Siècle*, Librairie Armand Colin, Paris.

Bullock, H. J. (1949) *Grammaire Française: methode orale*, Appleton-Century-Crofts, New York.

Chamberlain, B. H. (ed. 1887) *The Language, Mythology and Geographical Nomenclature of Japan Viewed in the Light of Aino Studies, Memoirs of the Literature College, Imperial University of Japan*, No. 1, Imperial University, Tokyo.

Chamisso, A. von (1837) *Über die Hawaiische Sprache*, Leipzig.

Chao, Y. R. (1968) *A Grammar of Spoken Chinese*, University of California Press, Berkeley.

Chomsky, N. (1965) *Aspects of the Theory of Syntax*, M.I.T. Press, Cambridge, Massachusetts.

Chomsky, N. and M. Halle (1968) *The Sound Pattern of English*, Harper and Row, New York.

Conant, L. L. (1923) *The Number Concept: its Origin and Development*, Macmillan and Co, New York.

Cook, W. A. (1969) *Introduction to Tagmemic Analysis*, Holt, Rinehart, and Winston, New York.

Corstius, H. B. (ed. 1968) *Grammars for Number Names, Foundations of Language Supplementary Series*, Vol. 7, D. Reidel, Dordrecht.

Cross, F. L. (ed. 1957) *The Oxford Dictionary of the Christian Church*, Oxford University Press, Oxford.

Darlow, T. H. and H. F. Moule (1905–11) *Historical Catalogue of the Printed Editions of Holy Scripture in the Library of the British and Foreign Bible Society*, The British and Foreign Bible Society, London.

Ellison, J. W. (ed. 1957) *Nelson's Complete Concordance to the Revised Standard Version Bible*, Nelson, Nashville, Tennessee.

Ertel, L. C., P. L. Garvin, F. C. C. Peng, and G. Reitz (1965) *Fulcrum Technique for Chinese–English Machine Translation*, Final Report under Contract AF30(602)-3462, The Bunker-Ramo Corporation, Canoga Park, California.

Evans, J. J. (1946) *Gramadeg Cymraeg*, Gwasg Aberystwyth, Aberystwyth.

Fornander, A. (1878) *An Account of the Polynesian Race, English and Foreign Philosophical Library*, Extra Series, Vols. 3, 6, 7, London.

Gallatin, A. (1845) 'Semi-Civilized Nations of Mexico and Central America', in *Transactions of the American Ethnological Society*, Vol. 1, pp. 1–352.

Gruber, J. (1967) *Functions of the Lexicon in Formal Descriptive Grammars*, Technical Memorandum TM 3770/000/00, System Development Corporation, Santa Monica, California (republished by Indiana University Linguistics Club, Bloomington, Indiana).

Hattori, S. (1964) *An Ainu Dialect Dictionary*, Iwanami Shoten, Tokyo.

Humboldt, W. von (1832–9) *Über die Kawi-Sprache auf der Insel Java*, in *Abhandlungen der Königlichen Akademie der Wissenschaften zu Berlin*, Berlin.

Jones, T. (1897) *A Guide to Welsh*, Hughes and Son, Wrexham.

Judd, H. P., M. K. Pukui, and J. F. G. Stokes (1945) *Introduction to the Hawaiian Language*, Tongg Publishing Co., Honolulu.

Katwijk, A. Van (1968) 'A Functional Grammar of Dutch Number Names', in Corstius (ed.), pp. 1–8.

Kluge, T. (1937–42) I. *Die Zahlenbegriffe der Sudansprachen*; II. *Die Zahlenbegriffe der Australier, Papua und Bantuneger*; III. *Die Zahlenbegriffe der Voelker Americas, Nordeurasiens, der Munda und der Palaioafricaner*; IV. *Die Zahlenbegriffe der Dravida, der Hamiten, der Semiten und der Kaukasier*; V. *Die Zahlenbegriffe der Sprachen Central- und Suedostasiens, Indonesiens, Micronesiens, Melanesiens und Polynesiens*, published by the author, Berlin.

Lamb, S. M. (1966) *Outline of Stratificational Grammar*, Georgetown University Press, Washington, D.C.

Laṣebikan, E. L. (1958) *Learning Yoruba*, Oxford University Press, Ibadan.

Mann, A. (1886) 'Notes on the Numeral System of the Yoruba Nation', in *Journal of the Anthropological Institute*, Vol. 16, pp. 59–64, London.

Menninger, K. (1969) *Number Words and Number Symbols*, M.I.T. Press, Cambridge, Massachusetts.

Merrifield, W. R. (1968) 'Number Names in Four Languages of Mexico', in Corstius (ed.), pp. 91–102.

Morris-Jones, J. (1922) *An Elementary Welsh Grammar*, Pt. 1, Clarendon Press, Oxford.

—— (1931) *Welsh Syntax*, University of Wales Press Board, Cardiff.

Norlev, E. and H. A. Koefoed (1959) *The Way to Danish*, Munksgaard, Copenhagen.

Peng, F. C. C. (1965) 'The Numeric System of Standard Chinese', Appendix III of Ertel et al.

Peng, F. C. C. and B. Brainerd (1970) 'A Grammar of Ainu Number Names', in *Lingua*, Vol. 25, No. 4, pp. 381–97.

Perlmutter, D. M. (1970) 'On the Article in English', in Bierwisch and Heidolph (eds.), pp. 233–48.

Pfizmaier, A. (1851) *Kritische Durchsicht der von Dawidow Verfassten Wörtersammlung aus der Sprache der Ainos*, Vienna.

Pike, K. L. (1967) *Language in Relation to a Unified Theory of the Structure of Human Behavior*, Mouton, The Hague.

Pott, A. F. (1847) *Die Quinare und Vigesimale Zählmethode bei Völkern aller Welttheile*, Dr Martin Sändig oHG, Wiesbaden.

Reibel, D. A. and S. A. Schane (eds. 1969) *Modern Studies in English*, Prentice Hall, Englewood Cliffs, New Jersey.

Ross, J. R. (1969) 'A Proposed Rule of Tree-Pruning', in Reibel and Schane (eds.), pp. 288–99.

Rowlands, E. C. (1969) *Teach Yourself Yoruba*, English Universities Press, London.

Sampson, G. (1970) *Stratificational Grammar*, Mouton, The Hague.

Sanders, G. A. (1968) *Some General Grammatical Processes in English*, Indiana University Linguistics Club, Bloomington, Indiana.

Saunderson, R. (1833) *An Introduction to the Welsh Language*, Bala.

Schane, S. A. (1968) *French Phonology and Morphology*, M.I.T. Press, Cambridge, Massachusetts.

Seidenberg, A. (1960) *The Diffusion of Counting Practices, University of California Publications in Mathematics*, Vol. 3, No. 4, pp. 215–300, University of California Press, Berkeley and Los Angeles.

Siromoney, R. (1968) 'Grammars of Number Names in Certain Dravidian Languages', in Corstius (ed.), pp. 82–90.

Smith, A. S. D. ('Caradar') (1925) *Welsh Made Easy*, Hughes and Son, Wrexham.

Y Bibl Cyssegr-lan, sef yr Hen Destament a'r Newydd (1620) Bonham Norton and John Bill, London. Reprinted and published by Eyre and Spottiswoode, London.

Index

For EU product safety concerns, contact us at Calle de José Abascal, 56–1°,
28003 Madrid, Spain or eugpsr@cambridge.org.